Understanding
Revolution

UNDERSTANDING
Revolution

Patrick Van Inwegen

LYNNE
RIENNER
PUBLISHERS

BOULDER
LONDON

Published in the United States of America in 2011 by
Lynne Rienner Publishers, Inc.
1800 30th Street, Boulder, Colorado 80301
www.rienner.com

and in the United Kingdom by
Lynne Rienner Publishers, Inc.
3 Henrietta Street, Covent Garden, London WC2E 8LU

Library of Congress Cataloging-in-Publication Data
Van Inwegen, Patrick, 1974–
    Understanding revolution / Patrick Van Inwegen.
        p.   cm.
    Includes bibliographical references and index.
    ISBN 978-1-58826-748-1 (hardcover : alk. paper)
    ISBN 978-1-58826-775-7 (pbk. : alk. paper)
    1. Revolutions. I. Title.
    JC491.V36   2011
    303.6'4—dc22
                                                    2010038599

British Cataloguing in Publication Data
A Cataloguing in Publication record for this book
is available from the British Library.

Printed and bound in the United States of America

The paper used in this publication meets the requirements
of the American National Standard for Permanence of
Paper for Printed Library Materials Z39.48-1992.

5   4   3   2   1

Contents

Tables and Figures

Tables

Figures

Acknowledgments

I would like to thank the following for their support and direct contribution to this book: my colleagues at Whitworth University, including Julia Stronks, John Yoder, Andrew Hogue, Jim Hunt, and those in several engaging faculty scholarship forums; a number of students, including Laura Adams, Michael Marchesini, James Spung, and the many students in the number of iterations of classes on revolution that I have taught, especially those who commented on rough drafts of my manuscript; and most important, my wife, Victoria, the love of my life.

Understanding Revolution

1

Understanding Revolution

Revolution is the sex of politics. —H. L. Mencken

H. L. Mencken's famous statement on revolutions is illuminating in two respects. First, revolutions can be viewed as the sex of politics in the sense that they give birth to nations. Out of revolutionary periods are born the countries that populate the modern international system. In this sense, they are literally a procreative act. But revolutions are "sexy" in the sense that they have all of the passion, intrigue, drama, ideas, heroes, villains, and crisis mentality that attracts students of social sciences. Revolutions are the subject matter of great works of art, literature, theater, and film—they are fascinating even for the nonspecialist.

Scholarly interest in the topic of revolution has produced a rich literature that spans the disciplines of sociology, history, political science, economics, philosophy, and theology.[1] This book reflects the vast research done on these amazing social phenomena. To begin, in this chapter I address two fundamental questions and introduce the remaining questions that structure the rest of the book. The two questions for this chapter are: Why do we study revolutions, and what are they?

Why Do We Study Revolution?

Excepting war, religion and romantic love, nothing in ordinary human experience has so inflamed the imagination of men, encouraged so many romantic illusions, or broken so completely with the ordinary routine of existence, as has been true of revolution. —Robert Ezra Park

1

Revolutions are fascinating topics for a number of reasons. Revolutionary situations are often dominated by larger-than-life figures. Some of these figures, such as Mao Zedong and Joseph Stalin, create a cult of personality; others, such as Augusto Cesar Sandino and Ernesto "Che" Guevara, become iconic figures for subsequent revolutionaries. These are people around whom legends emerge, about whom fables are told and countless biographies are written. They are heroes because they do what most others only dream of—they live their lives and direct their movements according to ideals that are much larger than themselves even though those ideals are not always brought to fruition.

Revolutions are an exciting topic of study because they focus our attention on key ideas and ideals. Revolutions are always struggles to create a better world. Heroic figures are a large part of revolutionary appeal because the people engaged in revolution are willing to risk everything to bring about larger sociopolitical changes. As the chapters on ideology discuss, revolutionary ideologies typically not only point out what is wrong with the current government but also suggest a better alternative and a way to move from one to the other. Part of the reason that revolutionary situations are dominated by heroic figures is that they pose a threat. Even more than during a conventional war, the very existence of a ruling regime is at stake. Wars often end with winners and losers, but the losers rarely are entirely purged from power, as is more typical in revolutions.

Revolutions mark key turning points in history. Because international relations have historically been dominated by states, it stands to reason that a change in who governs a state often leads to changes in international relations. France's radical changes in attempting to conquer Europe under Napoleon Bonaparte were a direct consequence of the revolution of 1789. Two hundred years later, with the fall of the Berlin Wall in 1989 and the crumbling of the Soviet Union in 1991, the international balance of power shifted from a Cold War to a new era of globalization.

Finally, the study of revolutions is fundamental to understanding the current world. Even though revolutions do not entirely determine the type of country that emerges and its relationship to others in the international system, they do set the course that countries follow. To understand why the Iranian president is not the sole source of foreign policy decisions, for example, one must appreciate the revolution that created the Iranian constitution. In a similar fashion, knowing about the independence movement that created the United States also helps us to appreciate the divided powers of the US government. Events in and immediately following the Cuban Revolution help to explain the long-standing animosity between the United States and Cuba. Even comparing the development trends of Southeast

Asian countries such as Indonesia and the Philippines is aided by contrasting the overthrow of their dictators in the 1980s and 1990s. James DeFronzo makes a compelling case for the importance of understanding revolutionary movements:

> An absence of public knowledge concerning the political histories and socioeconomic characteristics of other societies can permit a government to exercise an excessive influence over citizen perception of its actions in foreign lands. It is possible, for example, that U.S. involvement in Vietnam would not have occurred or at least would not have progressed as far as it did if the American people had been fully aware of the Vietnamese Revolution against French colonial rule, the loss of popular support for France's Indochina war effort, and the terms of the resulting Geneva peace settlement of 1954. Although the U.S. public was too poorly informed to prevent the tragedy in Vietnam, the collective memory of the Vietnam experience probably helped prevent direct U.S. military intervention in several countries in the subsequent years. (2007: xi)

In this sense, then, understanding revolutions can help countries avoid the mistakes of the past in similar foreign policy situations.

Beyond knowing the origins of modern states, understanding the current world also implies knowing how people in societies normally interact. In this way, revolutions are abnormal events that help us define what is normal. People normally follow their government (in terms of respecting the laws); revolutions instead involve people directly challenging their government. Societies normally operate with stable or slowly changing norms and values, whereas revolutions are often a time of radically shifting norms and values. Even economic interactions undergo significant fluctuation in revolutionary periods. In this way, studying revolution is like undertaking the psychological study of a deviant behavior in order to understand normal behavior. By studying the abnormality of revolutions, we get a better sense of what "normal" societies, economic interactions, and political regimes look like.

Defining and Distinguishing Revolution

We live in a world in which over half of the inhabitants of the planet live
in a country that has undergone a revolution in this century.
—Michael S. Kimmel

The purpose of social sciences is to more fully understand change and continuity within societies. Revolutions fundamentally involve change and are a part of what can broadly be termed social movements. Social movements, Charles Tilly argues, comprise three elements: (1) a campaign or public effort making claims on an authority, (2) means of political action, and (3) a public representation of the cause's worthiness, unity, numbers, and commitment (2004). They are coordinated attempts at creating some change in the existing system. This is obviously a broad field of which revolutions occupy the extreme periphery.

When we study social movements we are often interested in the types of changes that occur and the scope and speed of those changes. Revolutions tend to be the most radical kind of change a society endures; that is, they are positioned on the very edges of the spectrum of social movements. It is useful to look at what other types of events and activities are also included in social movements to better understand revolution.

Figure 1.1 arranges a number of types of social movements according to the rapidity of change as well as the intensity of these activities. The category of casualties, shown on the vertical axis, is chosen as a measure of intensity because of the assumption that people are typically not willing to kill or die for causes unless they are very important and no other way of achieving a goal is perceived. For example, the American colonists did not go directly to war with the British, but rather activists engaged in widespread noncooperation and nonviolent protests for years before any violence occurred. The lines surrounding the various types of events are meant to be fuzzy and oftentimes overlapping, because the general categories shown along the horizontal axis are theoretical concepts used to discuss actual events. The events are always going to be more complex than the theoretical concept used to discuss them implies. Thus, Gamal Abdel Nasser's coup in Egypt in 1952 probably resulted in more change than did the People Power revolution in the Philippines in 1986. Finally, the size and shape of ovals represents the scope of an event; for example, a civil war can create slow or fast change, but it always has high casualty rates.

There have been many attempts to define revolution, and, as we will see, many types of revolutions require slight alterations of the definition. A consensus of the bare minimum for what constitutes a revolution has begun to emerge, however, in the scholarly literature. Charles Tilly has written about a great many social movements, including significant works on revolutions, for more than thirty years. He provides the clearest definition of revolution that distinguishes between this type of social movement and the others discussed above. Building on his definition, I define revolution as *a forcible, irregular, popularly supported change in the governing regime* and then pull this definition apart into its constituent elements and implications.

First and foremost, revolutions are forcible events. The utilization of force entails getting someone to do something he or she would otherwise not

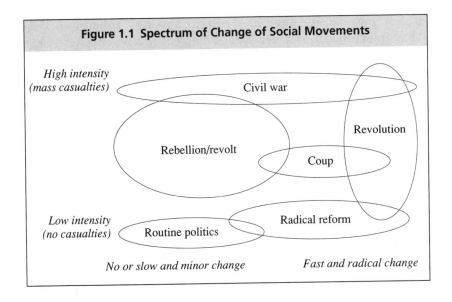

Figure 1.1 Spectrum of Change of Social Movements

do through threat of punishment or promise of reward (Keohane and Nye 2001). Force requires the exercise of power, which Max Weber defines as the "ability of one actor within a social relationship to carry out their will despite resistance" (1968: 53). Because governments do not want to relinquish power, force is required to take power from those who control the state. Force, in these terms, does not necessarily entail violence. If the group in control of the state is not forced to give up power, a revolution has not occurred. The merging of East and West Germany in 1990 is an example of when one state gave up power willingly to another. The East Germans gave up substantial power by unifying with West Germany, a process not typically viewed as a revolution. The "velvet divorce" of the Czech and Slovak Republics in 1993 similarly is not a revolution because the Czechs were not forced to give up their control over Slovakia but rather welcomed it.

Second, with the global spread in democratic governments, the definition requires a qualification that the change in leadership must be irregular, extraconstitutional, or noninstitutionalized. The toppling of state leaders and ruling parties is institutionalized in democracy. Rapid changes of power and control of the government within democracies are far from revolutions. Rather, they clearly illustrate democracy at work. Even highly irregular events such as an impeachment or the resignation of a president are part of the institutional process. For example, the resignation of US president Richard Nixon in 1974 did not constitute a revolution. In this case a head of state was forced from power (primarily by the threat of impeachment). The succession of the president was, however, institutionalized. Similarly, impeachment, votes of no-confidence, recall votes, and other means of removing an individual from office do not constitute revolutions because they take place within the institutionalized framework of the system; they are routine politics that do not alter the system.

Third, change in government must be supported by a substantial portion of the population. Support of a large political party, a distinct geographical section of the population, a large and powerful segment within the government (such as the military), or an economically defined segment of society (such as merchants, peasants, or farmers) could all be substantial segments of a population. The threshold of "substantial" is utilized to sort out those movements that are supported only by a few fringe elements of society or a few military generals. For example, a bloodless coup where one general replaces another as dictator does not necessarily constitute a revolution. This situation may be greeted with apathy by most of society and thus not meet the requirement that challengers be supported by a substantial portion of society. Further, support of the contenders must be more than a very small minority. For example, the East Timorese independence movement from 1974 until 2001 constituted a revolution only for East Timor rather than for the whole of Indonesia (just as if Chechnya were to secede from Russia, it would not constitute another Russian revolution). Indonesia occupied the half island, controlling all aspects of government. The secessionist movement was not aimed at the overthrow of the Indonesian state, however, but rather at a very small jurisdiction of that state. In contrast (and not coincidentally, at the same time), the popular demonstrations that led Suharto, then president/dictator of Indonesia for the preceding thirty years, to resign could be viewed as a revolution. The conflict in the latter case was for all of Indonesia, whereas in the former it was for half of a small island that had been a Portuguese colony.

A related, but not obvious, assumption of this forceful, popularly supported regime change is that the change in government must be domestically orchestrated. Invasions and occupations of a state do not qualify as revolutions even though they are forceful irregular seizures of the state. External actors often play a role in shaping a revolution; nevertheless it is primarily a domestic event. Thus, although the French alliance with the American colonies was crucial in supporting the war effort, the primary actors in creating the revolution were the colonists themselves. In contrast, the US actions of toppling the Taliban government in Afghanistan in 2001 or the Saddam Hussein regime in Iraq in 2003 are clearly not revolutions because they were externally imposed. Domestic actors such as the Pashtuns in Afghanistan and the Kurds in Iraq played a role in changing the state leadership, but they were not the primary contenders in these conflicts.

The clearest indication of a revolution is a change in who governs a country, both in terms of individuals and parties. A government is the leadership in charge of coordinating the various functions of the state, which Jeff Goodwin defines as "those core administrative, policing, and military organizations, more or less coordinated by an executive authority, that extract resources from and administer and rule (through violence if necessary) a territorially defined national society" (2001: 11). Thus, a government runs the state and provides for defense domestically and internationally, and it does this by extracting resources from society and monopolizing the legitimate threat and use of violence. The scope of its authority is limited to a politically defined geographic area with a population. The state is the sum of all these elements (government, geography, people, and institutions), whereas the government is the group who controls the state. This distinction is important because revolutionary actors compete with others to become the government and thus control the state. More than just the individuals in government must change, however; there needs to at least be an attempt at changing the system, or regime change. A regime is the larger framework of a government. Regimes are typically more enduring than governments, whereas states are more enduring than regimes. Regimes can be tied to governments, for example, the Franco regime in Spain or the Ba'athist regime in Iraq; but they do not need to be, as in the case of the democratic regime in the United States. A government is most often associated with a political party or party leader in democracies—the Tony Blair government in the UK or the Nicolas Sarkozy government in France. In this case, the government changes, but the regime continues. In patrimonial regimes, the regime and government are more likely to be the same; a change in one leads to a change in the other. Revolutions thus involve not just a change of the person or party in power but a wider change in the governing system.[2]

Because revolution is only one type of social event that occurs within a broad spectrum of change, it is useful to draw some distinctions among these other activities to highlight what constitutes a revolution. Routine politics is the starting point for any discussion on change. The assumption of routine politics is that conflicts can be resolved within existing institutions. An institution is an organization or activity that is self-perpetuating and valued for its own sake. Institutions incorporate a people's norms, rules, and values that give meaning to human activity. The method of resolving conflicts within a democratic republic is for elected representatives to debate an issue and come to some sort of compromise. In most modern democracies, this resolution depends on several institutions—a legislature, democracy, a free press, and political parties, just to name a few. In authoritarian systems, routine politics also involves the resolution of conflict within existing institutions, which may include the monarchy, a legislature, and political parties. The defining characteristic of routine politics is that it does not go beyond the boundaries of existing institutions or call for the destruction or radical change of those institutions.

Radical reforms go beyond routine politics in the scope and speed of their change. Some radical reforms may simply be the creation or destruction of an institution; for example, the government creates a new militia force or takes control of all media. Radical reforms can also be more encompassing and are similar to "revolution from above" (Trimberger 1978). These widespread changes are typically propagated by those in control of the government. For example, the shah of Iran (the ruling monarch), in an attempt to modernize his country, created a series of reforms to Westernize and restructure the Iranian economy in what is referred to as the White Revolution (though it was not a revolution). In 1963, he began with reforms that seized large parcels of land from aristocratic owners to redistribute to smaller farmers, nationalized pastures and forests to reduce nomadic herders, sold state-owned factories, allowed women to participate in politics, and established a literacy corps to run schools to reduce illiteracy. The key aspect that separates radical reforms from revolutions is that there is no challenge to control the state.

It is also important to note that although a reform can sometimes lead to revolutions (as the Iranian case suggests), at other times it may diffuse them. The British reforms of taxation and other legislation on the American colonies at various times encouraged reaction (as in the imposition of the Intolerable Acts) and at other times undermined rebellious action (as in the repeal of the various taxes and the Quartering Act in 1770). The intent of reform is typically to undermine opposition to a government. The idea is that a ruler allows public pressure to be dissipated by reforming something that the public does not like. Jack Goldstone argues that "successful reforms have several elements in common: they lead to meaningful (not just pro forma) involvement of different groups in political decisions; they strengthen the state sufficiently to meet pending challenges, usually by creating greater efficiency in revenue collection or state administration; and they do not raise the anger of prominent social groups or make enemies of them by imposing new burdens upon them" (1998: 416). Radical reforms typically go beyond this and are attempts by rulers to make changes that are not demanded by the public. Rather, they are changes intended to push beyond the existing system or radically restructure certain aspects of that system.

Rebellion or *revolt* (terms used interchangeably) typically refers to an unsuccessful version of revolution (*insurrection* is another synonymous term that has come into more popular use since the occupation of Iraq and

Afghanistan under US-led coalition forces in 2003). But it is more than just unsuccessful; as Mark Hagopian notes, it is an "angry, violent expression of the refusal of an individual or group to continue in its present condition" (1974: 11). Chalmers Johnson similarly defines rebellion as "the violent, spontaneous act of 'ordinary people' saying no! to conditions as they are" (1973: 8). It may be best viewed as the time when "the existing order of things no longer seems inevitable and change appears as a possibility" (Walton 1998: 414). This moment can then lead to a revolution, or if there is not a change in the government, it can dissipate. The reason that it is so often associated with the failure of revolution is that when a revolt leads to a revolution, the particular action becomes classified as one element of the larger movement. The Boston Tea Party of 1773, for example, is not viewed as a revolt because of later events that led to a revolution. It is subsumed as part of the beginnings of a revolution. In contrast, Shay's Rebellion of 1786, although it spurred significant changes (including the reconstruction of the conception of the federal government with a new constitution that eliminated the Articles of Confederation), did not lead to a revolution. As such, it is typically referred to as a rebellion or revolt. Because of this distinction, rebellions tend to be associated with less radical change (though the American example of Shay's Rebellion suggests that they can have a significant impact). They also tend to be associated with violence, though this is not necessarily the case.

A coup d'état, or coup, as it is often referred to, is the takeover of the government by a small group, usually from the military. Samuel Huntington outlines the distinguishing characteristics of a coup: "(a) it is the effort by a political coalition illegally to replace the existing governmental leaders by violence or the threat of violence; (b) the violence employed is usually small; (c) the number of people involved is usually small; (d) the participants already possess institutional bases of power within the political system" (1968: 218). Thus, there is a change in government that is unconstitutional and typically driven by violence. This is because coups are almost always orchestrated by the military or a faction within the military. This small group of military leaders typically seizes the power of government, and most of the institutions of the state fall in line. Cooperation with the coup leaders is often because the elites of the other institutions agree with the reason for the coup or because they fear repression if they do not cooperate. Because coups are typically driven by military leaders, they often justify the coup as part of their mission to defend the country. Typically they point to corruption or inefficiencies in the government as the rationale for their seizing power.

At its root, a civil war is a type of war in which the primary combatants are both from the same country. Conventional war is typically conceived as two countries' militaries fighting each other. The key distinction between war and civil war, then, is that rather than two countries fighting, it is two or more parties in one country fighting. Civil wars usually have the central government as one of the warring parties. The exception to this general rule is in states where there is no strong central government, such as in failed states. In contrast to coups, civil wars usually require more popular participation. Although the military may support a coup, they usually are not involved in fighting for the coup. If this were the case, it would be more likely that it is a civil war. This points to the last typical characteristic of civil wars: they usually have a certain threshold of organized violence. They are violent events, with the minimum casualties typically set at 1,000 battle deaths per year. These are people directly killed in fighting, and the figure does not include those who died because of starvation, malnutrition, disease, or other common corollaries of wars. Further, the violence must be organized, meaning that military structures of some kind engage in most of the fighting. This distinguishes between rioting and other types of violent demonstrations. Figure 1.2 shows the number of civil wars since the end of World War II.

Because *civil war* is a broad term used to capture a type of fighting, there are many variations of civil war. Typically the assumption of civil

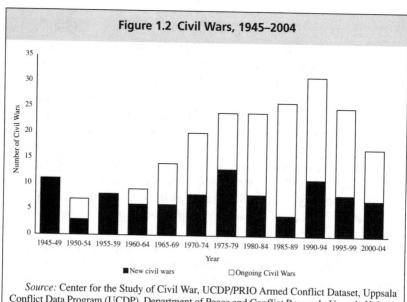

Figure 1.2 Civil Wars, 1945–2004

Source: Center for the Study of Civil War, UCDP/PRIO Armed Conflict Dataset, Uppsala Conflict Data Program (UCDP), Department of Peace and Conflict Research, Uppsala University and Centre for the Study of Civil War at the International Peace Research Institute (PRIO), Oslo, 2006, http://www.prio.no.

wars is that larger armies are fighting, as was the case in the US (1861–1865) and Chinese (1927–1949) civil wars. Civil wars can also occur, however, when the primary tactic is not conventional armies but guerrilla troops fighting a war of attrition, usually referred to as a guerrilla war. This involves the tactics of avoiding direct conflict with the opponent's military because they are much stronger and more likely to kill you (see Chapter 7). The fighting may be very drawn out, as in Chad, Colombia, and Myanmar, where civil wars have lasted for decades, or they may be relatively concise, as in the conflict in South Yemen in the first few months of 1986. They may be localized to one area, as in the Ugandan war against the Lord's Resistance Army in northern Uganda from 1987 to the present (though peace talks are currently under way), or may engulf the entire country, as in Bosnia (1992–1995). Ethnic wars are typically civil wars in which the defining characteristic of those fighting is drawn in ethnic or racial terms. These types of war may spill into genocide, the intention to systematically destroy a group of ethnically, religiously, or culturally distinct people, as was the case in Rwanda in 1995. Revolutionary wars are another type of civil war, where the fighting is aimed at creating a revolution. Civil wars may also be utterly devoid of any ideological motivations. The civil wars in Chechnya and Colombia (in the 1990s) both combined a secessionist or revolutionary movement with criminal activity that eventually swamped the movement and drained all the ideological content. These are all types of civil wars that share the defining characteristics of domestic combatants, with a large following where there is organized violence at a significant level.

As Nicholas Sambanis points out, "states avoid using the term [civil war] to play down the level of opposition to them. Thus, for example, the Kenyan '*shifta*' war of the 1960's against secessionist Somalis in the Northern Frontier District may have technically been a small civil war, but in the historiography of the country and in the minds of many Kenyans, it was just banditry ('*shifta*' means bandit) or a border conflict with Somalia" (2006). This caution is useful when analyzing any of the definitions given above. Coups, rebellions, civil wars, and revolutions all depend on someone labeling them after the fact. That someone is always the dominant power; as Winston Churchill noted, "history is written by the victors."

The discussion of these other types of social movements allows us to define revolutions in relation to these events. The definition of revolution I am using distinguishes one type of social movement from the others, though there is significant overlap in reality. Revolutions differ from routine politics in the level of change as well as the fact that they involve the change in government through nonroutinized forcible means. Unlike radical reforms that are pushed by a government, revolutions require an irregular change in the government. Revolutions differ from coups primarily in the extent of popular support and the scope of change advocated. As noted above, the distinction between rebellion and revolution is primarily that rebellions and revolts are not successful. Civil wars are distinguished by their level of organized violence, whereas revolutions have no such stipulation, as the many anticommunist nonviolent struggles in the 1990s showed. Historical cases are often difficult to classify; at one point an event begins with a coup, then later becomes a revolution that degenerates into a civil war. The purpose of defining revolutions is to highlight the tendencies that characterize what we refer to as revolutions.

Having defined revolution, I move now into a discussion of some types of revolutions in history.

Types of Revolutions

> *A reform is a correction of abuses; a revolution is a transfer of power.*
> —Edward Bulwer-Lytton

Just as there is a wide spectrum of activities within social movements, so there are many types of revolutions. Scholars, to further isolate what they hope to study, have defined revolutions as political, social, democratic, peasant, periphery, or several other types. The definitions of these suggest a particular type of revolutionary change or the key actors involved. Mirroring Figure 1.1, the types of revolutions can be arranged according to their intensity and the scope and speed of their change, as shown in Figure 1.3.

Political revolutions are what I have defined as revolution: a forcible, irregular, popularly supported change in the governing regime. They provide the widest latitude in incorporating revolutionary events without being so broad that they are synonymous with social movements. In contrast, social revolutions are broader in their impact. They are "rapid, basic transformations of a society's state and class structure; they are accompanied and in part carried through by class based revolts from below" (Skocpol 1979: 4). Samuel Huntington goes even further when he defines social revolutions as "a rapid fundamental and violent domestic change in the dominant values and myths of a society, in its political institutions, social structure, leadership, government activity, and policies" (1968: 264). As Jeff Goodwin notes, "What counts as 'rapid and fundamental' change, however, is a matter of degree, and the line between it and slower and less basic change can be difficult to draw in practice" (2001: 9).

Revolutions typically involve the most extreme tendencies of any type of social movement and social revolutions the most extreme tendencies of

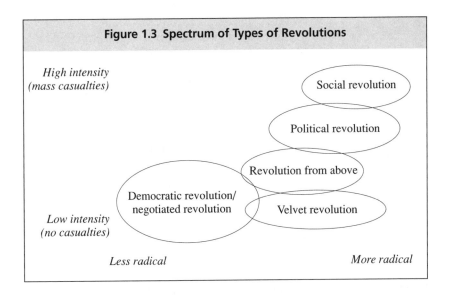

Figure 1.3 Spectrum of Types of Revolutions

revolutions. For this reason, they help to clarify much of what we are interested in understanding in revolution. If we want to understand the significance of revolutionary change, there is no better place to look than social revolutions. Social revolutions also have the drawback of being very rare, however. Figure 1.4 lists the major social revolutions over the past 200 years. What is striking is that there are relatively few social revolutions in history, and all but one were in the twentieth century. Although the list begins after the American Revolution, most scholars who analyze social revolutions do not include it as a possible case. They argue that the more significant economic, social, and even political restructuring required to be a social revolution did not occur in the United States until after the Civil War.

A revolution from above, another type shown in Figure 1.3, is an elite-directed transition from agrarian to industrial society that is guided by a relatively autonomous bureaucratic apparatus. This bureaucratic group usually originates from an increasingly nationalistic revolutionary leadership within the military. These revolutions involve modernizing the economic and to a certain extent the social and political structures of what are perceived as backward countries (by the modernizing elites). Ellen Trimberger argues that this type of revolution is only likely when four parameters are met (1978). First, the bureaucrats must be independent of the dominant economic class; that is, they cannot be beholden to conservative elements, and second, they must also be relatively cohesive politically. Third, they are spurred to action because they foresee a threat to their own interests, usually in the form of

Figure 1.4 Major Social Revolutions, 1789–1989			
France	1789	Ethiopia	1975
Mexico	1910	Angola	1975
Russia	1917	Mozambique	1975
Yugoslavia	1945	Cambodia	1975
Vietnam	1945	South Vietnam	1975
China	1949	Iran	1979
Bolivia	1952	Nicaragua	1979
Cuba	1959	Grenada	1979
Algeria	1962	Eastern Europe	1989

foreign countries' taking greater control of their resources, which leads to a more nationalistic sentiment. Finally, the international situation must be conducive to allowing military leaders to take power in a nationalist movement; if a country is too dependent upon an unapproving foreign power, this type of movement is very unlikely. There is debate about whether or not the crumbling of communist rule in Eastern Europe and the former Soviet Union constitutes a revolution or whether this type of revolution from above is as much a reform as it is a revolution—what Timothy Garton Ash calls "refolution" (1999). Refolution, he argues, originates in top-down elite reforms of a bankrupt system and takes place without the violent struggles common to past revolutions; as seen in the collapse of communism.

On the lower end of both the intensity spectrum and the scope of change in Figure 1.3 are democratic and negotiated revolutions. These are admittedly relatively newer phenomenon and as such have not been as thoroughly addressed in the scholarly literature. Democratic revolutions are "spontaneous popular uprisings—peaceful, urban-based, and cross-class in composition—which topple unyielding dictators to begin a transition process which leads to the consolidation of democracy" (Thompson 2004: 1). The outcome of the revolution—the transition from authoritarian to democratic regimes—is the key defining characteristic of this type of revolution. In contrast, a negotiated revolution, the most recent form of revolution, is one in which the toppling of the government is more likely to take place when opposition leaders engage the government in a process that yields revolutionary change than when armies of peasants storm the capital. The term *negotiated revolution* first was used for the transition in South Africa, then later applied to Hungary and generalized to this broader type by George Lawson (2005). Both democratic and negotiated revolutions are what Lawson calls "catching up revolutions" in that they seek "to join the prevailing international order . . . [they] seek liberation rather than utopia" (2005: 76). Unlike most social revolutions, they are not interested in creating a "new" social order, and they have no radical ideology; rather, they aim to implement the dominant international ideology: liberal (capitalist) democracy.

Throughout history, most revolutions have been violent or followed by civil wars. More recently, there have been a number of revolutions that were neither born of, nor led to, violent confrontations—as most visibly illustrated in the fall of communism in Eastern Europe and the Soviet Union. Velvet revolutions, the final type shown in Figure 1.3, are situations in which nonviolence is the dominant means of creating a revolution. The term *Velvet Revolution* was originally used just for the Czechoslovak revolution but came to include all of the nonviolent Eastern European revolutions. In my own study of this topic, I expanded it further to apply to all nonviolent revolutions (Van Inwegen 2006). The origins of the phrase come from dissident groups in Czechoslovakia who used music as a form of protest, meeting to play and hear banned rock music. This included the experimental music of the US rock group, the Velvet Underground, whose name reflected the spirit of the underground cultural scene (though it was not connected to Czechoslovakia). The velvet terminology was first applied to the goals of underground activists who sought change and eventually led to the revolution (Keane 2000: 351). Other terms have been used to denote similar processes, such as the Orange Revolution of Ukraine in 2004, the Carnation Revolution of Portugal in 1974, and the Rose Revolution of Georgia in 2003, though there is debate about whether or not some of these should be considered revolutions.

This typology is not meant to be exhaustive or entirely inclusive. Different scholars, for different reasons, have come up with typologies that have included other types of social movements. For example, Chalmers Johnson (1973) identifies the following types of revolution: jacquerie (reactionary), millenerian (aimed at creating heaven on earth), anarchist, Jacobin communist (nationalist), coup d'etat, and mass militarized insurrection (nationalist). Most of these overlap with the types I have described above, but they have not been used by other scholars. The common element of all these types of revolutions is that they result in attempts at rapid change of the government; the differences indicate the variety of revolutions in history.

Overview of the Book

He who serves a revolution plows in the sea. —Simon Bolívar

The reason for writing this book is to pull together as much of the relevant work on revolutions from a variety of disciplines as possible. This draws on sociology, history, economics, and political science. In each of these disciplines, there are further subdisciplines that have contributed to our understanding of revolutions. What all of these studies share in common is the assumption that we can know meaningful things about revolutions and that this knowledge can be cumulative. For example, a biography of John Adams can be used in a study on elite interactions in the American colonies, which may in turn be used as part of an economic analysis of the triangular trade system, which could be used for part of an investigation into the structural causes of the American Revolution. Each of these is a fundamental building block not only to our understanding of that particular event but also to the larger objective of understanding revolution. Because of the nature of social sciences, this does not mean that once a study is published on an issue, it has been resolved and there is consensus. Rather, some issues are hotly debated and often reflect larger intellectual debates that span the disciplines. For example, the relative importance of individuals versus structural elements is very contentious. Are revolutions the product of visionary leaders, or are they a function of the economic and historical context? This book will focus on areas of consensus, highlight the sides of debates, and chart the evolution of key debates in the literature to answer persistent questions about revolutions.

Having defined revolution and answered why we study it, the remainder of the book will discuss answers to key questions to help us better understand revolution. The earliest studies of revolutions were largely descriptive, drawing out similarities of the flow of revolutions. This tradition has continued and will be used in Chapter 2 to answer the question: How do revolutions happen? Answering this involves summarizing the variety of steps and stages that most revolutions go through. In the simplest version, there is a revolutionary situation in which the preconditions exist that make revolution likely. Some sort of catalytic event spurs mobilization of people against the government, and that leads to a clash between revolutionaries and the government. If the government wins, the revolution fails. If the revolutionaries seize power, there is a period of resolution when various groups vie to consolidate power and implement change.

Chapter 3 addresses one of the most fundamental and rigorously answered questions: What are the causes of revolution? A consensus has begun to emerge out of a contentious debate that there are structural preconditions that make revolution very likely, though not inevitable. The key structural factor appears to be the nature of the state, or more specifically the type of regime and its relationship with society. When a weak, patrimonial, repressive regime is in power, revolution is much more likely. There are also structural arguments that focus on class explanations as well as analyses that point to the international system, however. These analyses argue that revolution is more likely when countries modernize, when changes in the international balance of power open up opportunities, or when new ideas, money, and technology are introduced to the country.

Chapter 4 focuses on the role of ideologies in justifying revolutions by answering the question: What is the purpose of revolution? In short, the most common answers to this question have included: to create a government of the people that protects their inherent freedoms (liberalism), to create a state for our own people (nationalism), to create a classless society that will end exploitation (Marxism), and to create a state that conforms to the will of God (religious ideologies). In addition to developing the ideologies behind each of these answers, I will also summarize the work on the role of ideologies in revolution in Chapter 4. The scope of these ideologies is immense, and so the first two will be addressed in Chapter 4, and the latter two are covered in Chapter 5. To do this we will look at the development of the ideology as well as how revolutionaries have utilized and often significantly altered an ideology to fit their historical context. We will investigate the varieties of liberal ideologies used against colonial domination, communist rule, and dictators; nationalist ideologies in India and China; the adaptations of Karl Marx by Vladimir Lenin, Mao Zedong, and Fidel Castro/ Che Guevara; and the varieties of Islamic fundamentalism in the world today.

Chapter 6 addresses the question: Who leads revolutions? A wide variety of types of individuals participate in or support revolutions, but revolutionary leadership often comes from certain types or classes of people. This chapter investigates a spectrum of people, focusing on their revolutionary potential and the role they typically play. These groups include intellectuals, students, workers, peasants, ethnic groups, political parties, clergy, and capitalists.

To complete the analyses in the earlier chapters, which cover ideologies, structural contexts, and leaders, Chapter 7 answers two questions: Why do people participate in revolution? How do they participate in revolution? A variety of psychological and social psychological explanations for why people participate in revolutions are explored in the chapter. Within this basic flow of revolution, there is a spectrum of strategies that push the revolution forward. This spectrum ranges from nonviolent actions such as protests and noncooperation toward more violent actions such as guerrilla raids to full-scale civil wars. This, in short, is how people participate in revolution.

Chapter 8 deals with the aftermath of revolutions, answering the question: What is the result of revolution? As Chapter 2 shows, after the clash between revolutionaries and the government when the government is overthrown, there is necessarily a consolidation phase. This chapter looks at the types of consolidation and counterrevolutionary movements that have occurred as well as evaluates the tangible effects of revolution. Studies have shown that the ideologies espoused in the beginnings of revolutions are rarely implemented, casualty rates increase, there are significant effects on wealth, health, and social relations, and postrevolutionary states are much more likely to engage others in war.

Chapter 9 is a brief summary and discussion on the areas of consensus and continued debate in the revolution literature. Although there is relative consensus on the importance of structural factors, there continue to be debates about what constitutes revolution, the relative importance of structures versus agents, and the likelihood of revolutions in the future. There is agreement about the explanatory power of many of the theories developed in the literature but much less faith in the predictive power of these theories.

Each chapter ends with discussion questions related to the chapter, many of which encourage application to the case studies in the Appendix. The Appendix includes short overviews of some of the classic revolutions that have shaped the world's history as well as some more contemporary events. The reason for including these is to give a concise account of the key events and people so that readers can draw out further relationships to the concepts. Most scholarly work on revolutions assumes that the reader knows the basic outline of the revolution under discussion or that the reader can piece together the relevant facts as they emerge in the analysis. Although I agree that students are capable of this task, this book seeks to provide that information concisely. I have also attempted to balance between the great historical revolutions and more contemporary revolutions or revolutionary movements. In addition, the appendix includes a chronology of key events in the revolutions, the key individuals involved in the revolution, and some recommendations for further reading on that case.

Questions for Discussion and Reflection

1. How does the American Revolution fit the criteria of a social movement?
2. What is the relationship between radical reforms, rebellions, or revolts and coups d'état? Is it possible for a radical reform to discourage a rebellion but encourage a coup d'état, or vice versa?

3. What are the most important distinctions among rebellions, coups d'état, and civil wars? In what ways are they similar?

4. Once a successful revolution replaces an unpopular governing structure with one that is more widely accepted, what are the principal challenges that a revolutionary government might face?

5. Is a social/peasant revolution a more effective means of bringing about revolutionary change than a velvet/democratic revolution? Why or why not?

6. To what extent does the East Timorese battle for independence fit the definition of a revolution? Should it be considered a revolution? If so, what type of revolution (i.e., social, political, democratic, etc.)?

7. How did the actions of the Indonesian government help or hurt its ability to undermine a revolutionary or independence movement in East Timor? What comparisons can be made between the East Timorese fight for independence and the American Revolution?

Notes

1. As George Lawson notes: "Revolution is a constant feature of world history: a study of its etymology would have to include the Greek concepts of *epanastasis* (revolt) and *neoterismos* (innovation), the Arabic terms *inqilab* (to rotate) and *thaura* (to revolt), the notions of *mered* (rebellion), *kom* (uprising), *marah* (revolt) and *kesher* (plot) in classical Hebrew, and the Chinese word *ge-ming* (change of life, fate or destiny). Over the last two hundred years deriving in part from the work of Montesquieu, Voltaire and Rousseau, the concept of revolution has become more circumscribed, assuming a narrow meaning as a radical break from past arrangements. In this way, the English Civil War of the 1640s was reinterpreted as a revolution during the eighteenth-century, as was the Revolt of Netherlands and, later on, the American War of Independence. After the French Revolution, the concept took on a kind of transcendental, metahistorical tilt that universalized, naturalized and ultimately, mythologized, the revolutionary experience. Rationality, progress and liberty became inexorably tied to the concept of revolution alongside the idea of total, inevitable change" (2005: 52).

2. A caveat about control of the state is warranted: the change in government must be for a significant period of time. The seizure of the reins of power for a week only to be turned over to another group does not constitute a revolution. Tilly argues that a month of control is the bare minimum to consider an event as a transfer of power. Rapid changes in power either mean that a revolution is continuing to unfold or that a country is sliding into the category of a failed state.

2

The "Life Course" of a Revolution

Revolutions never go backward. —Wendell Phillips

Some of the earliest work on revolutions was aimed at comparing the processes of revolutions. Jack Goldstone, in his extensive review of the revolution literature, argued that there have been three generations of scholarship on revolutions. The earliest works were focused on the process of revolution, what Goldstone calls "the pattern of events found in revolutions" (1980). These tended to be historical accounts of the process of revolution as it unfolded. The second generation responded to this event-orientation by attempting to generate more general theories or explanations for why revolutions happen, from psychological and structural backgrounds. The third generation sought to develop this attempt at theory making by bringing in even more disciplinary depth. These generations of scholarship that Goldstone describes are the contours of an evolving debate in the revolution literature that focuses on how revolutions should be studied. Should research be focused on patterns and processes or structures? I will begin this chapter by reviewing the contours of this debate before turning to the question for this chapter: *How* do revolutions happen? The phrasing of this question leads toward the process side of the debate. Revolutions typically have a regular pattern or flow that can be charted and about which generalizations can be made that help us understand this complex phenomenon. This will set up the question for the next chapter: *Why* do revolutions happen? That will naturally lead to the structural causes of revolution.

The Agent-Structure Debate

Do not applaud me. It is not I who speaks to you, but history which speaks through my mouth. —Fustel de Coulanges

21

In trying to answer the question of how revolution happens, there are two typical responses. One is that people made a revolution happen (the "Great Man" idea of history, where influential individuals shape history through the force of their ideas and actions). The other is that the revolution was inevitable, given the existing realities. The second line of thinking has found much more support in the vast revolution literature, though it is never stated so boldly (social scientists rarely speak of inevitability). In common parlance, the French Revolution, for example, was bound to happen for a number of reasons: the state was too centered on an individual, the changing economic makeup of the country was shifting from agrarian-based to urban-based wealth, the new ideas of the Enlightenment emerged, and a number of fiscal and military crises weakened the state. In this context, revolution was very likely, regardless of who was the king, who lead the Parisians, and who inhabited the countryside. This, in social science parlance, is a structural explanation.

The debate over whether people or structures are more important in shaping history, or revolutions in particular, has more supporters of the structural argument, but the "agent-structure debate" continues (Wendt 1987; Berejikian 1992; Pagnucco 1993). An agent is someone who exercises some decisionmaking authority within a given context. In basic terms, an agent is a person who does something. The fulcrum of the debate is whether agents (individuals, groups, or other freethinking collectives) or structures (static factors that constrain agents, such as economics, domestic political systems, or the arrangement of international power) play a greater role in determining the outcome of events. Most political scientists agree that both agents and structures are important, but because of various limitations, they tend to focus on one or the other (Wendt 1987). This wider debate in the social science literature can be narrowed for the context of revolutions. Few argue that an individual made a revolution happen, but many have focused on the process of revolutions that is fueled by the actions of individuals. Thus, in this chapter, I will frame the debate in terms of processes (influenced by individuals) versus structures. Processes "have to do with the active choices and efforts of movement actors as well as of their opponents and other players in the conflict" (Goodwin and Jasper 1999: 29). The distinction between process and structure is best highlighted in Keohane and Nye's poker game analogy: "at the process level analysts are interested in how the players play the hands they have been dealt. At the structural level they are interested in how the cards and chips were distributed as the game started" (2001: 18).

In contrast, structures are factors that are "relatively stable over time and outside the control" of individuals (Goodwin and Jasper 1999: 29).

Thinking in terms of an architectural structure may be helpful. A structure, like a building, wall, or dam, is fixed; it cannot move. This does not mean that it is entirely permanent; all of these can be torn down, but this is a difficult process. If we continue with the idea of a building, we can imagine people living in a building. The structure does not make the inhabitants do anything, but it does confine what they can and cannot do. We cannot walk through walls, so to enter or exit a room, we would have to go through a door or window. In this sense, the structure has constrained our actions. We are not free to go where we please. To move to the context of revolutions, we are obviously less concerned with physical structures such as buildings, but the analogy is appropriate in terms of the constraints that social (political and economic) structures impose on the way people behave. The relevant social structures are not just customs or political ideas that a society has constructed (such as a constitution) but also the larger context. For example, Karl Marx argued that the proletariat, wage-earning, urban factory workers were the revolutionary class (2003). This did not provide for much support for Mao Zedong as he sought to create a communist revolution; there simply were not a lot of urban factory workers in China, compared to the vast peasantry. This is a structural reality; the economic structure of China during the first half of the twentieth century was primarily a peasant-based economy. That fact shaped Mao's reworking of Marxism to make the peasants the revolutionary class (a structural explanation). To better understand the likelihood of the Chinese, or any other, revolution, we need to first understand the normal process of revolutions.

Revolutionary Situations

Revolutions are not about trifles, but spring from trifles. —Aristotle

Charles Tilly's analysis of the process of revolutions breaks them down into three basic parts. Like a good story, there is an introduction that sets the stage for conflict (revolutionary situation), a crisis that causes the old regime to collapse, and then some resolution (consolidation of power by an opposition group). The introduction is what Tilly calls a revolutionary situation and is characterized by the convergence of three elements: (1) the appearance of contenders, or coalitions of contenders, advancing exclusive competing claims to control the state, or some segment of it; (2) the commitment to those claims by a significant segment of the citizenry; and (3) the incapacity or unwillingness of rulers to suppress the alternative coalition and/or commitment to its claims (1995: 10). The process of opposition formation, mobilization, and governmental incapacity is highly interwoven, but we will look at each element individually to highlight these elements of revolutionary situations.

For Goldstone, a revolutionary situation begins with intellectual dissent. This occurs when journalists, poets, playwrights, teachers, clergy, lawyers, technocrats, or others express discontent with the ruling regime. The role of these leaders is the topic of Chapter 6; here we focus on their abstract role in providing organizational leadership. This signals pervasive dissatisfaction with regime performance that undermines its legitimacy. Organization is required for individuals to come together to challenge the state. As Tilly points out, however, the concept of group is very inclusive (1978). To get a clearer understanding of what a group is, Harrison White distinguishes between categories and networks of people. Categories of people "share some characteristic: 'they are all female, all Sunni Muslims, all residents of Timbuktu, or something else'" (quoted in Tilly 1978: 62). In contrast, networks of people "are linked to each other, directly or indirectly, by a specific kind of interpersonal bond": attendants at a wedding, work or school colleagues, or people one talks to on a regular basis (White quoted in Tilly 1978: 62). A group, Tilly argues, is the combination of a category of people with a network of people: female Sunni Muslims to whom one talks on a regular basis, for example. "The idea of organization follows directly. The more extensive its common identity and internal networks, the more organized the group" (1978: 63). This is important to revolutions, as the level of organization of opposition groups can determine its effectiveness in mobilizing opposition.

The second element of a revolutionary situation is the attraction of support by a significant segment of society; people must be mobilized in opposition to the government. Tilly defines mobilization as "the process by which a group goes from being a passive collection of individuals to an active participant in public life" (1968: 69). There are two basic ways of mobilizing groups: *defensive* or *offensive*. In defensive mobilization, "a threat from outside induces the members of a group to pool their resources to fight off the enemy" (1968: 73). Peasants have historically been focused on this type of mobilization. Almost all peasant collective action is a localized effort to protect their access to land. They mobilize when that is challenged by the government or larger landowners. In contrast, offensive mobilization involves pooling resources in response to opportunities to gain new interests (1968: 74). In general, offensive mobilization is usually a top-down approach whereas defensive mobilization is grassroots driven. This is because of the resources of elites compared to those of the masses. As Tilly argues, "the rich are constantly mobilizing to take advantage of new opportunities to maximize their interests. The poor can rarely afford to. The poor and powerless tend to begin defensively, the rich and powerful offensively" (1968: 75). The type of mobilization is thus shaped by those who lead.

Mobilization is also shaped by those who participate. Tilly argues that opposition groups can be distinguished by their interests, organization, and control over resources. Interests are similar to goals; they are the reason that people come together in a group and are shaped by the ideology adopted by the group (see Chapters 4 and 5). Interests are important in that they will define how one group relates to another. The goal of much of the democratic opposition to Ferdinand Marcos's rule in the Philippines was to create a stable democracy with free and fair elections. In contrast, there were others in the Philippines, most notably the New Peoples' Army (NPA; a communist guerrilla group) and the Moro National Liberation Front (MNLF; a separatist Islamic group), who had very different interests. The goal of the NPA was to overthrow the regime, utilizing guerrilla tactics, and to create a Marxist regime. The goal of the MNLF was to declare independence of the island of Mindanao so that the majority Muslim island could retain its distinction from the rest of the archipelago. The reason interests are important in determining the likelihood of collective action is the tendency for groups with shared interests to work together to achieve those interests. Thus, the extent of a group's shared interests with others will shape interactions with those other groups. In the case of the Philippines, because of the Marxist orientation, the NPA was never able to gain much support from business elites, the military, or the church (all major segments of Philippine society). There was similarly little chance of cooperation among the MNLF and other opposition groups in the Philippines because of the MNLF's unique goals.

The second internal factor is the intensity of a group's organization. This is the extent of common identity and unifying structure among its members. The more intense that organization, the greater the chance of collective action. Finally, the resources that a group has control over determine its ability to effectively challenge other groups. The Catholic Church in the Philippines had extensive resources for mobilization, including its own radio station, newspapers, daily masses at churches, schools, hospitals, and a hierarchy to coordinate the administration of all of these. Contrast this with the resources of Fidel Castro's M-26 movement after it was decimated when it landed in Cuba. It had fifteen to twenty men with few weapons begging for shelter among the peasants in the mountains.

For revolutions to be successful, mobilization typically goes beyond one group or segment of society. Many scholars have argued instead that revolutions only happen when broad coalitions of groups form in opposition to the government. Misagh Parsa, in explaining the outcomes of revolutions, describes how coalition formation occurs (2000). He argues that coalition formation is first shaped by the fundamental nature of the state: the more exclusive the state, the more likely a broad coalition will form with more radical ideas. The radicalization, as discussed in Chapter 3, is caused by the exclusive nature of the state. If a state has a very narrow base of power, say the military and a foreign superpower ally, everyone else in the society is excluded from power. Moderates within the society will find that they cannot achieve even compromised goals and thus are pushed to increasingly radical positions. Even though a group's initial preference would be for moderate reforms, when the exclusive nature of the state ensures that those reforms never occur, the group may increasingly advocate more radical changes.

Second, coalitions are shaped by timing. Crisis situations encourage groups to downplay their differences to come together. A natural disaster, a political misstep, or a foreign invasion all can create this kind of crisis situation. The calling of the presidential election in the Philippines was a good example of this. Because there were only two months of campaigning, and even less time to meet the filing deadline, opposition groups had a stronger incentive to put aside their differences for a very short time to work collectively.

The Philippine Revolution, although demonstrating how crisis situations can help build short-term coalitions, also shows the limits to coalition building that can exist. Because the communist insurgency was gaining strength in the Philippines, the NPA had little incentive to moderate its message to attract support—its radical message and tactics (guerrilla warfare) were successful in doing so. This is one of the reasons why the United States pressured Marcos to hold elections. This also indicates an important phenomenon in coalition formation. Coalitions are more likely to form when ideologically driven challengers are relatively weak. In contrast, the Sandinista National Liberation Front (Frente Sandinista de Liberacion Nacional; FSLN) in Nicaragua was not very successful at challenging the government until it moderated its message and attracted support of the Catholic Church and even prominent business leaders. These groups would not have joined with the Sandinistas had they continued the standard radical Marxist rhetoric of eliminating private property and all forms of institutionalized religion. In the Philippines, the NPA continued to promote that message. As a result, there was never a coalition between the Far Left and democratic moderates to oppose Marcos.

This view of coalitions also helps to explain why there was not a revolution when Benigno Aquino was assassinated, despite the widespread frustration with Marcos. When Aquino was assassinated, because of the rise in power and popularity of the NPA, moderates within the Philippines were forced to choose between supporting a communist guerrilla insurgency with a radical ideology that they opposed or continuing to push for reform within a repressive regime. The moderates knew what to expect from Marcos but not necessarily from the NPA. When Marcos called the presidential elections in November 1985, the decision was then shifted from choosing between the NPA and Marcos to choosing between a democratic opposition and Marcos. The NPA, because of its radical ideology, did not participate in the election (and even encouraged people to boycott the election, though they were unsuccessful in this endeavor). As a result, the changing structure of how coalitions would likely form dictated the likelihood of revolutionary coalitions forming.

Third, broader coalitions are more likely when class conflict is limited (Parsa 2000: 240). When the masses target the wealthy, a coalition between the two is unlikely. Parsa argues that this helps to explain why the role of the state is so important. If the state is very involved in the economy (i.e., it owns a lot of banks, factories, or natural resources), then the state can become the target of the masses when the economy sours. This makes a coalition between upper, middle, and lower classes more likely, because no one class threatens the other's existence. In this case, there is less to fear from a potential coalition partner than from the government. When the state does not dominate the economy, however, class conflict is more likely and thus coalitions less likely.

The bridge between the second and third elements of revolutionary situations is the concept of opportunity. Opportunities allow for increased mobilization, and the government's response to mobilization provides for new opportunities for further mobilization. In this context, an opportunity is anything that encourages a change in perception that groups can utilize to mobilize against the government. This definition is intentionally vague because the opportunities that have arisen in revolutions are almost as numerous as the revolutions themselves. For example, the assassination of Aquino provided an opportunity for revolutionaries to mobilize people against the Marcos regime, as did his declaration of martial law, US pressure to hold elections, Marcos's calling of the presidential elections, the National Assembly's declaring him victor in a clearly fraudulent election, Aquino's call for noncooperation, the failed coup attempt, and so on. Each of these events provided an opportunity for groups to mobilize people.

In general, opportunities are created when the government is weakened or opposition groups are strengthened. The government can be weakened by a variety of external shocks: foreign wars (France 1789, Russia 1917), change in relationship with allies (Nicaragua and Iran 1979), or even revolutions in other countries (Eastern Europe 1989). Economic changes are often due to global markets. The price of grains in the global market in 2008 skyrocketed, meaning that many poor people had to devote any growth in their income to feeding their families. This led to food riots in Mexico and other countries, which encouraged revolutionary situations. Modernization theorists argue similarly that the expansion of the capitalist economic system to former colonial and underdeveloped regions of the world in large part explains their revolutionary potential. Even the Olympics have been cited as a possible catalyst to revolutionary situations. The revolution in South Korea in 1987 has been attributed to international attention that provided an opportunity for prodemocracy leaders to provoke the government. There was speculation that the 2008 Olympics in China might also prove fatal to the communist regime. The protests in Tibet in the months prior to the Olympics were an example of opposition groups taking advantage of the international media that the Olympics brought to China. Again, all of these opportunities arose outside of the state, but all of them weakened the government, encouraging revolutionary mobilization.

A government can also be weakened by domestic shocks. The most common are bad policies or reactions to opposition groups. For example, during the shah's White Revolution in Iran, one of the reforms that angered much of the population was changing the calendar from the traditional Islamic calendar to one where the year one began with the founding of the Persian dynasty. For a Muslim country, this lowered the public's perception of the shah and encouraged support for religious clerics. Sometimes the domestic shock is natural—an earthquake or the spread of a disease, for example. The natural phenomenon typically does not weaken the government (in the short term, it often actually strengthens the government's power, as people will "rally around the flag" in times of national disasters). The government's response, however, often does weaken the government. The earthquake that struck Managua, the capital of Nicaragua, in 1972 is a good example of this. The earthquake killed some 5,000 people and left more than half of the city's 400,000 residents homeless. In response, international aid was quickly offered and accepted by the Anastasio Somoza regime. Somoza used much of the money, however, to build houses for those loyal to him, or he embezzled the money outright. The tragedy of the earthquake quickly turned into a symbol of Somoza's corruption.

Another variety of opportunities that can arise is one that strengthens opposition groups. A particularly charismatic individual can make a group much more appealing. Leaders in the struggling young Nazi party in Germany recognized the oratorical skills of a German officer sent to investigate their activities and brought Adolf Hitler into their debates. His skills helped garner much more attention and popular support for the party. The adoption and promotion of a new idea or technology can also strengthen an opposition group. The use of the Internet by the Zapatistas in the southern Mexican state of Chiapas in the mid-1990s is an example of this. The group was able to spread its message and appeal for international attention to the plight of peasants being repressed by the Mexican military. Examples of revolutionary success in other countries can strengthen opposition groups. The success of the democratic opposition party Solidarity in Poland encouraged people in other Eastern European countries to support existing groups such as Charter 77. Support from foreign sources to opposition groups can also strengthen them. Arms supplied to the mujahidin in Afghanistan during the Soviet occupation helped them force a Soviet withdrawal in 1989. Chinese support for North Vietnam similarly helped to force French and then US withdrawal from South Vietnam in 1954 and 1973, respectively.

Opposition groups can also create opportunities. Most revolutionaries are not content to wait for an opportunity that weakens the state but rather will actively try to weaken it. Strikes, boycotts, protests, hostage takings, bombings, assassinations, demonstrations, and many other activities directed by opposition groups are intended to weaken the government. As Parsa argues, these actions weaken the government because they force the government to respond (2000). The old regime must respond and attempt to implement changes to stave off revolution. These reforms generally further undermine the regime. Typical reforms include liberalizing restrictions on the media, extending suffrage to new groups in society, or encouraging economic development. These backfire because they usually either provide for easier mobilization against the regime or because they create more dissatisfaction with the regime. If they respond with repression, it often serves to demonstrate the brutal nature of the regime. Either way, the government is weakened because it appears less legitimate; it has created "opportunities" for protest (Goodwin 2001; Parsa 2000). The shah's rule in Iran nicely illustrates this. In the summer of 1978, the shah introduced a series of reforms and liberalizations to try to reduce the number of protests. Rather than decreasing criticism of his repressive regime, it actually allowed the criticism to have a wider audience. "The proclamations then led to the expansion of the mobilization by the industrial working class and the population of smaller cities in the fall of 1978. Prior to the proclamation of liberalization, approximately seventy cities had experienced some form of collective action . . . some ten weeks later, roughly a hundred additional cities were rocked by anti-government collective action" (Parsa 2000: 90).

Figure 2.1 demonstrates a simplified version of the process of mobilization by opposition groups and by the government and how the general public responds to these opportunities. In the context of revolutionary situations, opposition groups have two basic choices: to provoke or to negotiate with the government. In response, the government can choose to respond or not. If it responds, it can either reform or repress. The general public

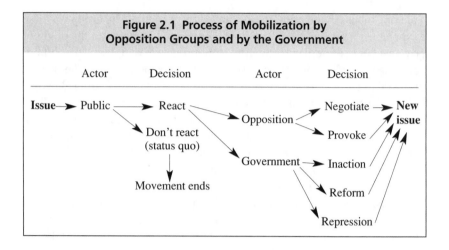

Figure 2.1 Process of Mobilization by Opposition Groups and by the Government

decides whether to react or not. The public's decision drives the other two because it demonstrates which side has been more effective at mobilization. If the government's reform or repression is adequate, the public stops reacting, and a status quo is maintained. If it is inadequate, the revolutionary situation continues. If the government chooses not to act, the issue may be resolved because the public's reaction does not last long enough to mobilize against the state, or it may be inflamed because the state is viewed as nonresponsive.

The revolution in Czechoslovakia is a good example of this. During most of the 1980s, any opposition provocation was met with repression, to which the public did not react. As a result, the opposition never moved beyond a revolutionary situation. With the change in Soviet policies demonstrated in Poland and Hungary, opposition groups again provoked the government. In this case, students marched in memory of a student killed resisting Nazi occupation. When the demonstration exceeded the planned route and headed toward Wenceslas Square in Prague, police officers stopped them. After a prolonged face-off, the police dispersed the crowd with billy clubs, water hoses, and tear gas. The relatively violent response to the clearly nonviolent students elicited significant reaction from the public. This fueled support that the opposition then mobilized for further demonstrations, which the government was unable to stop. This process continued until the government was no longer able to retain power. In contrast, the similar Tiananmen Square prodemocracy movement was sufficiently repressed by the Chinese government; after the crackdown, the public did not react.

The reason that coalitions are so necessary is that for their actions to be really disruptive, they must be of significant scope that the state is incapable of dealing with them. If intellectuals are able to reach out to coal miners to cooperatively strike, as was the case in Czechoslovakia in 1989, then the government is severely threatened. When the coal miners struck, they shut off power to the country. In a similar situation in Nicaragua, when almost every village confronted the National Guard with armed blockades, it was unable to continue to hunt down the FSLN. The coalition of the guerrillas with peasants, urban workers, and even key business leaders undermined Somoza's ability to effectively end the guerrilla war. This type of state in-action encourages both more disruptive action by the challengers and the likely defection of key elites, especially the military. When the military no longer supports the regime, its days are very often numbered.

Crisis and Collapse of the Old Regime

It was in us, in our hearts and minds that something started that changed the face of this earth. —Lech Walesa

Next there is often what Goldstone refers to as a "catalytic failure," an acute political crisis brought on by the regime's inability to deal with an economic, military, or political problem (2003). Tilly argues that challengers are instrumental in creating state weakness that leads to collapse. The transition of power from "multiple sovereignty to a new ruling coalition" marks a revolutionary outcome (1995: 14). Tilly argues that this "is more likely to occur if substantial coalitions form between challengers and existing members of the polity (that is, if some members or even some rulers defect from the existing government) and if the revolutionary coalition comes to control extensive armed force" (1995: 14). When this failure occurs, the old regime crumbles. In effect, this is when the revolution becomes a reality. How revolutionary the new society becomes is determined by how far the subsequent processes unfold.

Struggle for Control and Consolidation

The scrupulous and the just, the noble, humane, and devoted natures; the unselfish and the intelligent may begin a movement—but it passes away from them. They are not the leaders of a revolution. They are its victims.
—Joseph Conrad

After the old regime crumbles, Goldstone argues, there is significant competition among contenders for control of the state (2003). This only occurs after the old regime is gone because, for a revolution to occur, the opposition must be united. This unity is almost always brief, and contenders fight among themselves for control of the state. As Parsa shows, even though most of Nicaraguan society was joined in opposition to Somoza, they were united only in that opposition (2000). Thus, although the FSLN had significant support from broad sectors of society, as soon as Somoza left, that support declined significantly. At that point, in large part because of US interference, the country was plunged into civil war.

When the old regime crumbles, as the formerly united opposition begins to dissolve, the first to take power, Goldstone argues, are the moderate reformers (2003). They are the ones who typically have the least radical plan, and their primary basis of support was that they advocated getting rid of the old regime. The Russian Revolution illustrates this. When the tsar was toppled, the moderates in the Duma took power and began movements toward a constitutional republic. As we know from the Russian example, moderates are often consumed by radical challengers. Kimmel argues that this occurs because of the mobilization of society that is required for moderates to make any reforms (1990). This mobilization has two components. First, it raises expectations, especially for those who had been previously excluded from the government, that the government will be more responsive to their interests. Second, this leads directly to expanding the purview of government to include the interests of those marginalized individuals, especially peasants and urban workers. The combination of those two elements make reforms that were initially supported by the moderates seem too insignificant.

As moderates try to consolidate power with some of the old regime intact, radicals emerge to challenge this incorporation of the old guard. This constituted the October revolution in Russia when the Bolsheviks came to power. Goldstone argues that social revolutions occur when these radicals supplant moderates (2003). The radicals are able to do this because they become popular when moderates are unable to solve the problems of the old regime. They become popular because they continue the cause but also because they are willing to take more drastic measures to consolidate power. This creates a further surge in optimism, that "fuels the moral self-righteousness of the revolution's next stage" (Kimmel 1990: 50). When radicals come to power, they are much more repressive but also much more likely to make changes. This radical rule typically leads to coercion because order in this chaotic time is maintained only through terror.

In social revolutions, because political revolutions typically end with moderates consolidating power, the struggle between moderates and radicals heightens toward civil war. Counterrevolutionaries, or those who seek to restore the old regime, also often play a role in the struggle between radicals and moderates. This struggle accentuates military leaders, who then are much more likely to take power. Napoleon Bonaparte's rise to power in France nicely illustrates this dynamic. Throughout much of the French Revolution, Napoleon was not a key actor. It was only when the struggle between radicals and moderates was so intense during the Great Terror that military leaders became increasingly important factors in who would take power. Out of this, Napoleon emerged as the force who eventually seized power for himself.

Social revolutions eventually end with the defeat of radicals when a new pragmatism emerges. The revolution ends only when the government returns to a sense of normalcy after the radicals are killed or die and after more moderate forces return to power. This can take a long time; in most social revolutions, decades. For example, the radicalness of the Russian Revolution, as perpetuated by Joseph Stalin's terror, did not end until Nikita Khrushchev came to power in the mid-1950s. Although the Chinese Revolution, in many ways, ended in 1949 when the communists came to power, Mao's vision of perpetual revolution, as illustrated in his Cultural Revolution, meant that China did not return to a sense of normalcy until after his death in 1976. Under both Khrushchev in the Soviet Union and Deng Xioping in China, pragmatism returned to each country, effectively ending revolutionary fervor within the government.

In very general terms, we have answered the question of how revolutions happen: there is first a revolutionary situation that sets the stage; it is followed by a crisis that causes the collapse of the government; this ends in a struggle by opposition groups to seize control of the government and implement change. It should be stressed that this process is in no way inevitable or immutable. Many revolutions do not continue through all of the phases discussed. For example, the American Revolution never went beyond the moderates consolidating power. If a social movement does not go through the three basic phases, however, it is not really a revolution. Rebellions are revolutionary situations that never ripen to the crisis and collapse stage.

Questions for Discussion and Reflection

1. Compare the Tiananmen Square demonstrations with those in Eastern Europe just six months later. What explains the difference in outcome?

2. In the Appendix, look at when the key leaders of China who participated in the Tiananmen Square crackdown were born and compare that to

what was happening in China in their lifetime. How might this explain their reaction to the student demonstrations?

3. Read the Serbian Revolution summary in the Appendix. What opportunities were created by the government, opposition, and foreign forces?

4. Where do you stand in the agent structure debate? Which is a better explanation for the events in the Philippines?

3

The Structural Causes
of Revolution

*Revolutions are not made, they come. A revolution is as natural a growth
as an oak. It comes out of the past. Its foundations are laid far back.*
—Wendell Phillips

In this chapter I focus on the structures that give rise to revolutions. As discussed in Chapter 2, structures are factors that are "relatively stable over time and outside the control" of individuals, in contrast to processes that "have to do with the active choices . . . of movement actors" (Goodwin and Jasper 1999: 29). Given this definition of structures, it should be clear that they do not in themselves cause revolutions; rather, they make them extremely likely or unlikely. All structural explanations are stated in probabilistic terms. A revolution is very likely when you have a certain mix of structural factors. At the risk of swamping the reader with analogies, I will try one more: a fire. To have a fire, you must have heat, oxygen, and fuel (something to burn). Scholars of revolution, as well as political leaders, would love to find as simple a structural explanation for revolutions as there is for fires. If any one of these three elements is missing, there will be no fire. If all three are present in sufficient quantity, there is fire. Unfortunately for us, scholars have not found such clear answers to the origins of all revolutions. There are three very important (though much more complex) groups of structural factors, however, that have been the focus of most of the structural literature: states, class, and the international system. The rest of this chapter focuses on how the literature has developed our understanding of each of these structural factors and the role they play in making revolution likely.

States

All political changes originate in divisions of the actual governing power;
a government which is united . . . cannot be moved. —Plato

Theda Skocpol's work on social revolutions provided a significant shift from previous work on revolutions as processes and histories to her observations of revolutions as functions of structural conditions. In her seminal work, *States and Social Revolutions,* she argues, "In fact, in historical revolutions, differently situated and motivated groups have become participants in complex unfoldings of multiple conflicts. These conflicts have been powerfully shaped and limited by existing socioeconomic and international conditions. . . . The logic of these conflicts has not been controlled by any one class or group, no matter how seemingly central in the revolutionary process" (1979: 17–18). Because revolutions are so complex and the result of so many different contextually determined influences, we must focus on broad structural similarities that emerge when studying revolutions. One of the major theoretical additions that Skocpol's work introduced was the hypothesis that only when the state is weakened by an external crisis is it vulnerable to internal dissent, which it is unable to repress. Thus, the key structural factor for Skocpol and for most structurally oriented scholars who have followed her lead is the state.

According to Jeff Goodwin, a state is the "core administrative, policing and military organizations more or less coordinated by an executive authority, that extract resources from and administer and rule (through violence if necessary) a territorially defined national society" (2001: 11). It is important to point out that this is different from the government or a regime.

> [Regimes are] the formal and informal organizations, relationships, and rules that determine who can employ state power for what ends as well as how those who are in power deal with those who are not. The distinction between democracy, totalitarianism, and authoritarianism thus deals with the question of regime type. . . . Regimes are more permanent forms of political organization than specific governments [or rulers], but they are typically less permanent than the state. (Goodwin 2001: 12–13)

This distinction is important because the regime is what scholars are typically describing when they classify states (again as authoritarian or democratic). States are relatively enduring. As such, they exactly fit the conception of a structural element.

Jeff Goodwin has summarized the various types of state-centered analyses that attempt to explain how states create revolutions. The first is what he calls the "state-autonomy perspective," which emphasizes the separateness of state officials from other segments of society (social classes, civil society, and other states) (2001: 37). The point of focusing on the autonomy of states is to move away from Marxist analyses that argue that the state is merely a reflection of the interests of the dominant class. The state-autonomy perspective argues that the state is in fact autonomous; it has interests of its own. Borrowing from the old adage, "where you stand depends on where you sit," this perspective suggests that the state's interests are different from the interests of any other single class or of civil society. The second approach, the "state-capacity perspective," emphasizes the actual material and organizational capacity of states to implement policy (Goodwin 2001: 37). The resources a state typically has at its disposal include the military, taxing authority, police, and regulatory authority, all of which indicate the state's ability to meet challenges.

The third approach, the "political-opportunity perspective," argues that the state creates opportunities for action by challengers (Goodwin 2001: 38). It determines the challengers and their actions when it decides to repress, who to repress, whether to open up to reforms, and what types of reforms to create. For example, expanding the freedom of religion will shape the likely dissidents to emerge in different ways than if the government chooses to expand the freedom of speech. The point of this perspective is that the state creates the opportunity for challengers to act by the decisions it makes. The final approach that Goodwin discusses is the "state-constructionist perspective." This approach argues that the state creates identities, goals, strategies, social ties, ideas, and even emotions of actors in civil society that will pattern the form of challengers to the state. A nonrevolutionary example of how the state constructs these elements can be made over the issue of immigration. The state defines who is an immigrant, who is legal, and who is illegal (creating identities). A new law to redefine immigrants created by a government could shape the goal of protesters in that they respond to the actual legislation as opposed to the issue. The state determines the acceptable strategies that protesters may take by arresting those exhibiting violent behavior but potentially allowing peaceable marches.

Regardless of the approach taken, state-oriented analyses describe the kinds of states that are likely to have a revolution as distinct from those that are not. Jeff Goodwin's analysis of peripheral states during the Cold War is one of the best examples of this type of analysis and bears summarizing in some detail (2001). Goodwin classifies states along three criteria: the type of state organization, the type of political regime, and the infrastructural power of the state. A state's organization can be measured from bureaucratic to patrimonial. A bureaucratic state is one staffed by merit-based appointments of individuals in positions with clearly defined responsibilities. This is a very efficient form of administration. In contrast, the patrimonial system involves appointments based on political loyalty, kinship, ethnicity, or some other characteristic of who a person is and not what a person does. The responsibilities of administrators are not clearly defined or are ad hoc in nature, and thus this is not a very efficient system in terms of providing services. The regime types that Goodwin analyzes span from liberal/inclusive (democracies) to exclusive/repressive (dictatorships). The key feature of the liberal regimes is that they have multiple ways for drawing people into the political process, including voting, political parties, interest groups, and social movements. In contrast, exclusive regimes are more isolated from much of society. The third criterion, infrastructural power, refers to the ability of the state to carry out its projects and enforce laws even in the face of opposition. If we put these three spectrums together, with the patrimonial, exclusive, and weak states in the middle, we can visualize the types of countries that are likely to have a revolution (Figure 3.1).

Given these classifications, Goodwin is able to demonstrate how revolutions emerged in peripheral states during the Cold War. Patrimonial states are more likely to do things that encourage revolutionary activity. They will sponsor unpopular arrangements that support an exploiting class, making the state a legitimate target for action (Goodwin 2001: 45). They are also more

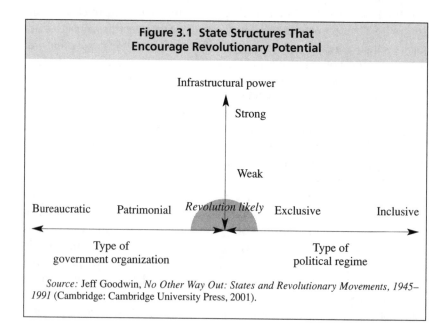

Figure 3.1 State Structures That Encourage Revolutionary Potential

Infrastructural power

Strong

Weak

Bureaucratic   Patrimonial   *Revolution likely*   Exclusive   Inclusive

Type of government organization   Type of political regime

Source: Jeff Goodwin, *No Other Way Out: States and Revolutionary Movements, 1945–1991* (Cambridge: Cambridge University Press, 2001).

likely to divide counterrevolutionary elites (those most likely to support the existing government). Because a patrimonial regime depends on personalized support, these dictators try to keep any segment of society from getting too powerful, as it might challenge their power. Ironically, this division of elites increases the likelihood of success of challengers to the state (2001: 49). Exclusionary regimes are more likely, by definition, to exclude important groups from the decisionmaking process. This means that they diminish the likelihood that opposition groups will push for reform, as they have no part of the government. Exclusionary regimes are also much more likely to use indiscriminate violence against mobilized opposition groups (2001: 47). This further discourages reform-minded opposition. If the state kills its opposition, it is unlikely that the remaining opposition will see the state as capable of reform and will adopt more radical tactics. A final conclusion is that if a state has weak infrastructural power, but it has done the previous things, it is unlikely to be able to stop radical change. If it is strong, then it will be able to continue jailing, killing, or otherwise repressing dissent (2001: 49). (See Figure 3.1.)

Support for Goodwin's state-centric analysis exists beyond the social revolutions that he studies. Of the forty-three cases of revolution (as defined in Chapter 1) with data since 1973, only three (Lebanon 1975–1991, Grenada 1979, and the Philippines 2000–2001) were labeled as free countries by Freedom House's rankings of civil and political liberties (2010). Twenty-three of the cases were labeled not free, with the remainder being only partly free. This validates the idea that countries that are more inclusive (an assumption of the civil and political liberties rankings) are less likely to succumb to revolution.

Parsa makes a similar argument, developing a key focus on the penetration of the state into the economy of a particular country (2000). Understanding the state's intervention in the economy is crucial because it makes any economic crises also political crises. Parsa proposes that it makes the state a legitimate target for any economic problems that exist in society. In an analysis similar to Goodwin's classifications, Parsa sees three types of states in terms of their penetration of the economy. A regulative state plays a limited role in the economy. It simply enforces laws and ensures the efficient operation of the market. This is the traditional role assigned the state in laissez-faire capitalism (e.g., the United States). An administrative state has a moderate level of penetration. Beyond regulating, it plans some aspects of the economy, enacts corporatist policies (state owned or supported industries, sectors, or businesses), and determines which areas should receive state subsidies (e.g., Japan). A hyperactive state has extensive penetration into the economy. In very real ways, it limits the scope of the market by owning or controlling vast resources, and thus is the primary economic actor (2000: 13–15) (e.g., Iran). This distinction is important in determining the likelihood of revolution, according to Parsa, because if the economy and the state are separate, conflicts in the market will likely generate calls from civil society for the state to intervene, requiring reform. If the economy and the state are unified, however, the reform option is less likely, and economic reforms will require reconstructing the state, fueling radicalism.

Timothy Wickham-Crowley calls this type of patrimonial praetorian regime a "mafiacracy." As in the case of both Cuba and Nicaragua, the very nature of the regime encouraged revolution because it encouraged a coalition of opposition. The Fulgencio Batista regime in Cuba, Wickham-Crowley argues, effectively excluded large portions of both the middle and upper classes from participation in the government. This created a "*large* reservoir of *moderate* discontent with the Batista regime, which must have been strongly 'magnetic' to the far smaller radical opposition. That magnetism worked both ways for, given their own lack of political alternatives, the moderates would find the radicals more attractive" (Wickham-Crowley 1992: 184). In the end, an alliance was relatively easy for radicals who were willing to downplay their radical rhetoric. In the cases of both Cuba and Nicaragua, key opposition groups did just that.

A more recent indicator that tries to capture the weakness of the state by analyzing twelve political, economic, military, and social indicators demonstrates the underlying theory of focusing on the state. The Fund for Peace and Carnegie Endowment for International Peace created The Index of Failed States that is published in *Foreign Policy* magazine (and available on its website) to indicate where conflict is most likely (*Foreign Policy* and the Fund for Peace 2010). The focus is on the potential for failed states because they are most likely to lead to civil war and international conflict. Although a failed state is not necessarily the same as a revolution, many of the underlying dynamics are the same.

The calculation of the ranking of the index gives a concrete example of the kind of criteria that make a state likely to have a revolution. The general variables identified by Goodwin, Parsa, and others are broader categories encompassing the twelve indicators of instability, which include such things as demographic pressures that measure the age distribution of a country, the number of refugees and displaced persons, the provision of public services, inequality, human rights, and the strength of the military. The indicators are measured by scanning thousands of news articles during a given year. A software package codes the articles for having or not having a factor and identifies the proportion of "hits" in the sample. The complexity of the analysis is an indication of the complexity of determining the likelihood of revolution in a specific case (as opposed to indicating the important factors in general). The news items are

> gathered from a range of publicly available print, radio, television and Internet sources from all over the world, including international and local media reports, essays, interviews, polling and survey data, government documents, independent studies from think tanks, NGOs and universities, and even corporate financial filings. . . . Quantitative data is also included, when available. Subject-matter experts then review each score for every country and indicator, as well as consult the original documents, when necessary, to ensure accuracy. (*Foreign Policy* and the Fund for Peace 2010)

The higher the number, the greater the instability and thus the greater the likelihood that the state will fail (or that there will be a revolution). As is true with all of the structural literature, the failed states index only suggests where a crisis is likely, not inevitable. Countries that have consistently topped the list (since its creation in 2005) include Somalia, Sudan, Zimbabwe, Chad, Iraq, Democratic Republic of Congo, Afghanistan, Côte d'Ivoire, Pakistan, and Central African Republic.

The primary critique of the state-centered literature is that what it gains in parsimony, it lacks in breadth. In its most simple form, the argument of the state-oriented literature is that revolutions occur because of the type of state that exists. Although this black-and-white version of a state-centered analysis is not the kind developed above, that is the fundamental argument. To get around the problems of some obvious glaring omissions (e.g., society, international context, culture, ideology), state-centered analysts try to integrate these elements into the focus on the state. Thus, Skocpol discusses external crises such as war that weaken the state to bring in the international context. Goodwin similarly discusses how states often create cultures of opposition through their policies to bring in culture and history.

Class

> *Revolution is simply "an insurrection, an act of violence by which one class overthrows another."* —Mao Zedong

A second structure that shapes the likelihood and outcome of revolution is the divisions and distributions of various socioeconomic classes within a society. In Marxist terms, classes are "clusters of people whose development or decline is predicated on particular historical circumstances, and who act together or against each other in pursuit of particular interests prompted by these circumstances" (Wolf 1999: xx). The historical circumstances are the relationship of an individual to the forces of production: does the individual work in a factory, on a farm, in his or her own shop, or on a board of directors of a corporation? Although strict interpretation of Marx would view classes as monolithic and thus leading to conflict of us against them, most applications of class analysis allow for significant divisions within and overlapping of classes. A peasant, for example, could be a day laborer during some parts of the year while a skilled craftsman and petit bourgeois other parts of the year. The utility of analyzing classes is based on the Marxist assertion that individuals typically behave according to their socioeconomic status. This makes intuitive sense, as peasants are assumed to behave differently than factory workers or intellectuals because their whole livelihood is radically different. Their class position structures their typical behavior.

Much of the early revolution literature came from and reacted to Marxist explanations of the epochs of history (Selbin 1993). A materialist explanation of history involves the unfolding of class struggle. A dominant class loses power when the mode of production changes, leading to broader social changes. An excluded class rises up and takes power. As Kimmel puts it,

> such a model [of class conflict] can best be understood by metaphor. In the class struggle model, a revolution is like a boxing match. Two fully mobilized classes get into the ring to slug it out. The winner is awarded, both literally and metaphorically, the "crown," political power, control over the state. (The state in this model is always the unitary prize captured and held by one class at a time, and the institutions of the state always act to promote the interests of that class.) (1990: 117)

This simplification is useful for understanding the element of struggle but for analogy only. There are no Marxists or class-oriented analysts who suggest there are only two classes and that everyone fits into these two classes. Even Marx acknowledged that peasants existed; in his mind they were a nonrevolutionary or even counterrevolutionary class. Thus, much of the literature that utilizes class structures as the focus of its analysis develops the different classes that exist in a given society and their impact on revolution.

Barrington Moore argues that the class arrangements that lead up to the modernization process determine the type of revolution and regime that follows (1966). Moore looks at the variety of classes and their character in premodern societies. These include the peasantry, aristocracy (land-owning elite), and the bourgeoisie. Bourgeoisie originally referred to urban residents (people who lived in a *bourg*), but it later was applied to any middle-class person—that is, not a peasant or an aristocrat. Later the term was "applied to the owners of business enterprises, especially those in manufacturing and trade" (Hamilton 1998: 47). This later sense is what is typically meant by Marxists when they talk about the bourgeoisie, though Moore's analysis is more akin to the conception of a middle class that owns property but that also typically works that property. Kimmel summarized Moore's conclusion on how class affects the origin and outcome of revolutions:

> If the aristocracy commercializes agriculture by evicting the peasantry and replacing them with hired labor, the aristocracy becomes part of the bourgeoisie and therefore favors democracy. At the same time, the forced eviction of the peasantry removes a potentially revolutionary or reactionary force from the land (the peasantry). This was the case in England. If the aristocracy keeps the peasantry on the land and forces them to hand over their produce for the market by intensifying traditional labor discipline, the aristocracy will favor fascism, which is a way of transferring traditional agrarian authoritarianism to industrial society. At the same time, the peasantry is utterly immobilized and removed from potential resistance. This was the case in Prussia and Japan. Finally, if the aristocracy leaves the land (coming to court in urban centers, for example) and its members become absentee landlords, the peasants will be allowed to produce directly for the market. Thus the aristocracy demobilizes itself politically, while the peasants are radicalized by their participation in the market and are thus mobilized for revolutionary activity. This is what occurred in China and France. (Kimmel 1990: 122–23)

This leads to Moore's famous dictum: no bourgeoisie, no democracy (1966). That is, the class structure that exists prior to modernization determines the path to modernity. The analysis here is on the nature of each class.

Eric Wolf builds on these ideas, focusing his analysis on the role of peasants in twentieth-century revolutions. His focus is on understanding peasant revolutions and how they arise. There are five structural elements that need to exist for a peasant revolution to occur. The first element is that revolutions are only likely when the state is highly despotic (as the state-oriented analyses would agree). Second, Wolf argues that peasant revolutions only occur in "newly capitalizing societies," that is, societies in which the economy is shifting toward the commodification of land, labor, and wealth (Wolf 1999: 279). These social changes create two elements that encourage revolution. Commodification, the third element, results in workers becoming alienated from the products of their labor, from themselves (as they view their time only in terms of money), and from others (who are viewed as competitors or assets). It also results in an ecological crisis, the fourth element, because land becomes privatized for production of cash crops at the same time that the population grows (because of new food acquired through foreign trade, improved transportation, industrialization that leads to specialization and better health care, all which decrease mortality). This change in the economic structures impacts three classes in particular, the aristocracy, new intellectuals, and peasants.

Peasant revolutions are increasingly likely when the rural, landed aristocracy become increasingly parasitic. Traditionally, the landed elite serve as the intermediary between the state and the peasantry in the feudal system. The relationship among the three (state, peasantry, and elites) is mutually beneficial, though the benefits obviously are larger for the upper classes. As the old elites become more parasitic, however, they extract more of the surplus of the land without reinvesting, creating a larger burden on the peasantry. Wolf argues that this occurs when these elites are absent landlords who live in the city but get all of their wealth from the country (1999: 285).

The new elites also play a key role in spurring peasant revolutions. Revolutionaries are always intellectuals; peasants are improbable revolutionaries. These intellectuals come from the new business class of professionals (doctors, lawyers, teachers) and even technocrats from within the government. When members of this group have limited advancement opportunities or are unable to be successful given constraints of existing society, they can become the leaders of revolutionary movements. They become the natural leaders of industrial workers and dissatisfied peasants who also have been socially dislocated owing to the economic changes spurred by capitalization. For example, Tsar Alexander II of Russia inadvertently increased the pool of likely revolutionary leaders when he created a substantial education campaign. His efforts resulted in a significantly larger educated class; enrollment in schools was five times higher in 1914 than just fifty years earlier, and it included more people from the peasantry, but there were no jobs for these newly skilled elites in the old social structure.

The fifth structural element is that the peasant class itself must be of a certain type for revolution to be likely. They cannot be too poor, or they will not have the resources sufficient to engage in collective action. But they also cannot be too wealthy, as they would not be motivated to participate; collective action would likely result in losing their privileged place. They must be what Wolf calls "middle peasantry," wealthy enough or autonomous enough to engage in collective action and poor enough to want change (1999: 290–292). This class is most susceptible to losing land in the process of capitalization and most likely to have links with the proletariat because relatives (children) often go to the city to work. Thus, peasant revolutions are only likely when all five of these conditions are met. When all exist, a revolution is likely to occur. This is a structural analysis because all of these conditions are outside the control of individuals. The class element is evident by Wolf's focus on peasants and the type of peasants that exists in a society as well as their relation to intellectuals and old elite (other classes).

A critique of class-centered structural analyses is that it strips away the autonomy of individuals and groups. When viewing society through the lens of class analysis, it is easy to see all actions as conforming to a notion of what is expected of a particular class. This is particularly problematic when evaluating the role of the state. Traditional Marxists argue that government is merely a tool of the dominant class in society, but the state-centered perspective shows that governments can be autonomous and often work against the dominant class's interests. Further, some of the utility that is gained by generalizing about class interests is lost when looking at particular revolutionary situations. A peasant in China may look very different from one in Cuba or Mexico. This often requires refining class groups into subgroups and further subsubgroups. Taken to the extreme, this undermines the whole idea of class with common interests; if every country and region has its own unique class structure, there are few generalizations to be made, and they become just groups and not classes.

The International System

> *A revolution can be neither made nor stopped. The only thing that can be done is for one of several of its children to give it a direction by dint of victories.* —Napoleon Bonaparte

This category of structural analysis is a more diverse collection of ideas that are related to international structures, the most prominent one being the modernization process. The international system, like states and classes, is a relatively static structure. There are changes, to be sure, but they are typically long in coming and never under the control of any individual, let alone any country. The structures discussed below are similar only in that they all originate outside of a particular country. The state and class structure of a country are, obviously, domestic structures. Like the domestic structures, however, these international structures have played a significant role in shaping the likelihood of revolution as well as the forms it takes.

Modernization

> *Every revolution evaporates and leaves behind only the slime of a new bureaucracy.* —Franz Kafka

Modernization is the movement of societies from traditional to modern. This division of societies was first described by Max Weber, who sought to understand the development of modernity by clarifying what was modern and what was not. One of the key elements of modernity, he argued, was the bureaucratic-rational form of society. A bureaucracy is an organization of individuals for the rational achievement of goals. Bureaucracies in government and civil society are the hallmarks of modernity. Rationality means that individuals behave according to "intellectually analyzable rules" (Weber 2003: 34). Bureaucracies are characterized by strict hierarchies, rules, and specialized functions. Because of this, they are able to coordinate work extremely efficiently. In a factory, bureaucratization means a worker repeatedly doing one specialized task that is essential to the manufacturing of a product. In government, civil servants play a similar role, whether it is the upkeep of transportation systems, the sorting of intelligence, or the tallying of votes in an election. A bureaucratic-rational society is one governed by rules that allow for the efficient conduct of business and personal relations. This means that the law, once created, applies to everyone equally.

This contrasted with the traditional society in which social relations were personal or familial. That is, one's relationship to another was defined in terms of who they were. The production of goods and services was done within a family and typically coordinated by a patriarch. Government was similarly structured around a ruling elite who had strong personal ties to the ruler. Their work was not specialized or "routinized" but rather was typically ad hoc. The person charged with a village's water distribution was chosen because of his relationship to the ruler, not because of his skill or training in that area.[1] Further, the law was a function of who you were in relation to others. Thus, the rules for a nobleman were different from those for a serf in terms of ownership of property, selling of goods, and other social activities. Moreover, a ruler would determine the nature of punishment for violations of these rules at his discretion. Weber saw this form of society as much less efficient in producing goods and services. He also argued that this type of government was much less stable and more prone to revolutionary challenges (state-oriented structuralists acknowledge their debt to Weber).

Weber's grand view of history was that societies generally moved from tradition to modernity, the foundational idea of modernization. Theorists look at the movement from traditional to modern societies as a structure that encourages revolutions. The existence of a traditional society means that revolution is likely because all traditional societies are in the process of moving toward modernity, and revolution is one way that this can happen (though it is not the only way: coups, democratic reforms, and other methods are possible). Once a society becomes modern, however, "revolution, in the sense of a forceful creation of entirely new formations of authority, [is] technically more and more impossible" because of the extent to which bureaucratization provides for the common good (Weber 2003: 36). There is wide latitude within that passage from traditional to modern, however, and that is where much of the modernization literature regarding revolution is focused.

Building on Weber's two ideal-type societies, Samuel Huntington argues that revolutions emerge in modernizing societies when there is a disjunction between the scope and pace of sociopolitical change and economic change. Huntington views revolution as the rapid and violent expansion of political participation outside of existing political institutions. As new groups in society emerge in the process of modernization, they will need to be brought into the scope of the state's authority so that they can exercise power in relation to their growing status (there are strong elements of historical materialism in modernization). If a government is able to make the necessary changes, it avoids revolution. If not, it is ripe for revolution. Huntington proposes that

> the two prerequisites for revolution are, first, political institutions incapable of providing channels for the participation of new social forces in politics and of new elites in government, and, secondly, the desire of social forces, currently excluded from politics, to participate therein, this desire normally arising from the group's feeling that it needs certain symbolic or material gains which it can achieve only by pressing its demands in the political sphere. . . . To be more precise, the probability of revolution in a modernizing country depends upon: (a) the extent to which the urban middle class—intellectuals, professionals, bourgeoisie—are alienated from the existing order; (b) the extent to which the peasants are alienated from the existing order; and (c) the extent to which urban middle class and peasants join together not only in fighting against "the same enemy" but also in fighting for the same cause. (1968: 274–275, 277)

As alluded to above, Barrington Moore makes a similar argument about modernization, stating that revolution is the product of the moving from traditional to modern societies. Moore's work goes beyond the study of when revolution is likely; he attempts to understand how class structures influence the path toward modernity. Moore argues that there have been three general paths of modernization, and a fourth option of weak modernization. "The first and earlier route through the great revolutions and civil wars led to the combination of capitalism and Western democracy" (Moore 1966: xxi). This is exemplified in the English and American civil wars as well as the French Revolution. The second path was driven by "revolution from above" in that there was no mass-based revolution that overthrew an existing regime. In contrast, the modernization push was driven by elites within the government, as exemplified by Germany and Japan. The reason for this, Moore argues, is that the "bourgeois impulse" was much weaker (1966: xxi). The fruit of this marriage between the old landed elite and the new business elite was fascism. "The third route is of course communism, as exemplified in Russia and in China" (1966: xxii). The distinguishing factor in this route was the utter lack of an urban class that could demand power. Each of these countries was dominated by peasants, who "subject to new strains and stresses as the modern world encroached upon [them], provided the main destructive revolutionary force that overthrew the old order and propelled these countries into the modern era under communist leadership" (1966: xxii). The final pattern that Moore discusses is not a pattern of modernization per se, but rather an indication of how some countries have not been fully pulled into the modern world. In the 1960s, when he developed his theory, India was the key example of this lack of progress.

The structure of modernization is apparent in Moore's analysis. Countries with different class composition will behave differently, but within the movement from traditional to modern societies. That is, the structure that none of them can avoid is the movement toward modernity. The fourth path (India) is simply an indication that not all countries have completed this trend. Huntington's and Moore's analyses also point to the implications for revolutions in the future: as more countries become modern, the likelihood of revolution will gradually recede. As Huntington argues, "revolution is thus an aspect of modernization. It is not something which can occur in any type of society at any period in its history. It is not a universal category but rather an historically limited phenomenon" (1968: 265). In this way, Huntington argues, modernization is a structural constraint to the possibility of revolution.

The primary problem with the modernization argument is that the process of social, political, and economic development that the argument describes is so complex and historically dependent that it is difficult to generalize. The basic idea of modernization is that countries go through a process that makes them look more like modern societies than traditional ones. This smacks of Eurocentrism, where modern is equated with the sociopolitical structures developed in Western Europe. But more important, the range of what currently constitutes modern is so vast that trying to align countries on a spectrum from modern to traditional is problematic. There may be agreement about clusters of countries on either end, but the countries in the middle, where revolution is most likely, are very difficult to place, indicating that it is nearly impossible to tell whether a country is in the early stages of becoming modern or at the later stages. The only clear indication is after the fact.

The Flow of Ideas, Money, and Power

*People make their own history, but they do not do so just as they please;
they do not make it under circumstances chosen by themselves, but under
circumstances directly encountered, given, and transmitted from the past.*
—Karl Marx

The movement of new ideas from one country to another is also an international force that is not controllable by any individual. Once an idea has taken hold, if there is communication among states, the idea will likely spread. The most powerful idea relating to revolutions is the concept of revolution itself. Revolutions, in the modern sense, are a product of the Enlightenment, which (as discussed in Chapter 4) views humanity as capable of progressive change. That is, by knowing the world and our place in it, we can elevate that place and create prosperity, happiness, and security. That idea was first demonstrated in the American and French revolutions. As Robert Snyder argues, "the French Revolution joined the idea of progress with the revolution's capture of the state . . . the revolution offered collective salvation and the embodiment of progress that would triumph worldwide" (1999). This idea spread throughout continental Europe, igniting an era of revolutionary movements.

In the twentieth century, Snyder says, revolutions also came to embody the idea of development. Unlike the American and French revolutions, twentieth-century revolutions embraced the idea that a country could undergo revolution and emerge a stronger, more developed state. "The Russian Revolution produced the second great myth: that through revolution a backward state could become more progressive and advanced than more prosperous and better-developed states. . . . Having been humiliated by colonialism, and being materially very backward relative to the West, third world revolutionary states believed that the revolution, based on the second myth, would make them more advanced than the Western states" (1999). This allowed revolutions to spread, not just to neighbors but also to similarly situated countries across the globe.

Like the spread of ideas, the flow of support, in terms of money, arms, and training, can also influence revolutions. Che Guevara, one of the leaders of the Cuban Revolution, saw his primary mission after leaving Cuba as exporting Cuba's success throughout the third world. Although few revolutionaries' international stature matched Guevara's, many governments worked to spread or contain the spread of revolutions throughout the third world. Angola provides a unique insight into this phenomenon. As a Portuguese colony, a variety of nationalist independence groups had attempted to mobilize Angolans to support independence. These movements, in part, led to a coup in Portugal in 1974. The new government moved quickly to transition its colonies to independent states. In the transition process, three of the former revolutionary groups in Angola declared independence and sought to control the government. As civil war broke out, support from a variety of countries propped up the indigenous groups.

> Foreign armies intervened in support of each side. Cuban troops and Soviet weapons aided the MPLA [Popular Movement for the Liberation of Angola]. Two regional countries, South Africa and Zaire, invaded Angola in support of UNITA [Union for the Total Independence of Angola] and the FNLA [National Front for the Liberation of Angola], respectively. The conflict was further complicated by the participation of mercenaries of various origins. The United States, still recovering from its defeat in Vietnam, avoided a frontal attack in Angola, choosing to provide support to the MPLA's adversaries through the CIA on the one hand and by supporting the South African invasion on the other, making Angola the most significant proxy war battlefield in the post-Vietnam era. (Mabeko-Tali 2006: 66)

Although the flow of money, training, and troops did not allow either side a decisive victory, it probably had the opposite effect of fueling a nearly thirty-year civil war.

In contrast, the French support of the colonists in the American Revolution was arguably the difference between a revolution and a rebellion. Throughout the revolutionary war, which began in 1776, the French had supplied arms to the colonists. In 1778, after the successful battle at Saratoga, the French signed an agreement of support against the British. They began fighting naval battles in Europe and throughout the Atlantic almost immediately. Their defeat of the British at the Battle of the Chesapeake in 1781 ensured that reinforcements and an escape route were cut off. A month later French land and naval forces combined with the colonial army to surround Yorktown, the last major battle of the war of independence. Following the loss of Yorktown, the English Parliament pushed for a treaty, which was signed the following year. Clearly the support of France played a decisive role in the American Revolution, without which it is likely that the rebellion would have been defeated by the British.

The involvement of foreign powers in each of these cases also illustrates the last international element that shapes revolutions: the international balance of power. The rise and fall of great powers and their relationships with each other have fueled revolutionary movements throughout the world. As the two cases above illustrate, the primary reason for becoming involved in each of the otherwise relatively unimportant revolutions was to reduce the power of a rival great power. This was true in the Cold War case of Angola and of the pre-Napoleonic conflicts between England and France.

The change of the balance of power in the international system after World War II had an impact on the incidence of revolutions. Snyder argues that the Cold War contributed to the proliferation of revolutions for two reasons.

> First, the heightened tensions between the United States and Soviet Union militarized international relations and states. This encouraged revolutionary and counterrevolutionary forces worldwide because the two superpowers aided their third world allies—including transnational ones, and because revolution and war are strikingly similar in the type of mobilization, beliefs, and organizations that they produce. Second, the radicalization of revolutions, particularly the Cuban, Iranian, and Nicaraguan revolutions, might not have happened without their conflicts with the United States. (1999)

Those conflicts were driven in part by a fear of the spread of communism that dominated US foreign policy during the Cold War. Further, when communism was no longer a fear, some repressive regimes lost their legitimacy with the United States. Both South Africa and Indonesia had been supported as bastions of anticommunism, and egregious human rights violations had been tolerated because of that stance. When communism was no longer a threat, both received significant pressure to reform, spurring successful revolutionary movements in South Africa, Indonesia, and the island of East Timor.

State, Class, and International Structures

It is impossible to predict the time and progress of revolution. It is governed by its own more or less mysterious laws. —V. I. Lenin

A number of structurally oriented works have integrated the analysis of state, class, and international structures with concepts such as culture and history to provide as holistic an explanation of revolutionary potential as possible. These typically involve a list of relevant factors, a flow chart, or both. Two examples will suffice, as most of the synthesis arguments come to similar conclusions, indicating an emerging consensus.

James DeFronzo's analysis of a wide variety of revolutions and revolutionary movements has found that there are five key elements that "if occurring simultaneously, appear to come close to constituting necessary and sufficient conditions for the success of a revolutionary movement" (2007: 10). They are (1) mass frustration that leads to popular uprisings; (2) a split of some elite leaders; (3) a unifying motivation that encourages cross-class coalitions, such as nationalism, anti-imperialism, or a truly despotic and brutal regime; (4) a catalytic event that paralyzes the administrative and co-ercive capabilities of the government; and (5) a global or historical context that encourages revolution, such as great powers being too occupied other-wise to meddle or be very interested in supporting the overthrow of the old regime (DeFronzo 2007: 10–11). DeFronzo uses this list to help explain why some revolutionary movements fail when others that appear very sim-ilar succeed. Table 3.1 lists a variety of revolutionary movements that did not succeed along with the missing criteria that explain their failures.

John Foran has a similar five-element theory for explaining revolutions in the third world but goes beyond the laundry-list strategy of suggesting the

Table 3.1 Revolutionary Movements That Did Not Succeed During the Time Periods Specified

	Mass Discontent	Elite Dissent	Unifying Motive	Government Crisis	Global Context
Russia, 1905	+	+	−	−	−
Zionist, 1897–1939	+	+	+	−	−
South Africa, 1912–1989	+	+	+	−	−
El Salvador, 1932; 1972–1991	+	+	−	−	−
Palestinians, 1936–1989	+	+	+	−	−
Guatemala, 1944–1954	+	+	+	−	−
Philippines, 1946–1956	+	+	−	−	−
Greece, 1947–1949	+	+	−	−	−
Hungary, 1956	+	+	+	+	−
Czechoslovakia, 1968	+	+	+	+	−
Chile, 1970–1973	+	+	−	−	−
Poland, 1980–1981	+	+	+	−	−

Source: James DeFronzo, *Revolutions and Revolutionary Movements,* 3rd ed. (Cambridge, MA: Westview Press, 2007), 19.

Note: A plus sign means that the factor was judged to have been present during the relevant time period; a minus sign means that the factor was judged to be absent.

necessary elements for revolutions to that of creating a relationship between the elements. That is, the elements are not detached structures but create a causal chain that encourages the likelihood of revolution. He argues that "five inter-related causal factors must combine in a given conjuncture to produce a successful social revolution: 1) dependent development; 2) a repressive, exclusionary, personalist state; 3) the elaboration of effective and powerful political cultures of resistance; and a revolutionary crisis consisting of 4) an economic downturn; and 5) a world-systemic opening" (Foran 2005: 18). The relationship is graphically demonstrated in Figure 3.2.

First, revolutions are most likely in a certain context: countries that have historically undergone dependent development. Dependent development is a situation in which economic growth occurs within the context of a colonizing or dominating economy. This means that countries that were exposed to capitalism through imposition in later historical time periods have a built-in crisis: the existing socioeconomic system is forced to compete with an external challenge of global capitalism. This first aspect is essentially an argument that revolutions are a product of modernization, but it alters the modernization argument to suggest that only when the modernization occurs in a certain way (dependent development) does a revolution become likely. As Foran puts it,

> certain Third World economies, at certain moments in their history, do undergo both rapid development—as measured by increases in GNP, foreign trade, and industrial or agricultural output—combined with the negative consequences of this process in the form of such problems as inflation,

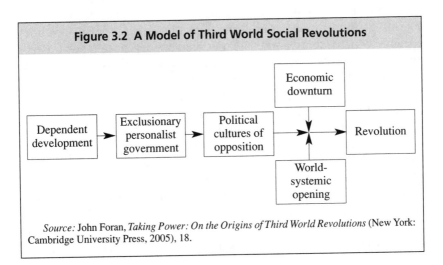

Figure 3.2 A Model of Third World Social Revolutions

Source: John Foran, *Taking Power: On the Origins of Third World Revolutions* (New York: Cambridge University Press, 2005), 18.

debt, growing inequality, or overburdened housing and educational infra-
structures, among many social ills. This historically specific process defines
in each case a changing social structure that creates social and economic
grievances among diverse sectors of the population, ranging from the
urban working, middle, and underclasses, to rural peasants, farmers and
workers, and crossing gender and ethnic lines as well. The argument, then,
is that a country's historical insertion into the world economy on dependent terms vis-à-vis core powers significantly shapes its social structure [to
encourage revolution]. (Foran 2005: 19)

This type of society (one undergoing dependent development) very
often has a government that is dominated by an individual. The reason for
this is that a strong central figure is required to "guarantee order in a rapidly changing social setting in which much of the population is suffering"
(Foran 2005: 20). Reflecting the state-oriented literature, when this type of
state exists, a revolution is much more likely. Collective military rule and
polyarchies are much more likely to avoid revolutions, even in societies
with dependent development. For revolution to be successful, however, a
coalition must emerge that, Foran argues, depends on a political culture of
resistance. This is an encompassing category of elements that include ideology, organization, and mobilization (all covered in other chapters). "Organizational capacity, lived experience, culture, and ideology come together
under certain circumstances to produce revolutionary political cultures" that
make revolution increasingly likely (2005: 21).

The last two elements involve an economic crisis and a permissive international context. The economic crisis is relatively easy to pinpoint, and
Foran makes the point that "economic downturns on the eve of revolutions
. . . are present in virtually all successful cases" (2005: 22). The global context for the third world countries that Foran investigates involves a brief
opening. Usually, third world countries are very dependent upon a larger
power. When something happens to change that relationship, even tem-
porarily, revolution is much more likely. "This may be the result of distrac-
tion in the core economies by world war or depression, rivalries between one
or more core powers, mixed messages sent to Third World dictators, or a divided foreign policy when faced with an insurrection. Mexico between 1910
and 1920 exemplifies the first two conditions; Nicaragua and Iran during the
Carter administration's human rights–oriented foreign policy the latter two"
(2005: 23). The change in the relationship weakens the government, which
is in many ways dependent upon the larger power, and thus provides an opportunity for opposition groups.

What are the structural factors that lead to revolution? If we take the
total of what the structurally oriented literature has developed, we find that

revolutions are rare for good reason. There is a relatively narrow space in which revolutions are likely to occur. The sum of these findings is listed below. Again, it is important to note that all of these are probabilistic statements; revolution is likely or unlikely, never assured or impossible. Also, these structurally supported statements are derived from the history of revolution. Thus, if the current context bears resemblance to history, then we are more confident in these statements. As the context changes, however, without new studies of new revolutions, we must be increasingly cautious.

Revolution is most likely when

The state is an exclusive, repressive, patrimonial regime that is weak and dependent upon foreign goodwill.

The class structure is dominated by landed elites who are increasingly parasitic and remote; newly educated elites do not have access to power in the system.

The international system is supportive of the move to more modern social, economic, and political arrangements; encourages access to ideological and financial support to revolutionaries; is dominated by great powers who support revolutionary movements, weaken dependent states, or are otherwise distracted by other great powers.

Revolution is very unlikely when

The state is bureaucratic, inclusive (liberal democratic), and strong.

The class structure is dominated by poor peasants and is divided.

The international system is closed to encouraging modernization, is open to encouraging the status quo, and is dominated by great powers that support existing regimes or discourage revolutionary actors.

Questions for Discussion and Reflection

1. Given the list of countries where state failure is likely, where do you think revolution is likely in the future?

2. Discuss the merits and drawbacks of modernization theory.

3. Wolf characterizes peasants in twentieth-century wars in which they played an important part. What do peasants look like today? Where are they?

4. To what extent is modernization a natural development versus a creation of Western civilization?

5. What should be the role of foreign governments in either encouraging or discouraging revolutions in other countries?

6. Compare the Tiananmen Square demonstrations with those in Eastern Europe just six months later. What explains the difference in outcome?

Note

1. Gendered language is intentionally used here, as traditional societies were almost always paternalistic. This further highlights Weber's view of these societies as much more dependent upon who you are than upon what you do.

4

The Role of Ideology, Part 1: Liberalism and Nationalism

Every revolution was first a thought in one man's mind.
—Ralph Waldo Emerson

Revolutions are fascinating events because they challenge us to see an ideal that is in the process of becoming a reality. As I will show in Chapter 8, although those ideals are rarely achieved, revolutions represent the rare times when individuals move beyond the "normal" political process in an attempt to create a radically new world. The ideals that often inspire the masses are revolutionary ideologies. This chapter and the next focus on the role of ideologies in justifying revolutions by answering the question: What is the purpose of revolution?

The debate over the answer to this question, the role of ideology, is one of the most contentious in the revolution literature. At its core, the disagreement is about whether radical ideas shape revolutions or whether they are more a function of the structural realities of a given situation. Although it is clear in the abstract that ideas matter, it is unclear whether or not they are the primary motivating force in revolutionary change. Thus, this chapter begins with a review of this debate. I then turn to investigating the dominant ideologies used in revolutions: liberalism and nationalism in this chapter and communism and religiously oriented ideologies (Islamic fundamentalism and liberation theology) in Chapter 5.

Scholarly Debate on the Role of Ideology

What we formerly called Revolutions, were little more than a change of persons, or an alteration of the local circumstances. . . . But what we now

57

*see in the world, from the Revolutions of America and France, are a ren-
ovation of the natural order of things, a system of principles as universal
as truth and the existence of man, and combining moral with political happiness and national prosperity.* —Thomas Paine

Before investigating the contours of the debate over the role of ideology, it
is useful to first define the concept. Ideology is a relatively coherent set of
ideas that explains how society should work. If we break the word into its
Greek components, it is literally the study or science of ideas. This has typically meant investigating the "-isms" of history: liberalism, communism,
fascism, and so on. What all of these have in common is an outlook on the
way that society should be structured. In this respect, ideology is different
from a theory, in that it goes beyond trying to describe what is or has been
observed and moves into the normative area of reacting to the existing by
detailing what should be. As such, it is an outline of the dominant values of
a society; a blueprint for attaining the goals, ideals, and policies; and an indication of the relevant tactics to be pursued by the state, political elites,
and the masses.

Ideology differs from religion in that the explanations that are given
are typically not grounded in faith. The term *ideology* began to be used as
a concept following the French Revolution, which explains the emphasis
on the study of ideas related to this world, as opposed to connections with
the eternal. Reacting to the dominance of the church, ideology was seen as
antifaith, whereas the church, religion, and faith are spiritual beliefs tied to
God that infuse ideas about reality. Ideology, in contrast, involves normative ideas about the sociopolitical structures as detached from any spiritual
reality. This reflects the Western humanist view that ideas are grounded in
materialism or even natural law but are not tied to a religious doctrine. This
division between ideas about social structures that are created using rational
analysis and ideas informed by faith makes sense in the historical development of Western Europe but is much less applicable to much of the rest of
the world, where there is less of a tradition of separation of church and state.
Thus ideology, as it is applied more broadly throughout the world, retains
the distinction that religious ideas are not typically considered ideological,
but the line between the two is blurred at best.

The debate over the role of ideologies has produced four basic arguments: they are irrelevant, they are like structures in that they shape people's
behavior, they are important in mobilizing people against the government,
and they are important in consolidating power.

The argument that ideology is irrelevant is grounded not in a dislike of
ideas or in thinking that ideas do not matter, but usually in more structurally

oriented analyses. Structures shape the outcomes of revolutions, not the beliefs of individuals. Skocpol has elegantly argued against the notion that ideology is an important component of revolutions (1994a). There are two key facets to her argument. First is the fact that ideologies are normative abstractions that can never be holistically put into practice. Responding to the argument that Enlightenment ideology set up the French Revolution, she argues, "we should not make the mistake of assuming that the talkers and the legislators could ever straightforwardly shape outcomes according to Enlightenment principles" (1994a: 206). Rather, revolutions are so complex that no one group or individual shapes the ultimate outcomes. Thus, the ideas advanced by these people cannot have a defining role. Wickham-Crowley echoes this sentiment when he asserts that "for China and Russia, the notion that revolutionaries consciously guided by communist ideologies brought down the old regimes is laughable: the Bolsheviks were underground and Lenin in Swiss exile when February food riots and garrison desertions brought down the old regime in 1917; Mao Zedong was but a child and the Chinese Communist Party not yet in existence when the Manchu dynasty collapsed in 1910–12" (1997: 41–42). The second part of Skocpol's critique is that there is no causal relationship between the ideology and the revolution. Modern revolutions, according to Skocpol, are fought by "contending armies rather than by Leninist parties, militant clerics, or well-read legislators" (1994a: 207). Ideologies do not cause revolutions, armies do.

Ideologies can, however, be viewed as similar to structures. The main argument of the structural perspective is that major events in history, such as revolutions, are a product of the larger context. Ideologies can fit into that larger context. William Sewell Jr. argues that the Enlightenment thinking shaped the context of the French and subsequent European revolutions (1985). This way of thinking was not a revolutionary ideology per se, in that it lacked a clear action strategy, but it redefined the perceived relationship of subject and sovereign. A "political culture of resistance and opposition" can be viewed as similar to an ideological perspective that encourages revolution (Foran 1997). Foran argues that formally articulated ideologies and manifestos often depend on the broader cultural context that is steeped in revolutionary or resistance history. An example of this would be the Sandinistas in Nicaragua. They were a Marxist group, but their name and success depended upon association with Augusto Cesar Sandino, the legendary anti-imperialist guerrilla of Nicaraguan history. Sandino's activity and popularity among the peasantry allowed the FSLN to immediately create parallels that helped to activate resistance. Thus, the ideology of the FSLN was shaped by the historical context, but by integrating this political culture of resistance, the ideology was able to strengthen support. Moaddel proposes a similar argument that the reason bazaaris and workers in Iran became revolutionary was that the Shiite revolutionary discourse transformed normal social discontent into revolutionary fervor (1993).

Ideologies can explain why people participate in revolutions (though this popular conception is generally not accepted within the structurally oriented scholarship). Revolutions are risky endeavors. "Other things being equal, people, like electric currents, take the path of least resistance. As Trotsky once put it, 'People do not make revolution eagerly any more than they do war. . . . A revolution takes place only when there is no other way out'" (Goodwin 2001: 26). The reason people do not rush to war or revolution is the very high cost (death) and the low likelihood of success (when confronting an organized military defending its territory). How, then, do we account for people ever taking up the revolutionary cause? One answer that Stephen Walt gives is that people are motivated "as much by moral commitments as by narrow self-interest" (1996: 24). There are "true believers" who are willing to give their lives for a cause (Hoffer 1951). Defining that cause is the domain of ideology. These "normative theories of action" explain existing social conditions and provide people with guidelines for how to react to them (Walt 1996). Most important, ideologies persuade individuals to act or participate in revolutions.

Walt argues that revolutionary ideologies do this in three ways. First, they convince followers that revolution is morally required. Ideologies do this by demonizing the existing government. For example, Ayatollah Ruhollah Khomeini, leading up to the Iranian Revolution, argued that the world could be divided into "oppressors (the superpowers, their allies, and their various puppets), and the oppressed (the victims of imperialist exploitation, such as Iran)" (Walt 1996: 213). The oppressors sought to "exploit our riches, our underground wealth, our lands, and our human resources" by "corrupting the minds and morals of the people" (Walt 1996: 213–214). The shah of Iran, viewed as a puppet enabling this exploitation, was thus an agent of evil. The fact that the government is portrayed as evil and incapable of change makes compromise impossible. Citizens are left with the choice of complicity with evil or revolution. The morality of revolution is important for a revolutionary ideology because it protects revolutionary leaders from appearing self-interested. The cause espoused is universal, and thus the revolution is not just about an individual taking power; it is a larger cause, something for the sake of humanity.

Second, despite their being portrayed as universally good, revolutionary ideologies also appeal to rational self-interest in that they convince followers that revolution will bring about significant benefits to average citizens. These may be somewhat generalized, such as good government or the ability to participate in the political process, but they must be substantial enough to offer an actual individual benefit. Without this assurance, there is no incentive to participate. It is not just that a participant will have helped rid the world of evil, but that the direct result of that will be liberty, equality, and humanity (in the French Revolution), a worker's paradise where class exploitation has ended (in the Russian Revolution), or the rule of God on earth ensuring salvation (in the Iranian Revolution).

Third, revolutionary ideologies convince followers that revolutionary success is inevitable. This is justified through scientific analysis (as Marxism argues) or the will of God (in both the natural law form that animates liberalism as well as in more explicitly religious ideologies promoting a theocracy). Revolutionaries in Latin America looked to history to suggest that communism was the wave of the future, as Marx had predicted. It had spread from Russia, to China, to Cuba, and the socioeconomic conditions of most Latin American countries were ripe for the continued progression. In each of these ways, revolutionary ideologies help to motivate people to participate. This is extremely important because, as Goldstone argues, the key to revolutions is a coalition of diverse groups to challenge the state; "the main role of ideologies in revolutions is to bring together diverse grievances and interests under a simple and appealing set of symbols of opposition" (1994: 14).

In addition to mobilizing people to participate in revolutions, ideologies can also be important in the consolidation of power after the existing regime has been overthrown. Goldstone (1994a) and Selbin (1993) argue that ideology does not become influential until revolutionary groups turn against each other in an effort to seize control of the now toppled government. Goldstone says that although ideologies are particularly fluid at this time (that is, they change rapidly), they are extremely influential in providing a framework for the rebuilding and reorganization of the state. Selbin argues that for revolutions to be successful, they must do more than build new institutions in the place of those torn down in the process of revolt; they must also consolidate power by convincing people to embrace the "opportunity to make a better life for themselves and their children" (Selbin 1993: 14). The primary way that this occurs is through dissemination of the revolutionary ideology. Ideology, espoused by visionary leaders, sells the "revolutionary project" to the masses; "[those leaders] seek to articulate and justify the desires of the population, kindle dramatic visions of the future, to justify the sacrifices of the present, and evoke the fervor of community—the sense of liberation from the alienated and atomistic past" (Selbin 1993: 79–80). In this way, ideology also plays a role in mobilization. It is not mobilization of the masses against the government but rather toward a new vision of the future after the government has been toppled. One of the key factors to note is that the group or coalition leading the charge against the government may not be the same group or coalition consolidating power, explaining the fluidity of ideologies in revolution.

There are a variety of roles that ideology can play in revolutions, whether in setting the context, mobilizing challengers to the government, or consolidating power after the fall of the old regime. Given the role that revolutionary ideologies can play, the remainder of this chapter and the next chapter summarize the dominant ideologies that have been successfully utilized in revolution.

Liberalism

We fight not to enslave, but to set a country free, and to make room upon the earth for honest men to live. —Thomas Paine

Liberalism as a revolutionary ideology has been prominent primarily in producing democratic states, or regimes that overthrew authoritarian states. It is the first and most pervasive of the revolutionary ideologies. Liberal ideology came about in the late 1600s, responding to what was perceived as the excessive growth of monarchical power. Liberalism was the predominant political ideology that came out of the Enlightenment of Western Europe. The crux of this long trend was a reevaluation of all accepted wisdom. The Enlightenment was based on the notion that we could understand the world around us through empirical observations that could lead us to change our behavior, making the world a better place. This took place first in the scientific fields, leading to new ideas about the way the heavenly bodies moved (aiding navigation), the way our bodies work (aiding medicine), the way gravity affects all matter (aiding mechanical engineering), and eventually the way that societies originated and are constructed. Each of these ideas challenged existing knowledge and power structures. With the Enlightenment, everything was up for reconsideration and empirical testing.

In the realm of societies, philosophers such as Thomas Hobbes and John Locke investigated the origins of society. They argued that "man" in a state of nature was self-interested, but as a result of this, life was "solitary, poor, nasty, brutish, and short" (Hobbes 1996: 84). To alleviate this, people created societies to regulate each others' behaviors, in a very limited sense. More specifically, they created a social contract by means of which they gave up some of their naturally derived freedom to get security from a sovereign ruler. John Locke, writing in the 1680s, developed the essential character of liberalism: that "all men are naturally in . . . a state of perfect freedom to order their actions, and dispose of their possessions and persons, as they think fit" (Locke 1690: 8). They voluntarily give up a very limited amount of freedom when they "make themselves members of some politic society" (1690: 24). This act of joining society is what others termed the social contract—every member of society agrees to the laws of that society by becoming a member.

Because of the focus on the state of nature and the issue of control over property, later philosophers portrayed this ideology as fundamentally conservative. Marxists have portrayed the Enlightenment as focused exclusively on economic interactions. Bronner counters that

> the idea of "interest" originally meant something more than economic gain. As the Enlightenment wore on, moreover, many became wary of egoism and its consequences: Adam Smith became concerned with moral sentiments, David Hume embraced tradition, Rousseau sought to introduce the "general will," Voltaire became ever more occupied with the sufferings of ordinary people, while Kant and his friends highlighted the role of moral philosophy. In truth, the general interest was never absent from enlightenment political thinking because it was never the stolid and conservative philosophy of a ruling class, but instead that of a class on the rise in need of coalitional support. (2004: 42)

The revolutionary element of the social contract developed by Locke and others is that when government no longer fulfills its duty to provide for the common good, individuals have the right to rebel against that government; the contract has been broken.

Locke's ideas met fertile ground in the North American colonies, where Thomas Jefferson clarified and applied this liberal ideology in the 1776 Declaration of Independence. The declaration so clearly and succinctly states the key themes of liberal ideology that it is quoted at length below.

> When in the Course of human Events, it becomes necessary for one People to dissolve the Political Bands which have connected them with another, and to assume among the Powers of the Earth, the separate and equal Station to which the Laws of Nature and of Nature's God entitle them, a decent Respect to the Opinions of Mankind requires that they should declare the causes which impel them to the Separation.
>
> We hold these Truths to be self-evident, that all Men are created equal, that they are endowed by their Creator with certain unalienable Rights, that among these are Life, Liberty, and the Pursuit of Happiness— That to secure these Rights, Governments are instituted among Men, deriving their just Powers from the Consent of the Governed, that whenever any Form of Government becomes destructive to these Ends, it is the Right

of the People to alter or to abolish it, and to institute new Government, laying its Foundation on such Principles, and organizing its Powers in such Form, as to them shall seem most likely to effect their Safety and Happiness. Prudence, indeed, will dictate that Governments long established should not be changed for light and transient Causes; and accordingly all Experience hath shown, that Mankind are more disposed to suffer, while Evils are sufferable, than to right themselves by abolishing the Forms to which they are accustomed. But when a long Train of Abuses and Usurpations, pursuing invariably the same Object, evinces a Design to reduce them under absolute Despotism, it is their Right, it is their Duty, to throw off such Government, and to provide new Guards for their Security. (Jefferson 2010)

This statement contains all of the revolutionary elements of liberal ideology that have been applied to revolutions since that document. The key elements are that individuals have natural rights to liberty. Governments are constructed to maintain the individual's ability to exercise that liberty, primarily in the form of mediating property disputes. Property is fundamental to exercising liberty, as it allows individuals to provide for themselves. When a government goes beyond providing this basic framework for mediation, it begins to usurp these natural rights. Thus, the power of the state should necessarily be limited. Again, this ideology is used exclusively against a powerful state that is seen as restricting liberties. In the 1700s, this was the ideology of the colonists in North America, of much of the French Revolution, and then in revolutionary movements throughout much of Europe. It continued to be influential in democracy movements through the twentieth century, even playing a role in contemporary revolutionary movements such as some of the "soft" revolutions of the former Soviet Republics (e.g., Ukraine).

In terms of establishing a new form of government, liberal ideology argues for a limited government that protects the rights of individuals. This has necessarily entailed two related elements: political and economic. Both of them emphasize the autonomy of the individual, but in different spheres. Political liberalism emphasized the autonomy of the individual in exercising rights upon which no government could impinge, whereas economic liberalism focused on the role of the individual operating within the free market. The institutionalization of these ideals has been republican democracy and capitalism. The republican democratic government allows the individual to shape the form of the government, with the exception that certain rights are always guaranteed (avoiding the prospect of mob rule). Capitalism entails individuals engaging in commerce in an open market where individual preferences determine supply and demand to create prices for the buying and selling of goods and services.

Liberalism more recently has continued to be influential in revolutionary movements against communism, dictatorial regimes, and the apartheid regime in South Africa. A brief discussion of examples of these movements illustrates the important power of liberalism as a revolutionary ideology.

Anticommunist: Vaclav Havel in Czechoslovakia

> *I really do inhabit a system in which words are capable of shaking the entire structure of government, where words can prove mightier than ten military divisions.* —Vaclav Havel

Liberalism was the dominant ideology used by the very diverse groups who opposed the continued rule by the communist parties in Eastern Europe and the Soviet Union. Vaclav Havel was the best known of a group of intellectuals opposing Soviet-imposed rule in Czechoslovakia. After a reform movement in 1968, referred to as the Prague Spring, the Soviet Union led the Warsaw Pact countries in an invasion of Czechoslovakia to install a new leadership more in line with the Soviets. The intellectuals formed around a group called Charter 77, formed in 1977 as a campaign to get the government to abide by the newly signed Helsinki Covenant on Human Rights. Havel was a playwright with an international reputation, and thus became one of the leading spokespersons of the movement to pressure reforms in what he called the posttotalitarian system. The group of intellectuals produced a rich literature, called *samizdat,* that was both illegal and widely circulated among intellectuals in Eastern Europe. It became the mechanism for discussing the liberal ideology for much of the anticommunist movements in 1989. The ideology that Havel developed embodied four key themes.

The roots of Czech dissident ideology are found in the phenomenological tradition that developed among intellectuals throughout the 1960s and 1970s. The crux of the phenomenological view of the world was that ideas exist apart from their expression in objective reality; as Tucker summarizes, "phenomenologists seek to intuit pure ideas" (2000: 10). This philosophy holds that there is truth that exists "irrespective of external circumstances" that can be "discovered through intuition" (2000: 10). This is important because it provides a way for dissidents to view the way the world ought to be, in contrast to the materialist-oriented Soviet-Marxist system. Havel highlights this distinction nicely. On the one hand is "the natural world" where "categories like justice, honor, treason, friendship, infidelity, courage or empathy have a wholly tangible content, relating to actual persons and important for actual life. At the basis of this world are values which are simply there, perennially, before we ever speak of them, before we reflect upon them and inquire about them" (Havel 1992a: 250–251). In contrast to this, Havel presents the "absolute of so-called objectivity: the objective, rational cognition of the scientific model of the world" (1992a: 252). This perspective "kills God and takes his place on the vacant throne so that henceforth it would be science which would hold the order of being in its hand as its sole legitimate guardian and be the sole legitimate arbiter of all relevant truth" (1992a: 252). Havel does not argue that technology is evil or that there are no benefits from modern science; he simply rejects the notion that science can give us answers to the most important questions.

The second element of Havel's ideology builds on the theme of Soviet moral vacancy. Havel argues that the totalitarian system represents the most extreme version of the scientific method applied to political systems. It is one logical conclusion of a bureaucratized state (1992a: 260). This basis on the rationalism pulls humans away from eternal realities. The eternal realm of ideas has no meaning whatsoever because words cease to have any meaning when they are defined and manipulated by the rationalist system. According to Havel, the larger manifestation of this was the lie that citizens in the Soviet system lived every day of their lives. The most damning aspect of the Soviet system was that it sapped the moral essence of humanity and left only a concern with material reality in its place.

If the greatest evil that a system can create is the lack of morality, then the third element of Havel's ideology is how to resist that system: by living according to a moral ideal. In Havel's "The Power of the Powerless," he writes that "the primary breeding ground for what might, in the widest possible sense of the word, be understood as an opposition in the post-totalitarian system is living within the truth" (1992b: 149). The most fundamental act of opposition then is to reject the ideology of scientific modernism. He identifies what "living in truth" entails:

> When I speak of living within the truth, I naturally do not have in mind only products of conceptual thought, such as a protest letter written by a group of intellectuals. It can be any means by which a person or a group revolts against manipulation: anything from a letter by intellectuals to a workers' strike, from a rock concert to a student demonstration, from refusing to vote in the farcical elections to making an open speech at some official congress, or even a hunger strike, for instance. If the suppression of the aims of life is a complex process, and if it is based on the multifaceted manipulation of all expressions of life, then, by the same token, every free expression of life indirectly threatens the post-totalitarian system politically. (1992b: 150–151)

The fourth aspect of Havel's revolutionary ideology is the communal aspect that it assumed. The act of living in truth is personal; one can be the sole opposition to an unjust system (Havel 1992d, 1992a). For justice to spread to others, however, individuals must focus their efforts on creating broader social change. Havel develops this point in a letter commemorating a doctor and political advocate. The doctor "realized early in his life that he could not confront human suffering solely as a good neighbor and doctor, but, if he was to remain true to his conscience, he had also to try to understand the social context of that suffering and discover a social way to eliminate it" (Havel 1992c: 366). Underlying the theme of living in truth is always the assumption that there would be a move from the individual dissident to create change in his or her community. Tucker concludes that "dissidents founded their political struggle for human rights on a concept of the good life as life in truth that should be promoted by the political community. Thus, they founded liberal politics on communitarian assumptions" (2000: 15). This version of liberalism was common among the Eastern European movements in 1989 and was a direct response to the existing regimes in many communist countries.

Antidictatorial: Chamorro in Nicaragua

No work of progress is good unless it is for the progress of the poor.
—Pedro Joaquin Chamorro

Although the Sandinistas eventually led the opposition to the dictatorial Anastasio Somoza regime in Nicaragua, there were also a variety of active prodemocracy opposition groups. In 1974, a number of them formed the coalition group Democratic Union of Liberation (UDEL), under the leadership of Pedro Joaquin Chamorro, the editor of an independent newspaper, *La Prensa*. Although UDEL did not seek elective office, it was organized to "constitute a permanent and public anti-Somoza front" (Berryman 1984: 69). The revolutionary ideology that Chamorro and others in the democracy group advocated can best be described as democratic within the nationalistic legacy of Latin American dissidents.

Chamorro outlined "a five-point program for democratizing Nicaragua, which included amnesty for all political prisoners, an end to martial law, political freedom, and the elimination of press censorship" (Chamorro 1996: 108). As with most dissidents in Latin America, Chamorro was heavily influenced by previous revolutionaries. These included Nicaraguan nationalists such as Augusto Cesar Sandino but also included the victors of the Cuban Revolution (Fidel Castro and Che Guevara). Chamorro led a delegation of young conservatives to Cuba in 1959 to get support from Fidel Castro, who rejected them as too conservative (Zimmerman 2000). Without Castro's support, Chamorro then organized the first air invasion in Latin

America from a base in Costa Rica where he had been training a hundred guerrillas for a coup (Edmisten 1990). This association with the Cuban Revolution does not mean that Chamorro was allied with the communists in Nicaragua. In his *Diary of a Prisoner,* he wrote, "I have fought against Communists. . . . They are and continue to be our enemies, but it is necessary to say that the same cause which produces them (at least in Nicaragua) is the same that produces movements like our own" (quoted in Edmisten 1990: 40). The cause was the dictatorial regime of Somoza.

The growing popularity of communist explanations of the necessity for revolution and interpretations of Sandino's legacy prompted Chamorro to distinguish his democratic push for change from that of the FSLN. He argued that "revolution is necessary not because the Communists say it is, but because revolution is necessary when there is no roof, bread, liberty, and work for the majority of people. It is also necessary that the revolution be Christian because only in this way can respect for individual dignity be maintained within community life" (quoted in Edmisten 1990: 41). Chamorro feared the popularity of the communists because of their perceived atheist ideology (which the FSLN downplayed to attract support). Nicaragua was deeply Catholic, as was Chamorro, and he feared that a communist revolution would lead to the destruction of the church. He also distinguished Sandino's legacy from that of the communists, in an attempt to further isolate them from the masses. In an essay in *La Prensa,* he argued that "it is not true that Sandino was a Communist, but he was a nationalist, which is different. . . . Sandino was not able to accept the internationalization that the Communists pursue because he essentially was a nationalist and a patriot, that is, the opposite of what fundamentally the Communists are" (quoted in Edmisten 1990: 53). This combination of nationalism in the legacy of Sandino and democracy sums up Chamorro's ideology, which took the key elements of liberalism and applied them to the Latin American context.

Antiapartheid: Mandela in South Africa

For to be free is not merely to cast off one's chains, but to live in a way that respects and enhances the freedom of others. —Nelson Mandela

The last example of a liberal ideology used in a revolutionary context comes from the South African struggle against the apartheid system. In 1948 the National Party, an Afrikaner-dominated political party, won national elections and began to implement white domination under a system called apartheid. Over the next decade, the apartheid government passed laws forbidding mixed marriages, required all citizens to be registered in one of the four racial categories, organized land ownership by race, established Bantustans or homelands for blacks and required that they live on the marginal lands of South Africa (which constituted only 13 percent of the landmass of South Africa), created separate educational systems, and ensured that only whites could vote. The liberal antiapartheid movement is somewhat ironic, as technically the ruling regime was democratic, with an elected parliament, president, and independent judicial system. South Africa was not democratic in the modern sense, however, as this system only applied to whites, excluding roughly 90 percent of the population. The ideology that infused the movement was, however, no less liberal in its goals. The opening lines to the Freedom Charter, written in 1955 to resist the newly created apartheid system, mirror liberal declarations of other countries: "We the people of South Africa declare for all our country and the world to know that South Africa belongs to all who live in it, black and white and that no government can justly claim authority unless it is based on the will of the people" (quoted in Lawson 2005: 121).

The African National Congress (ANC) was one of the key opposition groups to challenge the government. Throughout its long struggle it had received significant funding, training, and arms from the Soviet Union and other communist countries and had adopted much communist rhetoric. In 1988, the ANC agreed, however, to accept the need for a mixed economy, embracing the economic element of liberalism as well, and allowing the ANC to become more mainstream and to allay fears that they were a communist front organization.

> In early 1990, the Harare Declaration outlined the ANC's terms for the suspension of the armed struggle and the onset of negotiations [with the government]: commitment to a united, democratic and non-racial South Africa; universal suffrage; a codified bill of rights; the release of political prisoners; a lifting of the ban on the ANC and other opposition groups; the removal of troops from the townships; an end to the state of emergency; and the repeal of proscriptive legislation. (Lawson 2005: 133)

Finally, Nelson Mandela, the head of the ANC, summarized his liberal orientation when he was released from prison, repeating "the words he had first spoken at the Rivonia Trials twenty six years before: During my lifetime I have dedicated myself to the struggle of the African people. I have fought against white domination and I have fought against black domination. I have cherished the ideal of a democratic and free society in which all persons live together in harmony and with equal opportunities" (Lawson 2005: 135).

Table 4.1 lists groups that advocated liberal revolutionary ideologies at some point in their revolutionary campaign.

		Date of Revolution, Rebellion, or
Group	Country	Party Founding
Sons of Liberty	United States of America	1776
Charter 77	Czechoslovakia	1970s
Democratic Union of Liberation (UDEL)	Nicaragua	1970s
Estonian Independence Party	Estonia	1987–1991
Civic Forum	Czechoslovakia	1989
People's Front of Ukraine for Reconstruction	Ukraine	1989
African National Congress (ANC)	South Africa	1991–1994
United Democratic Front	South Africa	1983

Table 4.1 Groups That Advocated Liberal Revolutionary Ideologies

Nationalism

Utopianism is probably a necessary social device for generating the super-human efforts without which no major revolution is achieved.
—E. J. Hobsbawm

One result of the Enlightenment thinking that spawned liberalism was the concept of peoples as associated at a national level. A nation is a relatively large group of people who share common customs, origins, history, and frequently language. If they are organized under an independent government, they constitute a nation-state. Nationalism is usually viewed as pride in one's own people combined with the belief that those people should be sovereign. It becomes a revolutionary ideology when a group of people do not have sovereignty. The group seeks to create a nation-state by separating from an imposing force or taking control from a government that does not reflect the nation's interests.

The variety of forms that this can take is innumerable. For example, a people can argue that they do not have sovereignty because the absolute monarch has unjustly usurped it (as was the case in the French Revolution) or because imperialists have usurped it (as was the case in the Nicaraguan Revolution). The dominant ideology in each of these cases was liberalism and Marxism, respectively, but each revolution also entailed nationalist elements, as most revolutions typically do. Although the dominant ideology may espouse more universal ideals that are applied to people as a class or as autonomous individuals with liberties, every revolution seeks to over-throw the existing government in that regime first. The French may have re-volted for *"liberté, égalité, fraternité"* (liberty, equality, brotherhood), but the target of their action initially was the monarchy of France, and not any of their neighbors. The dissolution of the Soviet Union, even though osten-sibly guided by liberal ideology, was primarily driven by nationalist senti-ments. Boris Yeltsin's appeal was for a liberal democratic republic, but a liberal democratic republic for Russians. The revolutionaries of his cadre did not seek to maintain the Soviet Union under a democratic framework; they sought democracy for Russia. The facade of liberal democracy was even less apparent in most of the other republics as they sought to regain national sovereignty from the Soviet Union.

A version of nationalism can be formed around the ethnic qualities of a people. Ethnicity is a constructed, though relevant, set of attributes and so-cietal institutions that make one group of people culturally different from others. Ethnicity has been based on physical characteristics (such as race), language, religion, and lineage (though that may have produced no notice-able differences). The separation of Yugoslavia into its constituent republics was driven primarily by ethnic nationalism—the ideology that justifies in-dependence for an ethnically defined group of people. The divisions be-tween Croats, Serbs, and Bozniaks were drawn primarily along religious affiliation. Chechen rebels in southern Russia view themselves as distinct because they are Muslim. In contrast, the difference between the "blacks" and "Arabs" in the Darfur region of Sudan is driven more by lineage and the historic occupations of families. Those of "black 'African' descent . . . pri-marily practice sedentary agriculture and those who claim 'Arab' descent are mostly semi-nomadic livestock herders" (Straus 2005). A similarly difficult distinction fueled the revolutionary movement that in part sparked the geno-cide in Rwanda. Thus, even though ethnic nationalism does not share a long intellectual history stemming from Enlightenment thinkers, it has had no less an impact on motivating revolutionary activity or determining the out-come of countries' boundaries.

Two examples of prominent nationalist-oriented ideologies will help to clarify the role of nationalism in promoting revolutions.

Cultural Nationalism: Gandhi in India

What we have tested and found true on the anvil of experience, we dare not change. Many thrust their advice upon India, and she remains steady. This is her beauty: it is the sheet-anchor of our hope.
—Mohandas Gandhi

Mohandas K. Gandhi is typically remembered for his unwavering stance on the primacy of nonviolent action as the only legitimate means to achieve Indian independence. But the focus of most of his campaigns was independence, which he advocated using a nationalist ideology. "As Ainslie Embree observes . . . 'no other leader in history in his own lifetime has done so much to make a people into a nation'" (Steger 2000: 10). The nationalism that Gandhi espoused was what Steger calls "cultural nationalism." He distinguishes this from

> political nationalists, who typically strive for the creation of an autonomous state based on common citizenship, [whereas] cultural nationalists generate influential discourses of the nation beyond politics, [and] distrust state-centered models of their legal-rational roots in modernity. They emphasize the cultural realm of "the people" as a permanent life force that enunciates a popular "truth" in spite of domination and the corruption of elites. . . . Although the goals and techniques of cultural nationalists differ from those of their political counterparts, the former often become active in the political movements they inspire. (Steger 2000: 90–91)

Building on Tolstoy's *Letter to a Hindu,* Gandhi reasoned that there was only one way that 30,000 "rather weak and ill-looking" Britons could enslave 200 million "vigorous, clever, strong, and freedom-loving people" (quoted in Steger 2000: 92). The Indians must have allowed the British to enslave them, "for the sole purpose of advancing their own material interests" (2000: 92). That is, some Indians gained material comforts from being colonized. This leads to two fundamental elements of Gandhi's nationalism: purification leading to noncooperation. The soul of India had been polluted by Western materialism. As Steger summarizes Gandhi's Hind Swaraj (Indian Self-Rule or Home-Rule), Gandhi

> never hesitates to drive his stern message home, accusing his fellow citizens of having become indolent and "effeminate." Nurturing selfish thoughts of personal material gain generated by the perverted ethos of modern civilization, modern Indians habitually surrendered to their cravings for pleasure. Contented to hand over control of their nation to the foreign exponents of materialistic lifestyle, they had turned into sly sycophants and willing servants of the empire, thereby proving to the world that they were morally "unfit to serve the country." . . . The only way to reverse India's decline and shake off its self-imposed yoke of dependency was to bring about the moral regeneration of self and nation through the reappropriation of a virtuous way of life without parliaments, machinery, lawyers, and large cities. (2000: 92–93)

When Indians had individually purified themselves by rejecting Western comforts, only then could they achieve independence. By rejecting the Western lifestyle, casting off the British would then be easy. Thus, noncooperation was the primary tactic for forcing the British to leave India. It is equally important that Gandhi saw this form of nonviolent struggle as embedded in Indian civilization, and thus it represented a break from the militarist legacy of the West as well. The purpose, Steger argues, behind this focus on Indian civilization was nationalist:

> As one of South Asia's leading cultural nationalists, Gandhi confronted his audience with the myth of India's ancient civilization in order to introduce an alternative to present forms of nationalism. The goal was to create new patriotic values that nonetheless bore the stamp of age-old "authenticity." Imported into India and imitated by the Indians, Europe's shallow "obsession with history" was, according to Gandhi, responsible for the modern explosion of greed and disharmony that betrayed India's inherited tradition of elevating the unchanging moral truths over the fleeting achievements of history. Indeed, Gandhi's morality tales of ancient India performed most of the functions typically associated with political myths: the strengthening of group solidarity in the face of major challenges, the supply of compelling arguments for the abolition of undesirable institutions or conditions, the inspiration of group members with confidence in their destiny, the glorification of their past achievements, and the inauguration of a new symbolic order that engenders a sense of awe and fascination in true believers. (2000: 99)

In short, Gandhi's cultural nationalism was pure revolutionary ideology.

Chinese Nationalism: Sun Yat-sen

> *The principles of President Lincoln completely coincide with mine. He said: "A government of the people, elected by the people and for the people." These principles have served as the maximum of achievement for Europeans as well as Americans. Words which have the same sense can be found in China: I have translated them: "nationalism, democracy and Socialism."* —Sun Yat-sen

In contrast to Gandhi's cultural nationalism, Sun Yat-sen illustrates the more typical political nationalism that anti-imperialist movements often embody. Sun's nationalist revolutionary ideology is summed up in his "Three People's Principles," which are difficult to translate literally but are typically interpreted as nationalism, democracy, and livelihood. For Sun, nationalism was focused on "one single idea—foster a revolution to overthrow the Manchus and thereby regain China for the Chinese" (Chang and Gordon 1991: 97). Sun's nationalism viewed the Manchu dynasty as foreigners. In this way, Sun articulated a reasoning for China's oppression: foreign rulers (the Manchu) had propagated the bad policies of letting other foreigners take control of China's economy (by controlling the port cities). Sun's ideology, however, went beyond the typical removal of the dynastic leader to be replaced by a new dynasty (as was the pattern of Chinese history for the past two millennia). Rather, he "sought a new society with political, economic, and social changes. Sun clearly saw the need to have a 'plan to reconstruct,' to develop a genuine 'reform' (*kai-tsao*) program, even before taking action to destroy the old regime" (Chang and Gordon 1991: 97).

Sun's program was to encourage democracy, though he thought that China was not yet ready for full democracy in the Western sense. As such, he wanted to balance the power of the people (freedom and equality) with the power of the government, in order to avoid either extreme of anarchy and chaos or despotism and tyranny. To do this, Sun advocated (though never implemented) a "Five-Power Constitution." The constitution embodied Western liberal thinking with two added Chinese elements. The first three powers—the executive, legislative, and judicial branches—were identical to those in the US constitution that he studied. The last two branches incorporated Chinese institutions, two additional and equal branches of government. The examination branch would run exams so that civil service would be staffed by experts who were knowledgeable and not corrupt (hence the separate branch). The censorial branch was in charge of impeachments. "In China's traditional political experience, the right of impeachment was elevated and placed in a commission of censors with the authority to oversee the activities of high officials, including the emperor. Sun regarded this ancient system as an effective mechanism for checking the power of government and believed that it ought to be retained" (Chang and Gordon 1991: 113). The last of the three people's principles, livelihood, is the most vague and controversial. In some respects it is about development of a backward economy; in others it aligns closely with socialism. Because Sun did not as fully develop this aspect of his nationalist ideology, it is sufficient to say that he saw reforming the economy so that everyone had the ability to provide for themselves as a fundamental part of the revolution.

Table 4.2 lists groups that advocated nationalist revolutionary ideologies at some point in their revolutionary campaign.

Summary

Although there is debate over the role of ideologies in revolutions, we have seen that there are some common elements to revolutionary ideologies. All revolutionary ideologies set out to explain the problems with the current system and how a new one can be achieved. Further, they all convince followers that revolution is morally required and that revolution will bring about significant benefits to them. In addition, most revolutionary ideologies portray their vision as inevitable. After revolutions have moved into the consolidation phase, they can also shape the type of regime that emerges from the ashes of revolution. Both liberal and nationalist ideologies have demonstrated these aspects in the abstract as well as in the examples of how they were advocated by revolutionaries.

Table 4.2 Groups That Advocated Nationalist Revolutionary Ideologies

Group	Country	Date of Revolution, Rebellion, or Party Founding
Euskadi Ta Askatasuna (ETA; Basque Nationalist Party)	Spain	1895–
Irish Republican Brotherhood	Ireland	1858–1924
Indian National Congress	India	1885–
Boxers	China	1899–1901
Guomindang (GMD)	China	1912–1949
African National Congress	South Africa	1912–
Irish Republican Army (IRA)	Ireland	1919–1924
Rashtriya Swayamsevak Sangh (National Volunteers Organization)	India	1925–
Vietnamese Nationalist Party	Vietnam	1927
Nazi Party	Germany	1933–1945
Zionists	Palestine/Israel	1948
National Liberation Front (FLN)	Algeria	1962–1989
Quebec Liberation Front	Canada	1963–1970
Palestine Liberation Organization	Palestine	1964–
Grey Wolves (youth organization of the Turkish Nationalist Movement Party)	Turkey	1969
Provisional Irish Republican Army	Ireland	1969
Liberation Tigers of Tamil Eleam	Sri Lanka	1970s–
Kurdistan Workers Party	Turkey	1970s
Armenian Secret Army for the Liberation of Armenia	Lebanon	1975–1986
Sandinista National Liberation Front (FSLN)	Nicaragua	1979
Harkat ul-Mujahedeen	Afghanistan	1985
Hamas (Islamic Resistance Movement)	Palestine	1987–
Kosovo Liberation Army	Serbia	1990s
Chechen separatists	Russia	1996–2001
The National Revolutionary Front for the Liberation of Haiti	Haiti	2004

Questions for Discussion and Reflection

1. Distinguish religion, ideology, and theory. How do these differences reflect our own preferences?

2. Given your political context, what is your ideological orientation?

3. If you were to design a social contract for your society, what would be the limits and responsibilities of government?

4. Does liberalism depend upon a Christian worldview? If so, what are the implications for the spread of democracy?

5. Debate the potential positives and negatives of encouraging nationalism in the world today.

6. Should South Africa's transition to democracy be considered a revolution?

7. What parallels exist between Gandhi's nationalist ideology and Havel's liberal ideology?

5

The Role of Ideology, Part 2: Marxism and Religious Thought

Men's ideas are the most direct emanations of their material state.
—Karl Marx

Marxism

The Enlightenment thinking that spawned liberalism also gave birth to the twentieth century's most potent revolutionary ideology: Marxism. Karl Marx and Frederick Engels developed the ideas of communism and popularized them for generations of revolutionaries. Marx and Engels were born in Germany (in 1818 and 1820, respectively), where they both studied the ideas of Georg Wilhelm Friedrich Hegel (1770–1831). They were particularly attracted to Hegel's philosophy of history, on which much of Marxist analysis is built.[1]

Hegel argued that history was moving in a discernable direction with purpose. As history progressed, clashes between competing forces continually moved history forward. This process he called dialectic, the progress of humanity from one historical epoch to the next moved by conflict among competing forces. This occurs, Hegel explained, because virtually everything creates its own opposite: masters necessarily create slaves; wealth necessarily creates poverty. The direction of history, however, is toward a final synthesis. That is, the opposing forces would eventually come together to eliminate conflict. This was grounded in a religious understanding that God guided the direction of history.

Marx built on Hegel's ideas to create what he termed historical materialism (also referred to as dialectical materialism, indicating the debt to Hegel). Rather than being guided by the hand of God, for Marx saw God as created by humans, history was progressing because of an underlying economic reality. The fundamental force of Marx's theory of society was that economics determines our sociopolitical realities. The dialectic that drives history is a conflict between economic classes. A class is nothing more than a grouping of individuals by similar economic status, though there is a social aspect to class in that it is defined by others in the society.

Economics is the study of the production, distribution, and consumption of goods and services, which for Marx explained all social and political relationships. Production is the area that Marx focused on most, particularly because it is the beginning of the economic chain of goods and services and thus drives the other elements. Production, Marx argued, is dependent upon existing technology. If the only technology available is a stick and the natural flooding of a river, the production of food is going to be limited. With the development of new technologies, however, new and more goods can be produced. The advent of irrigation and selective breeding of crops, for example, allows for more food to be produced. Marx called this the forces of production, because technology drives the levels of what is available to be consumed. These forces of production lead to the dominant mode of production, the more abstract characterization of how the most valued goods and services are produced. If the leading technology is irrigation and oxen, the dominant mode of production in a society is likely to be agriculture. If new technologies allow for greater production, this will shift the mode of production. As technologies encourage specialization and trade of goods and services, the mode of production shifts. For example, the development of the factory where one person does the same task over and over in conjunction with other workers doing different tasks to create an item (a cart for example) led to greater production than all of those workers each making their own carts. The increased use of factories and machines to encourage this increased production led to the greater concentration of workers in cities.

The result of the dominant mode of production was thus the creation of a particular social system modified to augment that mode of production. Thus, we often talk about agricultural societies, industrial, and even postindustrial societies. The point that Marx makes is that each of these social systems is determined by the economic system (the production of goods and services). The social structures of an agricultural system are necessarily tied to the land and thus people live closer to the land, dispersed throughout the countryside. In contrast, because workers are needed in close proximity to the factories, industrial societies encourage urbanization.

In each of these economically determined social systems, there is also a government. Governments belong to what Marx labels the superstructures of society. Economics is the base or substructure of a society that determines the superstructure, the largely irrelevant dressing over the economic base. Marx often refers to the metaphor of a veil in this regard. Imagine that you have a chair, over which you drape a sheet. From the outside it looks as though the sheet has shape and form, but we know that the form is dictated by the chair. Should the chair be removed, the sheet would fall to the ground. Marx viewed superstructures as similarly misleading. Government, religion, culture, and nationalism were all superstructures that simply draped over the economic reality. From the outside they make us think that they are real and permanent, but they are economically determined. They are further molded and used by those benefiting from the economic structure to justify their superior place. Not unlike the sheet over the chair, they are meant to protect and preserve the underlying structure.

But, as Marx has shown, new technologies arise that lead to new modes of production that will necessarily force changes in society. This is where Marx's theory becomes relevant to revolutions. Marx views revolutions as a natural part of historical materialism in that they serve as the transition points from one economic system to another. Revolutions, he argues, arise when there is a gap between the base and the superstructure. The forces of production have changed the mode of production leading to social changes, but the superstructure resists change. This is because those in control of the government benefit from the existing system. The end result must be that the old system is smashed by the new one.

The proof of this inevitable cycle is in history. Marx argued that initially humans lived a form of primitive communism. This gave way to the domination of master over slave (as in ancient civilizations), then noble and serf (feudalism), and finally to the current stage of capitalism in which the bourgeoisie exploit the proletariat. The capitalist system is determined by the workers who sell their labor for wages (proletariat) to those who own the materials that the workers use for production (bourgeoisie). Given the history of class conflict and new economic systems yielding new social systems, Marx argued that history was moving toward the destruction of the existing capitalist system to be replaced by a new one. The French Revolution nicely illustrates Marx's ideas about change. Leading up to the 1780s, meaningful changes had occurred in the means of production; there had been a significant shift from wealth located in the hands of the aristocracy who controlled the countryside and the urban craftsmen. Eventually, this came to a crisis point when the merchants could no longer continue to grow, given the constraints imposed on them by the existing political system that favored the aristocracy. The nobility would not give up power, so the guildsmen mobilized the urban workers to overthrow the existing regime and create a new one structured to benefit them. This is when industrialization exploded in France, according to Marx, because the superstructure had been remade to match the changes in the economic base.

Like the French Revolution, the coming end of capitalism would take the form of the proletariat rising up to smash the bourgeoisie and seizing the means of production. This would necessarily be violent, as the capitalists, like the nobility before them, would not give up their wealth without a fight. Capitalism was unique, however, Marx argued, in that it had embedded in it the seeds of its own destruction as well as the ability to end class conflict.

Marx said that there were three immutable laws of capitalism that collectively created the conditions for the end of class conflict. The law of falling rate of profit stated that through competition, prices are pushed down, but so are profits. Looking at three gas stations on an intersection, assuming the quality is the same, most people will go to the least expensive one. This will push the neighbors to lower their prices to meet the lowest price, which means that profits will also be reduced. This is important to Marx's theory, because if profits are continually declining owing to competition, owners must do something to increase profits, such as increase productivity. This leads to reinvesting capital in new technologies, allowing fewer workers to do more work. Second, the law of disproportionality states that, because of the anarchic nature of markets, there will always be the possibility of overproduction. That is, a business cannot sell everything it has produced. This has led to boom-and-bust cycles that encourage social instability. This is crucial because these cycles, if the market is unregulated (a big if, to be sure), will intensify and provide for a ripe environment for revolution. Finally, the law of concentration of capital states that capitalism tends to create a growing gap between owners and workers. This is caused by the fact that as businesses compete, some will fail. Those who fail will be bought out by more successful companies, thus reducing the number of owners and increasing the supply of potential workers. But as new technologies make production possible with fewer workers, the supply of workers will go up, reducing the wages they can demand. The successful businesses will continue to buy out more and more unsuccessful ones to the point at which there will be very few owners controlling all the others who are selling their labor at an increasingly lower rate.

Combined, these three laws of capitalism provide for its demise but also lay the foundation for the end of class conflict. Because of the technological advancements that capitalism creates and the virtual elimination of classes (as most of humanity is forced into the proletariat), a relatively simple shift is all that is required to end the cycle of exploitation. In a very short period of time, the proletariat will be able to destroy the capitalists (who are few in number) and take over the means of production to provide for their common good. Rather than the surplus value going to the bourgeoisie, that time spent producing surplus will be available for workers to do with as they please. This economic system is communism, about which Marx said relatively little.

Marxist ideas have been expanded and adapted to a wide variety of situations and used as a sophisticated analytical tool (much of the structuralist literature of revolutions owes a debt to Marxist thinking). The theory as a revolutionary ideology has also evolved at the hands of a variety of thinkers and activists. As was the case for Marx himself, many of the key developers of his theories of revolution have been revolutionary activists. Thus, it becomes difficult to determine what is advancing the ideology to make it intellectually more refined as opposed to bastardizing it to justify a grab for power. I will not become involved in that activity, but rather will present some of the relevant theoretical additions that have been made in the context of successful revolutionary movements.

Leninism

Sometimes history needs a push. —Vladimir Lenin

Marx's writings had a sense of urgency to them that the coming revolution was imminent. Thus, as time passed after his death, Marxists were forced to try to explain why that revolution had not occurred, why exploitation continued, and why the workers had not revolted. Writing in the last decade of the 1800s and first of the 1900s (prior to his role in the Russian Revolution), Vladimir Lenin developed three key elements of Marx's theory.

First, Lenin explained the delay in revolution by arguing that capitalism has an intermediate step before leading to socialism in the historical progression toward communism. In his 1920 "Theses on the National and Colonial Questions," Lenin clearly identified Western imperialism as the highest form of capitalism and explained why the seeds of destruction that are planted in capitalism had not yet taken root. In effect, imperialism delayed the horrible consequences of the three laws of capitalism. It had done this by exporting the exploitation through colonization. Lenin argued that "the acquisition of colonies had enabled the capitalist economies to dispose of their unconsumed goods, to acquire cheap resources, and to vent their surplus capital" (Gilpin 1987: 39). This allowed for capitalism to slide into democratic socialism with relatively strong unions that encouraged the expansion of worker rights in the developed capitalist economies. This meant that the workers, although still exploited, were in effect bought off, meaning the revolution was very unlikely.

Second, because of this highest stage of capitalism, Lenin argued that a vanguard party was necessary to create class consciousness and lead a revolution. Lenin saw that the proletariat tended to develop unions and fight for reform rather than revolution. Thus, for revolution to occur, there must be a committed revolutionary organization educated in Marxist theory to fully understand the progression of history.

> As he wrote, "give us an organization of revolutionaries and we shall over-turn the whole of Russia." The bourgeois intelligentsia, aware of the needs of the proletariat, had a responsibility to lead the class struggle, imparting their knowledge to the workers through propaganda and agitation. . . . For Lenin, the vanguard party should be made up of "professional revolu-tionists": a small, committed band of well-organized revolutionaries op-erating a central apparatus, and a wider network of fellow travelers. (Lawson 2005: 55)

Third, Lenin also refined the notion of historical progression. He argued that history is not the slow-moving wheel of progress, but that revolutions are a big bump that gets it rolling. Lenin stated:

> The fundamental law of revolution is as follows: for a revolution to take place it is not enough for the exploited and oppressed masses to realize the impossibility of living in the old way; for a revolution to take place it is essential that the exploiters should not be able to live and rule in the old way. It is only when the lower classes do not want to live in the old way and the upper classes cannot carry on in the old way that the revolution can triumph. This truth can be expressed in other words: revolution is impos-sible without a nation-wide crisis affecting both the exploited and the ex-ploiters. (quoted in Lawson 2005: 56)

Thus, without a catalytic event, there can be no revolution.

Leon Trotsky, a contemporary of Lenin and, like Lenin, an active par-ticipant in the Russian Revolution, added one further refinement of Marxist thought that had profound implications for its use in the third world. Trotsky argued that the socialist revolution would occur in the semiperiphery rather than in the industrial core (England and Germany) because the states that experienced firsthand the long-term, organic evolution of industrialization, urbanization, and agrarian reform ushered in by modern capitalism had slowly adapted to the system. This "privilege of historic backwardness" that the semiperiphery existed in allowed underdeveloped states to overtake pre-viously more advanced countries in leaps as they adapted the new technolo-gies developed in the core (Lawson 2005: 56). As Lawson notes,

> the consequence of combining large-scale industrial modernization with a predominantly rural, peasant-based subsistence economy was instability. Without intermediate buffers to guard against uprisings from below, rul-ing classes were vulnerable to surges of discontent. As Trotsky observed

of Russia, "whereas in the dawn of history, it was too unripe to accomplish a reformation, when the time came for leading a revolution, it was over-ripe." (Lawson 2005: 56)

Thus, the catalyst of the revolution would have to be the semiperiphery and work back into the core. Despite the change of location, however, the process that Lenin and Trotsky envisioned was the same—the workers led by the vanguard that created a dictatorship of the proletariat that paved the way for communism. These ideas are crucial, as they form the core of what revolutionary leaders in Asia and Latin America utilized to foment revolution in their countries.

There has been significant debate about Lenin's implementation of Marx's, and even his own, ideas in Russia. Soon after World War I, Russia was plunged into a civil war between the Bolsheviks and reactionaries who sought to reinstitute the tsar (with foreign aid). This exacerbated the economic ruin of Russia. In response, Lenin opened up the economy to allow for less state control and an increasing role of a competitive market. In 1921, under the New Economic Policy (NEP), peasants were allowed to sell surplus for a profit, regulations on small enterprises were lifted, and restrictions on foreign trade were liberalized. All of these policies sought to encourage economic development by utilizing the market to more efficiently allocate resources. Lenin argued that he was not giving up on socialism because the state would continue to control the "commanding heights" of industry: rail, coal, and electricity.

Major changes came to Marxist theory as revolutionaries moved into increasingly less-developed economies. As Marxism spread to other countries, it was clear that the theoretical formula would not work in peasant-dominated societies. Joel Migdal has argued that

> communists gained adherents among peasantries not because of the inherent attractiveness of communist thought, but because communist parties were the most effective groups in undertaking the tasks of organizing peasants for land reform and protecting traditional village communities from state or landlord depredations. Communism's major effect has not been to induce revolutions but to provide an ideology for reconstruction after the old regime has fallen. (Migdal quoted in Goldstone 1994b: 14)

Thus, as revolutionaries advocating Marxist ideology became active in Asia and Latin America, they reworked key elements to fit their context. In doing so, two primary legacies emerged—the Maoist and the Latin American versions. Both of these emphasized similar elements, but they did this largely independently and in response to similar socioeconomic contexts. Figure 5.1 depicts this lineage.

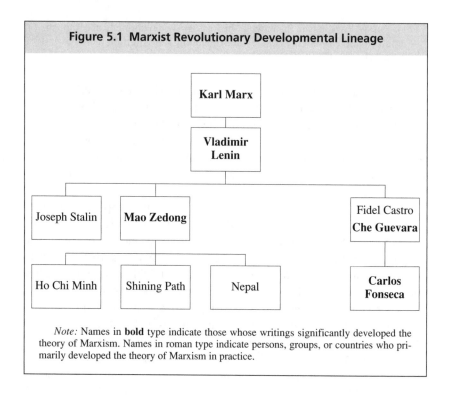

Figure 5.1 Marxist Revolutionary Developmental Lineage

Karl Marx

Vladimir Lenin

Joseph Stalin   **Mao Zedong**   Fidel Castro **Che Guevara**

Ho Chi Minh   Shining Path   Nepal   **Carlos Fonseca**

Note: Names in **bold** type indicate those whose writings significantly developed the theory of Marxism. Names in roman type indicate persons, groups, or countries who primarily developed the theory of Marxism in practice.

Maoism

If you want to know the taste of a pear, you must change the pear by eating it yourself. If you want to know the theory and methods of revolution, you must take part in revolution. All genuine knowledge originates in direct experience. —Mao Zedong

Two structural realities that Mao Zedong had to deal with in the Chinese context were not in existence in Russia or in the Europe around which Marx developed his theories: an agrarian economy and foreign domination. Thus, the major additions to Marxism-Leninism are largely in response to these realities. Mao reversed the supposed direction of revolutionary action. As discussed earlier, Marx argued that the proletariat was the revolutionary class. The proletariat worked in urban factories that dominated the economy, and Marx believed they would rise up and take control of the factories and extend their control outward; change moved from the city to the countryside and was led by workers. Mao reversed this. The peasantry was the revolutionary class for Mao; they would lead the revolution in the countryside, surrounding the cities and eventually strangling them. To do this required a much different tactic than urban strikes. Mao developed the idea of a prolonged war in which the peasantry would lead a sustained campaign in the countryside. This required a peasant army that would be led by a vanguard party.

Mao's revolutionary struggle was not to overthrow an existing regime so much as it was to eliminate foreign influence. By the time Mao became active (in the early 1920s), the Qing dynasty had already collapsed, and China had been wracked with a decade of civil war. This had led to the further "opening" of China to imperialist powers that Mao and others sought to force out. Like Gandhi, whose nationalist ideology called on Indians to reject Western materialism, Mao blamed the Chinese for what he perceived as their cultural weakness and the root cause of their inability to resist imperialist powers. Unlike Gandhi's embrace of his culture, the solution Mao advocated was a radical reconstruction of society away from the Confucian values that constituted Chinese culture. Mao sought

> direct confrontation that broke previous rules through outrages and violence. Struggle, he felt, built courage and character in a people who, Mao believed, were by inclination and culture too passive and accepting. . . . Struggle *(douzheng)* consisted broadly of a politically motivated direct act against another person in massive violation of social conventions. . . . The whole object of struggle was to smash prevailing social inhibitions in such a dramatic and traumatic way that the participants (both the activists and the targets) could never again reestablish their prestruggle relationship. (Lieberthal 2004: 68–69)

From this broken society could emerge a new vision of humanity akin to Marx's conception of a classless society. Thus, for Mao, ideology was crucially important in molding the new relationships that would emerge. In this way Mao built even further on Lenin's ideas of a vanguard party in promoting revolutionary development. Mao believed that "properly motivated people could overcome any material odds to accomplish their goals" (Lieberthal 2004: 63). This explains the Great Leap Forward campaign of 1958–1961, the product of Mao's belief that with focused action, China could surpass the industrial countries in such things as steel production within a span of several years (the experiment failed miserably, leading to a famine that claimed some 30 million lives). This and other campaigns were intended to transform "the ways people thought about key issues and social relationships" or to change the basic forms of production (2004: 66). The campaigns were led and developed through the concept of the "mass line."

> The basic idea was that officials in direct contact with the masses should always remain close enough to the people to understand their fundamental

desires and concerns. These officials would report their understanding up the hierarchy to provide the leaders a good sense of what the people would welcome and implement and what they would not. The top leaders, with their superior understanding of the laws of history and of China's overall conditions, would then reach appropriate decisions that would push forward the revolution in a strong but realistic fashion acceptable to the masses. As the resulting orders for new initiatives were issued, the local officials would try to involve the people in implementing these directives in order to win popular commitment through popular participation. (Lieberthal 2004: 64)

Maoist groups, that is, those who have adopted Mao's additions to Marxism-Leninism in theory and practice, have emerged in a number of places. A group in Peru that emerged in the 1970s, Sendero Luminoso (the Shining Path), advocated Mao's ideas of prolonged guerrilla warfare as the only way to overthrow the government. They became active in fighting the Peruvian government in 1980 when they burned ballot boxes in the first elections since 1964. The leader, Abimael Guzman, a former philosophy professor at a university in the central Peruvian Andes, sought to implement Mao's ideas in Peru. Throughout the 1980s, Sendero gained control over much of the southern half of Peru, adopting Mao's strategy of cultivating relationships with the peasantry to surround the urban areas. They also adopted the brutal tactics derived from the notion that power comes from the barrel of a gun. Sendero targeted not only the army and police but also government employees at all levels, other leftist groups, workers who did not participate in the strikes organized by the group, peasants who cooperated with the government in any way, and middle-class inhabitants of Peru's main cities. In response, the Peruvian government launched a massive campaign against the group that involved paramilitary forces as well. In the battle, almost 70,000 people were killed, half of them at the hands of Sendero (the military and paramilitary forces also killed thousands) (Truth and Reconciliation Commission of Peru 2003). The fighting ended when Guzman was captured in 1992, and Sendero has been largely inactive since then.

The Communist Party of Nepal adopted the strategies and tactics of Sendero Luminoso, thus perpetuating Mao Zedong thought in Central Asia. In 1996 the party launched the Nepalese People's War that mimicked the tactics outlined by Mao. Within a few years, it had taken control of much of the rural areas of Nepal. In 2002, the Maoists attacked an army barracks, which spurred the military into action (up to this point, the matter had been seen as the province of police forces). With the military involved, the conflict escalated significantly, until a stable cease-fire was signed in November 2006, which allowed the party to become a part of the government. In the course of the fighting, almost 13,000 people were killed (4,500 by Maoists and more than 8,000 by the government) (Douglas 2005).

Latin American Marxism

> *I began revolution with 82 men. If I had do it again, I'd do it with 10 or 15 and absolute faith. It does not matter how small you are if you have faith and plan of action.* —Fidel Castro

Marxism has been used in many revolutionary movements in Latin America, spurred primarily by the successful overthrow of the Fulgencio Batista regime in Cuba by Fidel Castro's initially small band of guerrillas. Castro's revolutionary ideology that was used to lead M-26 (a group of Cuban exiles organized by Castro in Mexico) was ironically decidedly non-Marxist. As Wickham-Crowley shows, Castro gained support among peasants and workers because he was seen as a moral alternative to the increasingly immoral Batista (1992). Most of Castro's "ideology" was focused on the idea that Batista was a cruel, torturing, illegitimate thug who impoverished Cuba. The only real plan Castro offered for change was "to restore the 1940 Constitution and to hold free elections" (1992: 176). It was not until after Batista left and Castro consolidated power that the Marxist elements became more important (and those not until after confrontations with the United States in 1960 and 1961).

In contrast, Ernesto "Che" Guevara, born and educated as a medical doctor in Argentina, had become increasingly open to Marxist ideas as he traveled throughout Latin America and increasingly saw revolution as the only viable solution to mending the ills of the peasantry. In 1953, he went to Guatemala to support the Jacobo Arbenz government in its effort to redistribute land to reduce domination of US-owned businesses. While there he rejected joining the communist party but studied Marx. Within a year, the US Central Intelligence Agency (CIA) supported a military coup against Arbenz, and Guevara fled to Mexico. There he met Fidel Castro and helped to organize the M-26's failed invasion of Cuba, which he survived; he went on to become one of the prominent leaders of the guerrilla war that overthrew the Cuban government. Reflecting on his experiences in Cuba, Guevara wrote extensively on the nature of guerrilla warfare. He sought to replicate the Cuban success in Democratic Republic of Congo (then Congo-Kinshasa) and Bolivia (where he was captured and executed).

Guevara's Cuban experiences led him to add two key elements to Marxist revolutionary ideology. First is the further refinement of the idea of a vanguard party with the notion of *foco* (Spanish for focus). Focalism or *foquismo* was the idea that a small fast-moving paramilitary group would provide the focus for popular discontent against the government. Revolution could come about by the actions of a very few committed and well-trained individuals. This idea was inspired by Guevara's experiences in the 1959 Cuban Revolution. Mainline Marxists had thought that such a small force was antithetical to the ideas of Marx, viewing it as Blanquism, named after the French revolutionary Auguste Blanqui. Engels defined blanquism: "a relatively small number of resolute, well-organized men would be able, at a given favorable moment, not only to seize the helm of the State, but also to keep power, by energetic and unrelenting action, until they had succeeded in drawing the mass of the people into the revolution by marshalling them around a small band of leaders" (quoted in Wolf 1999: 269). As Wolf puts it, "this view was anathema to most Communists. Even Lenin had written that 'the uprising must be based on the revolutionary upsurge of the people'" (1999: 269).

After 1961, *foquismo* was the guiding variant of Marxist ideology with which the majority of revolutionaries in Latin America identified.

> No matter the sociological label we pin on the sudden spread of a new idea . . . the process is the same: conversion from one way of looking at the world to a radically different one, the adoption of a different frame of reference. In adding guerrilla warfare to its cultural repertoire, the Latin American left did not expand its previous repertoire so much as it narrowed it down, leading to the splitting off of a new left wing of the left, with a repertoire of but two elements: rural guerrilla warfare and urban terrorism. (Wickham-Crowley 1992: 33)

The spread of *foquismo* was so complete that even liberal-oriented revolutionary groups adopted it. In Nicaragua, the leading liberal opposition figure, Pedro Chamorro, sought an audience with Castro before planning an assault on the Anastasio Somoza regime. Chamorro was rebuffed as too conservative but then trained a group of guerrillas for the first aerial guerrilla attack in Latin America with a result similar to that of Castro's initial voyage on the *Granma,* the ship that carried the M-26 from Mexico to Cuba. One key difference in Nicaragua was that all of the guerrillas were killed or taken prisoner.

Guevara's second primary addition to Marxist theory was the expansion of the concept of praxis, the complex process of action followed by reflection that then informs further action. Much of Marxism-Leninism focuses on the fact that the proletariat lacks class consciousness; that is, the workers do not know that they are exploited. The way to lift this veil of ignorance is to be exposed to Marxist theory. Once workers understand the historical progression of human societies as moved by economic changes, they can appreciate the class differences that currently exist. Having this knowledge, they will then work to overthrow the capitalist class. Lenin argued that part of the reason for having a vanguard of the proletariat is that most workers will not be able to appreciate the richness of Marxist theory. Thus, the intellectuals would lead the movement in the name of the workers; however, they must fully understand Marxist theory and the current economic conditions to be successful. Guevara disagreed with the importance of understanding Marxist theory. Although he agreed that it was useful, he thought that action was more important. The ideology would not bring revolution, guerrillas would. This ties into his *foco* theory but expands it. As he argued, "revolution is not an apple that falls when it is ripe. You have to make it fall." Guevara continued, "the revolution can be made if the historical realities are interpreted correctly and the forces involved are utilized correctly, even if the theory is not known" (quoted in Hodges 1986: 174–175). The act of challenging the government would spur the kind of reflection that would lead to Marxist understandings.

The only other successful Marxist revolution in Latin America was led by the Sandinistas (the FSLN) in Nicaragua.[2] In 1959, Carlos Fonseca, a young member of the Nicaraguan Socialist Party (Partido Socialista Nicargüense; PSN) traveled to Cuba to learn from the example of the Cuban Revolution (though he was not well known enough to get an audience with the leadership). After participating in a failed guerrilla campaign, he returned to Cuba to study the legacy of Augusto Cesar Sandino in light of the Cuban experience (Zimmerman 2000).

Fonseca's development of Marxist ideology completes the trajectory away from Marxist thought, as it incorporates more of the contemporary context as well as the Latin American tradition. Fonseca was killed in 1976, three years before the FSLN seized power in Nicaragua, but he was the intellectual father of the movement (Zimmerman 2000). There were four key elements to Fonseca's ideology, both as it was portrayed prior to the revolution and as it was utilized after the FSLN gained control of the government. Only one of these aspects is Marxist, an indication of how far Marxist groups had drifted from the original theory.

The first and most prominent element of Sandinista ideology was its debt to Sandino. The rebel was the leader of a guerrilla army that sought to win peasant support to eventually overthrow the government. Sandino was an impassioned nationalist whose rhetoric incorporated resistance to foreigners and hostility toward imperialism, including condemning the abusive aspects of capitalism (Selbin 1993: 85). In this sense, he was a kindred spirit of Marxist ideas but was never involved in a communist group.

Sandino was also a kindred spirit of the rhetoric of Karl Marx, as a letter from Sandino to the US forces in Nicaragua indicates: "Come on you pack of drug fiends, come on and murder us on our own land. I am waiting for you on my feet at the head of my patriotic soldiers, and I don't care how many of you there are. You should know that when this happens, the destruction of your mighty power will make the Capitol shake in Washington, and your blood will redden the white dome that crowns the famous White House where you plot your crimes" (quoted in Zimmerman 2000).

The second element of Fonseca's ideology was the use of historical materialism to understand the economic and historical situation in Nicaragua. Marxist analysis of class and the historical progress of capitalism provided a viable explanation as well as a rectification for this inequality. This explanatory power of Marxist historical analysis was attractive to both revolutionaries (such as the FSLN) and those simply seeking reform (such as many within the church). According to Fonseca's Marxist historical analysis, "the national and international conditions that currently prevail make it possible for at least a sector of the Nicaraguan people to initiate armed struggle, conscious that they are trying not simply to achieve a change of men in power, but a change of the system—the overthrow of the exploiting classes and the victory of the exploited classes" (Fonseca 1982: 29). This analysis was based on the fact that the ideas of Marxism had finally come to Nicaragua and prepared a group capable of leading a revolution. This explains why Sandino and other previous struggles were not successful (they lacked Marxist theory as a guide). Nicaraguan revolutionaries would not suffer the fate of Sandino because the context for revolution had ripened, as demonstrated by the Cuban Revolution. Although Fonseca himself was already studying Marxist ideas, the success of the Cuban Revolution was a watershed event for all Latin American revolutionaries.

The third element of Fonseca's ideology was clearly derived from the Cuban example and Guevara's additions to Marxism-Leninism. Following Guevara's lead, the FSLN was inspired to remain focused on bold attacks against the National Guard. Fonseca himself admitted in 1975 that this had led to an initial overreliance on armed action: "The view we had at that time [1963] of the Cuban experience was that all it took was launching the armed struggle to call into being an uprising on a mass scale. . . . A little more careful attention to the experiences of the Russian and Chinese peoples in their revolutions would have helped us avoid in part our exclusive preoccupation with the armed revolutionary struggle" (quoted in Zimmerman 2000: 79).

The fourth aspect of Fonseca's revolutionary ideology was the practicality of it. Fonseca knew that the FSLN was unlikely to win a revolution that alienated all sectors of the bourgeoisie or the Catholic population of

Nicaragua. As the revolution progressed and it became apparent that the United States might intervene if the FSLN took power without support of the bourgeoisie, the FSLN created a group of influential but apolitical leaders to call on Somoza to resign and to give support to the FSLN. The leadership of the FSLN also downplayed the Marxist origins of the group in interviews. A 1977 interview with the *New York Times* indicated that they had abandoned their struggle for a Marxist victory through prolonged popular war in favor of a more immediate popular insurrection supported by broad sectors of the population. "Those who think we'll be going straight to communism are wrong. Our basic program is not Communist. It is a threat to no one who favors a just society" (Fonseca quoted in Faroohar 1989: 187–188). In one of his earliest writings, Fonseca declared "himself an open-minded Sandinista. . . . 'In my thought I welcome the popular essence of the distinct ideologies of Marxism, of Liberalism, of Social Christianity'" (quoted in Hodges 1986: 188). As the church began to reflect the reforms of Vatican II, Medellin, and liberation theology (topics discussed in detail later in this chapter), Fonseca realized that both Marxism and Christianity worked to alleviate the plight of the poor. In 1970, when the FSLN captured a radio station, he began his broadcast: "Two thousand years ago there appeared a redeemer who said that his brothers were those who did the will of one in heaven from whom proceeded justice and truth" (quoted in Hodges 1986: 269). He then went on to draw parallels among the FSLN, Sandino, and Christ—all martyrs for the struggle of justice.

Summary of Marxism

Though still in the Marxist lineage, it is clear that the adaptations of Marx's ideas have required significant revisions to be useful in the many places that Marxist groups have emerged to challenge the government.

Table 5.1 lists groups that advocated Marxist or Socialist revolutionary ideologies at some point in their revolutionary campaign.

Religious Ideologies

The crime of liberation theology was that it takes the Gospels seriously. That's unacceptable. The Gospels are radical pacifist material.
　　　　　　　　　　　　　　　　　　　　　—Noam Chomsky

Even though Marx viewed religion as the opiate of the masses and thus fundamental to people's not creating change, there are several religious ideologies that have been the basis for revolutionary activity. Religious

Table 5.1 Groups That Advocated Marxist or Socialist Revolutionary Ideologies

Group	Country	Date of Revolution, Rebellion, or Party Founding
All-Union Communist Party (Bolsheviks)	Russia	1917
Communist Party of Cuba	Cuba	1923
Communist Party of Vietnam	Vietnam	1930–2008
Lao People's Revolutionary Party	Laos	1930
Tudeh Party of Iran	Iran	1941–1953
Communist Party of China	China	1949
Sudanese Communist Party	Sudan	1946–1971
Popular Movement for Liberation of Angola	Angola	1956–
Revolutionary Armed Forces of Colombia (FARC)	Colombia	1960–2008
Liberation Front of Mozambique (FRELIMO)	Mozambique	1962
Front de liberation du Quebec	Canada	1963
Communist Party of Indonesia	Indonesia	1965–1966
Irish Republican Army	Northern Ireland	1970s
Kurdistan Workers Party	Turkey	1970s
Peoples Democratic Party of Afghanistan	Afghanistan	1978
Sandinista National Liberation Front (FSLN)	Nicaragua	1979
African National Congress	South Africa	1980s
Sendero Luminoso (Shining Path)	Peru	1980–
Farabundo Martí National Liberation Front (FMLN)	El Salvador	1981–1992
Communist Party of Nepal	Nepal	1994

ideologies often mirror nationalism (both religion and nationalism overlap in that they are tied to language and culture) but maintain a distinction in terms of the relevant group. Nationalism focuses on a people, whereas religious revolutionary ideologies derive their ideas from a religious tradition, confined to those believers. Unlike national ties, religious ideologies have the possibility of conversion, however. Thus, it is like nationalism in that it seeks to gain political autonomy for a particular group; it differs from nationalism, however, in that it justifies this autonomy in a religious tradition that has the potential to be universal. In this regard, religious ideologies may be more easily transferable to others. To take Iran as an example, there are many Muslims in countries other than Iran, but not Iranians; thus Islamic fundamentalism may be applicable in other areas where Iranian nationalism would not. A variety of religious ideologies have influenced political movements but have not been used to justify or encourage revolution. I will focus on the two religious ideologies that have played an important role in several revolutions and revolutionary movements: Islamism (or Islamic fundamentalism) and liberation theology.

Islamic Fundamentalism

The ink of the scholar is worth more than the blood of a martyr.
—The Prophet Muhammad

Islamic fundamentalism is an ideology steeped in the Islamic faith, with two particular aspects. First, the fundamentalism implies a selective, instrumental reading of the Quran. The point of this selective reading is that the fundamentalists believe that others have strayed from the Quran, whereas it should be the sole source of authority as Allah's word. Second, fundamentalism "involves the mobilization of popular or other support in order to implement at the political and social levels a model of the ideal state and of social practice" derived from the Quran (Halliday 1998: 263). Halliday argues that this typically focuses on aspects of the social order that are under threat, such as the position of women, ritual purification, and correct diet. This second element has demanded the imposition of *shari'a,* or quranic law. *Shari'a* is not an explicit set of instructions, but is derived from the Quran, sayings of Muhammad, and interpretation. It deals with all aspects of day-to-day life, including politics, economics, and social issues.

The very idea of revolution is somewhat foreign to the historical experience of the Muslim world and thus was revived (or created) by modern scholars. The civil conflict that tore apart the Muslim community in the mid-seventh century (when a civil war erupted over succession, ending with the Sunni and Shia split) led most religious leaders to advocate "a sort of pessimistic realism: even an evil ruler is better than anarchy" (Bergesen 2008: 7). Then, throughout Muslim history, religiously justified fighting was traditionally against non-Muslims and thus led by the established political leader within the Muslim community. Challenging that leader was largely without precedent. Sayyid Qutb, one of the predominant fundamentalist writers during the 1950s and 60s, created an Islamic justification for revolution. "Qutb built upon Ibn Taymiyya's (1268–1328) justification for fighting the Mongol rulers who had conquered Baghdad but were practicing Muslims" (Bergesen 2008: 8). Taymiyya reasoned that although they followed the guidelines of Islam, this was not enough. He introduced a new criterion:

> A Sunni Muslim ceases to be one when he fails to keep (or in the case of a Muslim ruler, apply) the *shari'a*. . . . Now, in Qutb's application, Nasser's government, while composed of faithful Muslims in terms of their private religious practices, was not actually a true Muslim regime because the government did not apply the shari'a. Hence they were fair game for the application of the doctrine of *jihad;* and hence fair game to be overthrown. . . . As a disciple of Qutb's would later comment: "One cannot account for the first Muslim Empire unless one takes into consideration the prophecy of Muhammad; the groundwork for the French revolution was laid by Rousseau, Voltaire, and Montesquieu; the Communist Revolution realized the plans set by Marx, Engels, and Lenin; Nazism grew out of a soil labored by Hegel, Fichte, and Nietzsche. The same holds true for us as well," . . . grounds for resistance, revolt, and revolution were being set in Islamic, not Marxian or socialist, terms. (Bergesen 2008: 8)

Beyond these generalizations, there are two predominant strains of this revolutionary ideology that follow the dominant split within Islam: Shia and Sunni. Although there are a variety of Islamic fundamentalist movements, only in the Iranian Revolution was this ideology used to consolidate power following a revolution. It has been implemented by coup leaders (in Sudan) and existing leaders (in Egypt and Pakistan) but was a revolutionary ideology only in Iran. Iran is somewhat unique among Muslim countries in that it is one of the few with a majority of Shia Muslims. The Shia had historically philosophically avoided direct involvement in politics, opting for moral guidance instead (Joffe 2006). This changed with the rising prominence of Ayatollah Ruhollah Khomeini in Iran in opposition to the shah.

The ideology that much of the masses heard from Ayatollah Khomeini, the most vocal opposition figure in the revolution and eventual supreme leader, was relatively nationalist, populist, and rooted in the Islamic faith. Khomeini was a proponent of the elimination of both Soviet and US influence in the Middle East with the slogan: "not Eastern, nor Western—Islamic Republican." Khomeini portrayed the shah as merely a puppet of Western interests, going back to British control over Iran and followed by US influence in propping up the shah. Combined with the anti-imperialist rhetoric was a strong populist undertone. One example of the fiery populist rhetoric has Khomeini addressing the shah: "And those who have filled foreign banks with the wealth produced by our poverty-stricken people, who built towering palaces but still will not leave the people in peace, wishing to fill their pockets . . . are these not parasites?" (DeFronzo 2007: 285).

The most important element of Khomeini's Islamic fundamentalist ideology was the notion of *velayat-e faqih*. This "rule of the just Islamic jurist" was something that all Muslims required so as to have order in their lives and was based in the Quran, Khomeini argued. A truly Islamic government, "dedicated to social justice—and thus the interests of the oppressed—should be monitored and guided by a jurisconsult who reflected the perfection" of the twelfth imam (quoted in Joffe 2006: 459). Khomeini called for the creation of a theocracy—rule by God. Those most schooled in Islamic law would be best able to interpret God's will in contemporary Iran. Khomeini argued that the Quaran and the books of the *hadith* were dominated by ways to organize society.

> The ratio of Quranic verses concerned with the affairs of society to those concerned with ritual worship is greater than a hundred to one. Of the approximately fifty sections of the corpus of *hadith* four sections relate to matters of ritual worship and the duties of man toward his Creator and Sustainer. A few more are concerned with questions of ethics, and all the rest are concerned with social, economic, legal, and political questions—in short, the gestation of society. (Khomeini 1981: 29)

But the laws of the Quran, *sha'ria,* were not sufficient for ordering society. As Khomeini argued:

> We believe in government and believe that the Prophet (upon whom be peace) was bound to appoint a successor, as he indeed did. Was a successor designated purely for the sake of expounding law? The expounding of law did not require a successor to the Prophet. He himself, after all, had expounded the laws; it would have been enough for the laws to be written down in a book and put into the people's hands to guide them in their actions. It was logically necessary for a successor to be appointed for the sake of exercising government. Law requires a person to execute it. (Khomeini 1981: 36)

Thus, the Quran contained the laws that would govern society, but someone was needed to execute these laws. Who better understood the laws than religious clerics? Thus, Khomeini argued that clerics would function as the just Islamic jurist inherent in *velayat-e faqih*. Clergy were thus imbedded in all branches of government, and their checks and balances were structured so that the popularly elected politicians were accountable to the clergy. Khomeini also designed the system with a supreme leader who could "provide advice to the parliament and the president and has the power, at the rare times he may deem it necessary, to overrule the government or any part of the government" (DeFronzo 2007: 303). Khomeini appointed himself supreme leader and retained the position until his death.

Khomeini's ideology was delivered in universalistic terms, arguing that the overthrow of the shah was only the beginning. As Walt notes,

> Khomeini rejected existing state boundaries as "the product of the deficient human mind" and emphasized that "Muslims are one family, even if they are subject to different governments and even if they live in regions remote from one another." Accordingly, he called for active efforts to spread the revolution far beyond Iran's borders, declaring that "we have in reality, then, no choice but to . . . overthrow all treacherous, corrupt, oppressive, and criminal regimes." (Walt 1996: 214)

Although the ideology declared universal appeal, "it was not philosophically related to the dramatic intellectual changes taking place within Sunni Islam" and thus was not utilized in other revolutionary movements (Joffe 2006: 459).

The second branch of Islamic fundamentalism, and the one that is much more widespread, developed in Sunni religious circles. This version is the one actively advocated by most revolutionary movements in the Middle East today, including groups such as Al-Qaida. This brand of fundamentalism originated in reaction to the French colonization of Arab lands in the mid-1800s. To challenge Western domination, Jamal al-Din al-Afghani argued that, by understanding the true nature of the rule of those immediate successors to the prophet Muhammad, "contemporary success and modernization could be achieved that would be consonant with Islamic values" (Joffe 2006: 455). In this regard, the ideology was reactionary, as it harkened back to the glory days of the empire. But it has been interpreted in light of the modern context, that of colonial or postcolonial domination. From this was revived the concept of jihad or struggle. As Joffe notes, "*jihad* for most Islamic theologians is a process of internal strife designed to achieve personal purification and betterment. Originally, however, it also meant warfare sanctioned by Islam. Initially it was warfare to expand the Islamic world, but for the past five hundred years at least, if not longer, it has meant a defensive war to protect the *umma* [Muslim community] and region it occupies" (2006: 458). There are two types of jihad within this context: "to harass the enemy in order to discourage attack upon the Islamic world, and *jihad* actually to defend it against attack" (Joffe 2006: 458). The second or defensive type of jihad illustrates the motivation behind revolutionary movements in Afghanistan (during Soviet, US, and North Atlantic Treaty Organization [NATO] occupation), Bosnia, Chechnya, and Kosovo. It has also been expanded to include those governments that, although clearly Muslim, do not comply with the strict moral and legal code that fundamentalists adhere to. This ideology provides for both the target and motivating force for Islamic fundamentalism: "A defensive *jihad* against Western influence and intrusion is a moral duty. An inner-directed *jihad* against corrupt Muslim governments that connive with Western influence is an imperative to protect the Muslim world. . . . This, in essence, is the ideological imperative for the Islamic extremists who make up movements such as al-Qaeda and its associates and who form the core of 'Islamic fundamentalist revolution' today" (Joffe 2006: 458).

Much of the current Sunni Islamic fundamentalism stems from Qutb's relatively simple three-part revolutionary ideology. Qutb argued that first and foremost, the Quran provides a template for structuring society. This is the ideal that humans are supposed to bring about. Second, the ideal clearly does not exist, as most societies (none at the time of his writing) embody fundamentalist views of *shari'a*. Thus, the existing sociopolitical structures are viewed as barriers to achieving the fulfillment of God's plan. In this way, governments that do not rule by *shari'a* actively oppose the will of God. This, then, leads to the third element, the requirement to create groups to oppose these governments and societies, destroying the barriers to the will of God. "In short, there is (1) a goal to be realized, (2) obstacles to be overcome, and (3) a means to overcome these obstacles and realize that goal" (Bergesen 2008: 14). This basic idea underlies much Sunni Islamic revolutionary ideology.

The more recent version of this revolutionary Islamic fundamentalism has been developed by two groups: Al-Qaida (literally "the base"), which is best described as a "network of networks," and the Taliban (Joffe 2006). Al-Qaida was created by Osama bin Laden "for the thousands of largely foreign Islamic volunteers who came to Afghanistan during the 1980s to fight against Soviet troops" (Joffe 2006: 464). The base coordinated the training of these volunteers and directed weapons and funds to actively resist the Soviet occupation. The leadership was centered around Abdallah Azzam, a Pakistani, and Osama bin Laden, who was recruited by the then-director of Saudi National Intelligence, Prince Faisal bin Turki (Joffe 2006). The CIA also was active in supplying the group with money and training. When the Soviets withdrew in 1989, funding for the resistance was cut off, and by 1991 most of the foreign volunteers were expelled from Afghanistan and Pakistan. Al-Qaida served as a connecting network for these trained volunteers. Osama bin Laden returned to Saudi Arabia, but was expelled in 1991, "in response to the Saudi realization that he could mobilize up to 35,000 men, when he offered them as shock troops against the Iraqi presence in Kuwait" (Joffe 2006: 460). Soon after, Al-Qaida began organizing attacks in support of its Islamic fundamentalist ideology, most spectacularly the September 11, 2001, attacks in the United States.

The ideology of Al-Qaida was formed in the experience of resistance in Afghanistan and then applied to a larger context, drawing on intellectual leaders in Pakistan and Saudi Arabia. Azzam, one of the original leaders of Al-Qaida, refined the two notions of jihad mentioned earlier: one offensive and the other defensive (Joffe 2006: 458). The latter was "an individual responsibility, as important as the observance of the five pillars of faith. The war in Afghanistan was of the second kind, thus obliging Muslims to ensure that the Soviet invasion should not succeed" (2006: 458). With the successful end of the Soviet occupation, it became clear that there were many other areas similarly occupied such as Chechnya, Bosnia, and Kosovo. Further, there was a realization that the occupation by foreign powers was not the only type of affront to the rule of Allah. Nominally Islamic countries that relied upon Western support were viewed as little better than puppet regimes. Thus, Al-Qaida's mission was broadened to the liberation of all Muslims, according to their fundamentalist interpretation.

Unlike Al-Qaida, the Taliban in Afghanistan was not active in spreading a broader revolution. Rather, it sought just the opposite: the implementation of an Islamic fundamentalist state in Afghanistan. Initially the ideology focused on simply restoring morality to a country torn by the rule of competing warlords. It even suggested that it would step aside once good Muslim rule was restored. Once in power, the Taliban implemented a mix of extreme *shari'a* law and Pashtun tribal customs. The rule that it imposed is classic reactionary rule, attempting to recreate (according to its interpretation) the rule of the prophet. A spokesman for the Taliban explained the system of government as follows: "The Sharia does not allow politics or political parties. That is why we give no salaries to officials or soldiers, just food, clothes, shoes and weapons. We want to live a life like the Prophet lived 1400 years ago and *jihad* is our right. We want to recreate the time of the Prophet and we are only carrying out what the Afghan people have wanted for the past 14 years" (Rashid 2001: 43). The rule that it imposed was the strictest interpretation of *shari'a* law in the Islamic world; it outlawed the education of women under age eight, most media (film, television, and music), dancing, hanging pictures in homes, and clapping during sports events and enforced strict dress codes for both men and women.

The Taliban came to power over the course of two years as it moved from controlling an area in southern Afghanistan in 1994 to entering the capital, Kabul, in 1996. The Taliban initially fought with the mujahidin (literally fighters) and thus were also funded in part by a number of governments supporting any movement that resisted Soviet occupation of Afghanistan.

When the Soviets withdrew in 1989, the Kabul government (that had been propped up by the Soviets) remained in power until 1992, when the mujahidin toppled the government. Thus, since 1979, there had been almost nonstop fighting in Afghanistan. The Taliban came to power with the intention of ending conflict by firmly implementing Islamic rule. This rule came to an end in 2001 when the United States invaded and established a new government.

Liberation Theology

A person learns to swim in the water, not in a library. —Paulo Freire

Liberation theology has been one of the dominant ideologies of many Central American revolutionary movements since the 1970s. The ideology grew out of significant changes advocated in the Roman Catholic Church from the Second Vatican Council (1962–1965; also known as Vatican II). The point of Vatican II was to investigate the role of the church in the modern world. Vatican II created three key innovations for the church in response to changes of the modern world. First was recognizing the growing gap between rich and poor and taking a clear stand that the gap was unjust. Second, Vatican II argued that biblical interpretation must be understood contextually, through current events. The church had previously advocated a more permanent focus: that the Bible is what it is, and its meaning does not change. This was particularly important in relation to the first innovation focused on the needs of the poor, for it required looking at Jesus' relationship with poor people. The Vatican II stand was that to understand biblical passages, people need to look at the current system and be more like Jesus. Third, Vatican II allowed openness to assigning some authority and responsibility to laity (although there was still a primary role for priests and bishops, the lay people could be more active). These changes had revolutionary implications in Central America, an overwhelmingly Roman Catholic area.

Throughout most of Latin American church-state history, the two have been mutually supportive. Up to the 1960s, the clergy supported the regimes, which in turn supported the independence and wealth of the church. This relationship changed in the 1960s and 1970s. As part of the openness to laity encouraged in Vatican II, the church in Latin America sought broad inputs from society about how it could address the needs of the poor. After three years of reflection, discussion, and analysis, the leadership of the church in Latin America met at the Second Council of Latin American Bishops in Medellin, Colombia, in 1968. The meeting sought to interpret

Vatican II in light of the Latin American situation. This included a dialogue with social scientists and secular experts, including Marxist interpretations on the reality of dependency in Latin America. Out of this Medellin Council came two crucial theoretical concepts for revolutionary movements in Latin America: liberation theology and *concientizacion*. Liberation theology sought to interpret the Bible and understand Jesus' role but only after making a commitment to the fundamental change embodied in liberation. This ideology built on a critical and selective reading of Marx, to suggest how the goal of the kingdom of God could be built within history. *Concientizacion* was a learning process in which, by working alongside the poor, missionaries could come to understand more deeply their situation and, in turn, bring the poor to an understanding of the causes of their conditions and the possibilities for change. The goal was not evangelization but rather to know poverty and help those in poverty combat the roots of their condition. The point of this was to bring about an awareness that poverty was not divinely ordained but rooted in the prevailing political and economic arrangements that, being human creations, could be altered. The practice of this was set out in Paulo Friere's *Pedagogy of the Oppressed,* in which he described liberation as "not a gift, not self achievement, but a mutual process" (2006: 7). These were radical ideas compared to the dominant ideology just a decade prior that advocated suffering as redemptive and salvation as the source of alleviating suffering. The old notion encouraged going along with the existing system, whereas liberation theology advocated radical reconstruction to alleviate poverty in this world.

The result of this change in the stance of the Catholic Church was a burst of grassroots organizing aimed at alleviating poverty. Very quickly the governments were identified as the major source of much of the poverty in the region. Whether because of the antigovernment groups' pushing for institutional reforms or because of their mobilization efforts, the result was that many more of these groups became much more active and even successful in some instances (Nicaragua in particular).

Unsuccessful Religious Ideologies

Religious ideologies are a lot like nationalist ideologies in that they are much more particular to a people, time, and place. Arguably Marxist and liberal ideologies are not context dependent; religious and nationalist ideologies historically have been, however. This overview of religious ideologies has included only ones that have been part of a successful revolution that led to attempts to replicate it elsewhere. There are others that have been utilized less successfully that have not spread beyond the initial country. Two short examples help to illustrate this point: the Taiping Rebellion in China from 1851 to 1864 and the Lord's Resistance Army in Northern Uganda from 1986 to the present. The Taiping Rebellion was like many challengers to the Qing Dynasty in that it sought to take over control of the crumbling state. It was unlike most other challengers in that it was motivated by a dynamic leader espousing a new vision for China (not just a new dynastic order) that was based on his reading of the New Testament and a visionary dream in which God told him he was Christ's younger brother. The ideology with which Hong Xiuquan led his "Taipings" argued that the Confucian system was morally bankrupt, as it lacked a framework for including God's rule on earth. Hong led a million soldiers to capture significant parts of the middle of China, including Shanghai and the Yangtze river valley. In the sixteen-year struggle between the Ming Dynasty and Hong's Taipings, between 20 and 40 million lives were lost. Although some of the reforms that Hong advocated regarding women's equality were picked up by the communists when they came to power a century later, the ideology that Hong developed died with the rebellion.

A contemporary revolutionary movement to overthrow the Yoweri Museveni government in Uganda espouses a similar religious ideology in that it is based on the interpretation of the Bible to create a radically new government. The Lord's Resistance Army of Northern Uganda is led by Joseph Kony, whose ideology is based on implementing the Ten Commandments as the governing law for Uganda. There are claims by former soldiers that he received instructions on where to fight from the Holy Spirit and that he speaks in tongues. His soldiers are instructed to make the sign of the cross with oil on their foreheads, shoulders, and guns to avoid being killed in battle (BBC News 2006). Kony's and Hong's ideologies share similarities in that they are dependent upon a charismatic leader who takes religious elements in a new direction. Neither ideology has been duplicated by others or has been successful in taking control of the state, which distinguishes them from Islamic fundamentalism and liberation theology.

Summary of Ideologies

This chapter concludes the review of various ideologies that have been used in justifying revolution. Liberalism, nationalism, Marxism, and religious ideologies have been developed by philosophers and scholars as ways to understand what is wrong with existing systems as well as to point to the possibility of new ways of structuring society. As these two chapters have shown, these revolutionary ideologies also depend a great deal on the historical context of those leading the revolutions; the grand ideologies of revolution are not separated from the act of revolution. Because these are ideas that are acted out in different societies, significant refining and adaptation occurs. The permutations of Marxism best illustrate this. Originally Marxism explained exploitation and class conflict in the most developed parts of the world to show the historical progression of economic and social change. By the time these ideas were adapted to China and Latin America, the focus was on the countryside of the least economically developed parts of the world and a group of committed individuals who would force the change.

Questions for Discussion and Reflection

1. In what ways does Marx's theory help explain today's world?

2. Do Lenin's and Trotsky's additions to Marxist theory solve the problem of Marx's inevitable revolution not materializing?

3. Does Lenin's NEP undermine his ideas about communism?

4. In what ways does the Russian Revolution support and refute Marxist theory?

5. In what ways did Fonseca's ideology depart from Marxism?

6. How does the experience of various leaders shape their ideologies (e.g., Lenin, Mao, Fonseca, Chamorro, and bin Laden)?

7. To what degree is Islamic fundamentalism a product of Islam versus a reaction to Western influence?

8. One of the central developments of Vatican II dealt with how people cope with injustices such as poverty. Compare this change in Catholicism's stance with that of other world religions.

Notes

1. Because the revolutionary ideology is called Marxism, for the remainder of the chapter I will refer to Marx as having created the argument. Engels played just as great a role, however.

2. The namesake of the Sandinistas, Augusto Cesar Sandino, was also an intellectual and tactical precursor to Castro's M-26. The lineage is as follows: Sandino was active in resisting imperialism in Nicaragua up to the 1930s. Alberto Bayo, a former Cuban military leader who had studied Sandino's tactics and written a manual on guerrilla warfare, lived in Mexico and trained Castro, Guevara, and the rest of the M-26 guerrillas prior to their invasion of Cuba.

6

The Sources of Revolutionary Leadership

The first duty of a revolutionary is to get away with it. —Abbie Hoffman

Structures establish the likelihood of a revolutionary situation arising, but they also shape those who are likely to emerge as leaders of revolutions. The focus of this chapter is on clarifying who leads revolutions. There are a variety of types of people who have typically challenged governments. This chapter discusses the most prominent challengers, the ideal type of individual, and then the role that these leaders typically play in revolutions. It builds on the structural class-oriented analyses to investigate intellectuals, students, workers, peasants, ethnic groups, political parties, capitalists, and clergy.

The list of domestic nonstate actors may at first seem overly inclusive, as it includes groups that are often not typically associated with revolutionary movements. For example, Marxists view religion as the opiate of the masses. It seems odd, then, to consider the leadership of religious institutions as potential leaders of revolution. As Figure 6.1 demonstrates, religious leaders are typically conservative in most societies. Thus, we would expect more radical segments of normal society (a normal society being one that is not afflicted with a revolutionary situation) to be the most likely to engage in challenging the state and the more conservative elements to be the least likely. As we shall see, however, all have played a role in shaping the course of revolutions.

Intellectuals

It does not require a majority to prevail, but rather an irate, tireless minority keen to set brush fires in people's minds. —Samuel Adams

103

Figure 6.1 Spectrum of Domestic Challengers

Radical			Conservative
Intellectuals	Workers	Peasants	Capitalists
Students		Ethnic groups	Clergy
		Political parties	

Intellectuals are individuals who primarily work with their minds as opposed to their hands, a situation that typically requires a higher level of education. Beyond this, intellectuals are also often typically viewed as "cultured members of society who are vitally concerned with the 'larger' social, political, and philosophical issues of the day" (Meisner 1998: 243). This helps to distinguish intellectuals from what are often referred to as white-collar workers, who also primarily work with their minds more than their hands in the service sector or management. The result of intellectuals' efforts are "works of literature or art, interpreting history, conducting scientific research, or educating the young" (Selbin 2006: 255). As a result, intellectuals are usually the most public voice rationalizing the status quo, but paradoxically they are the best trained to criticize flaws in the current system.

Intellectuals' skills require extensive education and thus are different from the skills of much of the rest of society. As Wolf argues, "these skills are only in the rarest of cases traditional within [developing societies]; they are much more likely to have been learned from the West or from Western-type educational institutions. . . . Moreover, these skills are based on literacy, of specialized acquaintance with a corpus of literature which departs from the traditions of the country and suggests new alternatives" (1999: 288). This depth of education exposes intellectuals to ideas that are foreign to the traditional ruling ideology as well as providing them with skills necessary for organizing others. As Selbin indicates, intellectuals are not a monolithic group:

> the most relevant for revolution are academics (including professors and students, sometimes at the secondary as well as at the university level) and "public" intellectuals, who can vary greatly depending on the society but may well include prominent writers and thinkers (Lenin, Trotsky), those with legal (Castro) or academic (Cabral) training, medical people

(Che Guevara), or respected or revered religious figures such as priests (Camilo Torres or Gasper Garcia Laviana), shamans, pastors, rabbis, imams (Ayatollah Khomeini), lamas, elders, etc. (2006: 255)

Intellectuals are often viewed as the bellwethers of revolutionary situations. As discussed in Chapter 1, revolutionary situations are signaled by the "transfer of allegiance of intellectuals" (Brinton 1965). Intellectuals are usually the first to stop following the government. They are more likely to be critical of what they perceive as inadequacies of the existing regime. If intellectuals, en masse, latch on to a competing ideology, this is usually one of the first indications that a revolutionary situation is emerging. They provide the revolutionary ideology as well as the organizational connections that allow other groups in society to come together to either challenge the state or to craft a new government in the face of collapse of the old regime.

The rest of this section consists of short sketches of the lives of some prominent revolutionary intellectuals that demonstrate some of the remarkably similar characteristics and experiences. As Wolfenstein argues, there are common elements of child socialization, adolescence, and young manhood that have encouraged a particular revolutionary personality among the subjects of his study. In his study, he finds "that each man had a complex and 'unusually ambivalent relationship with his father' which became decisive in his personality and predisposed him toward revolutionary activity" (quoted in Kimmel 1990: 70). Most revolutionary leaders also come from the wealthy elites of society and thus are very well educated, often including study or travel in foreign countries. They are typically blocked from full access to political power, however. Wolf argues that this is the hallmark of the revolutionary elite in modernizing societies. When the political structures do not allow these newly educated elites a position of stature, they encounter significant frustration. "For such 'marginal men' political movements often provide a 'home,' of which they are otherwise deprived by their own skill, their social positions, and their divorce from traditional sources of power. . . . What they need is a constituency; and that constituency is ultimately provided by the industrial workers and dissatisfied peasants whom the market created, but for whom society made no adequate social provision" (1999: 289). In other cases, the marginalization is caused not by modernization but by other sociopolitical barriers that keep them from occupying their higher status.

Thomas Jefferson was born on April 13, 1743, in the Virginia colony, then under British rule, to a prominent colonial family with substantial landholdings. When he was fourteen, his father died, leaving him 5,000 acres and dozens of slaves. For two years, he attended the College of William and Mary, where he was exposed to the writings of John Locke, Francis Bacon, and Isaac Newton. Five years after graduation, Jefferson was admitted to the bar in Virginia and actively practiced as a lawyer until 1773. During this time, he often defended Albemarle County in the Virginia House of Burgesses, and after the passage of the Coercive Acts he wrote a series of resolutions that argued for the natural rights of colonists to govern themselves (beyond the constitutional or government-granted rights). He was elected to the Second Continental Congress that was organized to debate independence and was appointed to the committee to draft the statement of independence. He was the primary author of the Declaration of Independence of the United States of America, which sought to establish the reasons that the colonies should be able to govern themselves. Following the declaration, Jefferson returned to Virginia and was elected to the House of Delegates, elected as governor, and appointed minister to France (1785–1789). Under the new constitution he served as the first secretary of state under George Washington, vice president under John Adams, and then as president from 1801 to 1809.

Mohandas K. Gandhi was born on October 2, 1869, in Porbandar State, then a part of British India. His father was a government official in the colonial state, serving as prime minister. Gandhi was a mediocre student in school but was sent to study law at University College London at the age of nineteen (in 1888). Having passed the bar, he returned to Bombay to set up a legal practice, which failed; he eventually took a job representing an Indian firm in South Africa, which was also part of the British Empire, in 1893. There Gandhi was exposed to significant racism toward the Indian community and became active in pressing for their rights as British citizens. Gandhi's notions of *satyagraha* or "truth-force" were further refined in what he termed his "experiments" with nonviolence. His successes at gaining concessions from the South African colonial government brought him significant attention in India. When he returned in 1915, he was quickly brought into the Indian National Congress but always played more of an advisory role. It was not until the late 1920s that Gandhi became active on the national scene as a force actively promoting independence. In 1930, the Indian National Congress declared Indian independence, which was quickly followed by Gandhi's Salt March, a campaign to use noncooperation to force the British out of India. Although the campaign ended with significant reforms of British rule, the rule continued nonetheless. With the coming of World War II, Gandhi advocated a new "Quit India" campaign to force the British to leave. The British repression of the campaign of noncooperation was significant, but as the war came to an end, the British indicated that independence was likely. In response, Gandhi called off the Quit India campaign and began negotiations with the British. The talks broke down on whether India would be divided along religious lines between Hindu- and Muslim-dominated areas or unified (as Gandhi advocated). India was granted independence in 1947, and the new governments of Pakistan and India became a reality in 1950. Gandhi was assassinated by a Hindu nationalist in 1948 at the age of seventy-eight.

Vladimir Ilyich Lenin was born to an educated family in Russia in 1870. When he was sixteen, his father, a successful Russian official in public education, died; when Lenin was seventeen, his eldest brother was arrested and hanged for participating in a terrorist bomb plot threatening the life of Tsar Alexander III. Lenin enrolled at the university and became interested in Karl Marx, even participating in student protests, and was subsequently arrested and expelled. He later finished his education and practiced as a lawyer for some years. Throughout this time he was increasingly involved in revolutionary propaganda efforts, joining a local Marxist group. As a result, in 1895, he was arrested, imprisoned, and exiled to Siberia for five years. For the next fifteen years, he spent most of his time writing in exile in Europe, though he was actively in contact with socialist groups in Russia. After the 1917 February Revolution occurred, he returned to Petrograd in April with the help of the German government, who hoped he would stir up discontent and thus weaken the Russian forces fighting Germany at the time. He led a Bolshevik uprising against the provisional government in July, which failed, so he fled the country. Lenin returned in October to lead the Bolshevik coup that overthrew the provisional government and took power in mid-November.

Ho Chi Minh was born in the northern area of Vietnam in 1890, in what was then French Indochina. His father was a low-level magistrate and teacher. Ho went to school, learning French, and then set off for France to pursue an education at the French Colonial Administrative School, but he was not accepted. He traveled as a kitchen helper and worked a variety of menial jobs in the United States and England before returning to France, where he lived from 1919 to 1923. There he embraced communism and petitioned the Western powers at the Treaty of Versailles talks for Vietnamese independence from France. In 1921, in Tours, France, he helped found the French Communist Party and thereafter spent much time in Moscow. Between 1923 and 1941, Ho traveled unceasingly, with his longest stay in Hong Kong, where he was imprisoned by the British for two years. Throughout this time he was active in promoting communism. In 1941, he returned to Vietnam to lead the independence movement. Ho declared the independence of Vietnam on September 2, 1945. Within weeks, nationalists from China had invaded and eventually worked with the French to force Ho to concede French authority over Indochina. This began the long war for independence. In 1950, in a meeting with Joseph Stalin and Mao Zedong, Ho secured Chinese support for Vietnam's independence struggle against the French. By 1954, the Vietnamese forces (Vietminh) had largely defeated the French occupation, leading to the Geneva Accords, which outlined French withdrawal and an eventual national election for reunification of North and South Vietnam. Although the French agreed, the United States and South Vietnamese did not sign the accords. Ho became president of the newly independent North Vietnam, a communist one-party state. Under his appointees, the struggle for reunification with the south continued. The United States withdrew from South Vietnam in 1973, and the north invaded in 1975, reunifying the country, six years after Ho's death.

Fidel Alejandro Castro was born August 13, 1926, on a sugar plantation in the Oriente Province of Cuba. His father was relatively prosperous from work in the sugar industry but was married to another woman at the time of his son's birth. As a result, the boy lived much of his childhood as an illegitimate child raised in foster homes. When Castro was seventeen, his father and mother were married, and Castro took his father's name. In 1945, Castro enrolled in law school at the University of Havana and became politically active. In 1948, Castro traveled to Bogota, Colombia, where he was involved in a student conference to oppose US imperialism in the Western Hemisphere and foment discontent. While there, riots broke out, and the students played an active role in what became more than thirty years of violent conflict termed La Violencia. Castro married Mirta Diaz Balart, who came from a wealthy family, and graduated with a law degree in 1950. He quickly opened his own practice and in 1952 ran for a seat in the Cuban parliament. Before the elections were held, however, Fulgencio Batista, a general in the Cuban military, led a coup that deposed the elected president. The remainder of the Cuban Revolution and Castro's role in it is covered in the Appendix.

Vaclav Havel was born in Prague, Czechoslovakia, on October 5, 1936. At the time, Czechoslovakia was an independent democratic republic, but three years after his birth, it was invaded by Germany. Following World War II, democratic elections in 1946 brought the Communist Party of Czechoslovakia to power on the Czech side (the Democratic Party won on the Slovak side), and the communists quickly consolidated power. Because Havel's family had strong and well-known bourgeois ties, Havel was not allowed to study beyond the required education. Havel spent most of the 1950s as a laboratory assistant, taking night classes (he was not allowed to enroll in any school that had a humanities program) and completing his military service.

In 1959, he began work as a stagehand and studied drama in Prague. In 1963, his first full-length play, *The Garden Party,* received international acclaim. In 1968, the Warsaw Pact countries invaded Czechoslovakia to end what had been dubbed the Prague Spring. Reformers within the Communist Party sought to open up the party to limited economic and civil liberties. The Warsaw Pact countries quickly stopped the reforms and replaced most government workers with "right-thinking" Soviet loyalists. During the invasion, Havel provided radio commentary on Radio Free Czechoslovakia. Almost a decade after the crackdown, Havel's dissent remerged to the public life with the creation of the group Charter 77, which petitioned the government to abide by its commitments to the Helsinki Accords, guaranteeing civil rights. While going in and out of jail, house arrest, and short detentions, Havel continued to write, often on the subject of the posttotalitarian state. As the events of 1989 began to unfold in Eastern Europe, Charter 77 became a focus for antistate activity in Prague. The group reorganized itself into Civic Forum, which advocated local, nonstate associations of citizens to govern themselves. A coalition of these groups demonstrated throughout Czechoslovakia, under Havel's leadership. His negotiations with the Communist Party paved the way for a swift dissolution of the old regime, to be replaced with a democratic government, which elected him as president.

Students

Revolution is a serious thing, the most serious thing about a revolutionary's life. When one commits oneself to the struggle, it must be for a lifetime. —Angela Davis

Very few revolutions in the twentieth century did not have students as an active and forceful part of the revolutionary process. They are one of the most revolutionary-minded groups in society, but they also have not played a significant role in leading revolutionary activity beyond the initial stages. The typical student is young, unmarried, exposed to new ideas, and unemployed. This sets students apart from the rest of the population in some important ways. They are very similar to intellectuals, at least as long as they are students. Like intellectuals, students are distinct from society and are exposed to new or different ways of thinking. The typical college student is often away from family for the first time in his or her life, and thus the exposure to new ideas is all encompassing. The combination of new ideas and separation from family life has encouraged the radicalization of students.

Compared to the rest of society, students have tended to be much more radical—whether they were nationalist, liberal, or socialist. Islamic students in both Iran and Afghanistan were much more radical than the society around them. The Taliban, an Islamic fundamentalist group that came to power in Afghanistan, is so named because its members were formed in the madrassas (Islamic schools) across the border in Pakistan. *Talib* means student, and the plural version in Arabic is *taliban*. Most communist revolutions were led by groups whose origins were in students who pushed for more radical change than their older and more established counterparts who organized political parties. Followers of Mao Zedong and the Sandinistas (in Nicaragua) and Sendero Luminoso (in Peru) are all examples of revolutionary Marxist groups originating in schools. Some of this tendency toward radicalism is also explained by the changing demographics of students. In the latter half of the twentieth century, universities increasingly expanded to incorporate more middle-class backgrounds (Parsa 2000). This brought in more and more students who were not from the traditional elite and thus were much more open to new ideas about restructuring society (Mannheim 1936).

Students are in many ways separate from society while they attend school. As Barrington Moore argues, "protected enclaves within which dissatisfied or oppressed groups have some room to develop distinctive social arrangements, cultural traditions, and explanations of the world around them" are fundamental to the development of a revolutionary group (1978). Universities, with regional variations, have been just this kind of autonomous enclave (Latin American universities are especially autonomous). This autonomy also particularly shelters students from the experiences of the lower classes of society. University students "tend to lean toward 'voluntarist extremism' because only exceptionally do they have a 'practical grasp of the thought patterns . . . of the 'underprivileged' or even personal contact with the mass of the people.' In Herbert Blumer's terms, they have a 'romantic morale' rather than 'practical morale'" (Wickham-Crowley 1992: 36). Wickham-Crowley says that the isolation of university students is "thus a door that swings both ways"; students enjoy sanctuary but must leave the sanctuary for their ideas to take effect, which requires adjustment to fit the new audience. Often, there is a severe disconnect between the students' views of society and society's view of itself.

The autonomy provided by universities encourages more radical behavior in students. Most of the bonds—including marriage and children, employment, and property ownership—that encourage individuals to not participate in risky revolutionary activities do not exist for students. This means that students have very little to lose—what can the state take away? This has made students the most active participants in social movements in general, and in revolutions in particular. Students have little to lose, so they have little to fear by acting out against the government. In addition to being exposed to new ideas that might encourage revolution, they also have many significant tools to help them organize revolutionary activities. These include the very structure of universities in most societies: they have separate housing where students live in relatively close proximity to each other. Further, university students typically have access to technologies that allow the spread of communication. As technologies have developed, the relevant ones have changed, but they have gone from lecture halls and public spaces for meeting, to supplies for poster making, to copy machines, to fax machines, to computers with Internet access. All of these have helped students to communicate with nonstudents as well as each other.

Finally, although students are typically fairly well respected in most societies, they are also the most likely to be repressed, a combination that encourages the spread of revolutionary activity. Even where significant portions of the population attend universities, students are generally viewed as making themselves and society a better place. They inhabit the centers of knowledge in most societies, which are also respected. Thus, when they speak out about an issue, they often are given more leeway and seen as genuinely interested in the betterment of the nation. Because they have relatively little to gain or lose in revolutions, they are often viewed as the least biased, compared to workers, business elites, or others who may significantly benefit from changes in government. Because students are the most radically active group in society, however, if any repression occurs, it is likely that they will bear the brunt of it, at least initially. At the beginning of the Czechoslovak Revolution of 1989, it was primarily students who participated in the demonstrations against the communist government. Thus, when the police cleared the streets of demonstrators, it was mostly students who were injured. When the rest of Prague saw police beating students protesting for a better government, they viewed the police as increasingly illegitimate.

Despite the access to communication and the willingness to actively engage in struggles, students have traditionally not played a key role in the leadership of revolutions beyond the initial stages of protest. According to Parsa, there are three primary reasons why this is true (2000). First, students typically make up a relatively small proportion of society. Second, as noted above, they are typically unemployed and do not own property. Thus, they have nothing that they can withdraw to coerce the government. They do not buy much, because they are unemployed, and thus are unable to exercise power through boycotts. They do not work, so they are unable to engage in meaningful strikes. Students actually often engage in strikes by not attending school, as was illustrated in the 1989 Tiananmen Square movement in China. Unlike strikes by taxi drivers (Philippines 1986), sugarcane cutters (Cuba

1959), oil workers (Iran 1979), ship builders (Poland 1988), or coal miners (Czechoslovakia 1989), however, if students engage in strikes, normal activity for most of society does not stop. In this way, they are not able to force the government to respond, something other strikes are able to accomplish. Third, students, because of their radical ideologies, are less likely to form the broad coalitions that are necessary to effectively challenge the state. Thus, students are likely to spur initial activity, but it is other groups in society that are typically the ones to make change occur in revolutions. Students' work in the 2001 Serbian Revolution was unique in how influential the students were in mobilizing resistance to Slobodan Milosevic.

Workers

> *Let the ruling classes tremble at a Communistic revolution. The proletarians have nothing to lose but their chains. They have a world to win.*
> —Karl Marx

The Marxist tradition views workers as the revolutionary class. Marx saw the growing divide between the proletariat (workers) and the bourgeoisie (owners) as driving the class conflict that would end capitalism. But who are the workers? In Marxist theory, the proletariat are more than just workers. They are a particular type of worker—those who sell their labor for wages. In this way, they have further extended the commodification of everything that is inherent in the capitalist system. Their time and skill are turned into money, meaning that they are soon viewed as nothing more than inputs into the industrial process. The proletariat work in factories, doing primarily unskilled labor. One worker is no better or worse than another at running complex machinery, for all they are required to do is maintain the machine. According to Marx, the expansion of technology to mechanize and centralize the means of production would increasingly reduce wages of the proletariat so that they would eventually become impoverished, unfulfilled, cogs in the wheel of production. As mechanization reduced the need for manual labor, the wages of the proletariat would be driven down, increasing their exploitation. Crammed together in urban societies, working in massive industrial factories, and extremely exploited, this class, Marxists argued, was ripe for revolutionary activity. A spark, created by intellectuals, would ignite this revolutionary class to overthrow the entire capitalist system.

A broader conception of a worker is anyone who works for wages. Typically, though not necessarily, a worker lives in an urban area. For example, it is appropriate to view the sugarcane cutters of Cuba prior to the 1959 revolution as rural workers. They were not peasants, they did not own their own land, and many of them migrated between urban areas and the countryside on a seasonal basis (Wolf 1999). In contrast to the typical Marxist view, workers need not be employed in very large factories. This is typically the case, but they may also be employed in smaller factories or work as semiskilled laborers in a particular craft. The key defining variable for workers is that they are not entrepreneurs. That is, they do not earn money from something they create or a service they render. They earn money from someone who owns a business that makes something or provides a service. This distinction is important, not because it is an indication of the income of an individual but because it has historically indicated their attachment to the continuity of the system. Wage earners have no fixed assets that can be taken over by someone else, in contrast to capitalists.

Workers are often one of the more radical elements of society. Although not as radical as students or intellectuals, they are prone to following their radical tendencies. Because they do not have the attachment of owning property for their income, they are more inclined than capitalists to follow more radical changes. The effect of this radical predisposition does not translate into revolution unless some other element is present. Parsa argues that this radicalization can be a force that either encourages or actually discourages revolutions from occurring (2000). The difference, according to him, is whether or not the state is heavily involved in the economy. If the state is very involved, then the target for radicalized workers is the state. This creates the opportunity for other classes, especially the capitalists, to join the workers in seeking to change the government. If the state is not very involved in the economy, then the target for radicalized workers is the economy itself. Capitalists and others are much less likely to join with workers in attacking the economy, because it will more likely be at their expense. Thus, the position of the state affects the likelihood of coalitions forming and thus the likelihood of revolution being successful. In contrast, Gould argues that workers do not become organized unless they are "integrated into larger-scale organizations that specifically highlighted their wage-earning status—as in the national workshops in France in 1848 or the soviets in Russia in 1917—at the expense of narrower, craft-based collective identities" (2006: 528). Without this larger guidance, workers tend to be more likely to form unions that will actually compete in some ways with each other, undermining their revolutionary potential.

In addition to being radical, workers—unlike the students—have significant resources at their disposal to effect change. Workers, by definition, are an essential element in the production and distribution of goods and services. Thus, when they engage in a strike or work stoppage, they have much greater potential to affect the entire economy. If workers are viewed as cogs in the wheel, they have the ability to make the machine cease working by removing themselves from the wheel. Further, workers, because they are usually urban and thus in the same physical location as governments, are able to more quickly take advantage of political crises. As Gould argues,

> at moments of political uncertainty and crisis, the willingness of organized urban groups to be vocal in pressing their demands, to the point of physically invading the buildings where deliberative bodies meet, has had a powerful effect on the course of revolutionary politics. . . . It is no accident that nations whose capital cities are also major industrial centers have been more susceptible to radical revolutionary change than have those whose capitals are dominated by financial, cultural, or administrative institutions. (2006: 528)

At the same time, because workers are a part of the system and all of their income comes from their labor, they are less likely to engage in strikes or work stoppages. Unlike students, who have little to lose, individual workers have much to lose. They could be fired or their employer could be forced out of business. Because workers, unlike students, typically have families to support, the implications are greater. It is for this reason that Parsa views workers as opportunistic revolutionaries (2000: 163). When it is likely that they will not be repressed, they are open to collective action. When their actions are likely to be met with retribution, they are more likely to be good workers.

The primary drawback of strict Marxist conceptions of workers, even if we allow for the broader definition above, is that they have rarely been a revolutionary force. The theory makes logical sense but has not proven to be historically accurate. As many have pointed out (e.g., Skocpol, Wolf, and Gould), revolutions in the modern period have been driven more by peasant uprisings than by worker revolts. The French, Mexican, Russian, Chinese, Cuban, Algerian, Vietnamese, Nicaraguan, and other revolutions "have all been predominantly rural in origin, even if urban workers and intellectuals took part" (Gould 2006: 527). Further, the workers who have played a role in revolutionary movements have generally been the opposite of the ideal-type proletariat envisioned in Marxist theory. Rather than increasingly unskilled, impoverished, and unattached persons, Goldstone finds that those workers who participate in revolutionary activity are generally better off than most of their cohorts:

> Whether we look at the residents of growing cities in eighteenth-century France or twentieth-century Mexico, we find they are not isolated, ignorant, disoriented masses. Instead, urban migrants tend to be better educated and more highly skilled than the compatriots they leave behind in the

countryside, generally have family contacts already in the city, and maintain frequent contacts, through circular migration, with rural kin. Moreover, when we examine the backgrounds of the participants in riots and revolutionary tumults, whether in eighteenth-century towns or in twentieth-century American ghettos, we find that the rioters tend to be among the better educated residents of their communities and are more likely to be long-term residents than recent arrivals. These urban rioters are generally laborers or artisans for whom swings in prices and employment have a powerful impact, rather than the poorest, hard-core unemployed. (Goldstone 1994b: 11)

Peasants

It was the class struggles of the peasants, the peasant uprisings and peasant wars that constituted the real motive force of historical development in Chinese feudal society. —Mao Zedong

A peasant is someone whose existence is tied to agricultural production. Peasants are a class of people, and thus are defined, like workers, capitalists, and intellectuals, by the relationship of the individual to the means of production. The peasant is, above all else, an agricultural laborer. Peasants usually are not primarily wage workers, however. That is, although they usually pay taxes or rent, the decisions about planting, cultivating, and utilizing crops are determined by them. For most of history, most peasants have been primarily oriented toward subsistence with a minimal amount of produce going to market. This generalization has within it a wide variety of rural lifestyles. Peasants may be very primitive or relatively advanced in their use of agricultural technology: they may have significant income from nonagricultural sources such as weaving, spinning, and metalwork; they may be relatively separate from government intrusion or may be heavily taxed and conscripted to serve in the military; they may be exclusively rural or have significant experiences in cities and even foreign countries (typically as a soldier) (Markoff 1998).

Eric Wolf's *Peasant Wars of the Twentieth Century* was a landmark study of the role of peasants in modern revolutions. In it, he explores the paradox of why peasants are an unlikely source of revolutionary activity, while at the same time most of the major social revolutions have involved peasant participation. Peasants, Wolf argues, are unlikely revolutionaries for six reasons. First, they are primarily solitary workers. They work their land alone, typically with only their immediate family for support. This decreases the chances of networking that might spread ideas. More important, the solitary nature of their work encourages peasants to view each other as potential competitors for what little goods are sold in the market. Second, peasants are very structured, hard workers in that the planting cycle demands routine and constant work. Wolf argues that "the tyranny of work weighs heavily upon a peasant: his life is geared to an annual routine and to planning for the year to come" (1999: 289). This is part of the appeal of wage labor in urban areas; there is the potential for leisure time that does not exist in the peasant life. This makes getting together to plan revolutionary activity difficult.

Third, peasants are in some ways isolated from economic crises that impoverish others. Because they are tied to the land and most of their production is for their own consumption, as long as there are no natural disasters, they are insulated from market fluctuations. It is these disruptions that make other classes most likely to advocate change. This insulation is augmented by the fourth characteristic of peasants, which is that they have extensive kinship ties that provide for a social safety net. Because they are rural and thereby removed from government, they have relied upon kinship ties to provide for each other in times of economic distress. This further separates them from society. Fifth, this exclusion is reinforced by traditions that dictate that political decisionmaking is the domain of elites. Peasants view politics with suspicion and prefer to have others make those decisions that do not seem to affect their lives much. The sixth characteristic of the peasantry that makes it unlikely to be revolutionary is that their interests "crosscut class alignments" (Wolf 1999: 289). That is, "rich and poor peasants may be kinfolk, or a peasant may be at one and the same time owner, renter, share-cropper, laborer for his neighbors and seasonal hand on a nearby plantation" (1999: 289). This means that the peasant can identify with both owners and workers, making them unlikely to support either in class conflict.

The irony, given all these reasons why peasants typically do not make for a revolutionary class, is that they were historically required for the really fundamental shifts from feudal to capitalist societies in the twentieth century. They have been the key force, especially in communist revolutions. This is even more ironic given what Wolf describes as the peasant utopia: "The free village, untrammeled by tax collectors, labor recruiters, large landowners, officials" (1999: 294). In other words, what they want most is for everyone to leave them alone—anarchy. What they have historically been most important in creating is massively intrusive state bureaucracies that have stripped away private property.

To understand why peasants, despite being inherently conservative, have been a key to many revolutions, Wolf says that we must further classify the types of peasantry that exist. There are three types of peasants, in terms of revolutionary potential: poor, middle, and rich. We might view this as the Goldilocks principle of peasants. First there are the poor peasants who do not have the resources sufficient to engage in collective action. They are typically moving toward becoming wage laborers, as their land, if they own or rent any, is not sufficient to provide for them. On the other extreme are the rich peasants who have extensive resources for collective action, but not the motivation. Participation in collective action would likely result in losing their privileged place. "As employer of the labor of others, as money lender, as notable co-opted by the state machine, he exercises local power in alliance with" the government and thus will not actively challenge that government (1999: 291).

The middle peasantry, in contrast, is the ideal type for supporting revolutionary activity. These peasants have the means to support themselves and thus are "tactically free" in that they can retreat to their own land in times of crisis. Because their control of land was still relatively low, they typically strongly favored the redistribution of land. This "desire for land often encouraged radical politics" (Snyder 1999). It should be noted that the justification of land redistribution, for peasants, has historically been driven by a restoration of land rights. That is, peasant support for communist policies has been a reaction to what they perceived as landlords taking their land (Scott 1976). The goal of redistribution, then, was to reclaim lost lands, not to eliminate private property.

The middle peasant also has more extensive ties to urban workers, as "[he] stays on the land and sends his children to work in town; he is caught in a situation in which one part of the family retains a footing in agriculture, while the other undergoes 'the training of the cities'" (Wolf 1999: 292). This connection, which allows urban discontent to spread to rural areas, is the crucial link in revolutions involving the peasantry. "Though urban disorders have often been at the leading edge of revolution—in Paris in 1789, in Petersburg in 1917, in Tehran in 1980—no revolution has succeeded solely on the basis of rioting and seizure of the political capital by the populace. The state can isolate and defeat revolutionaries in the capital city if the revolutionaries lack support in the provinces and the countryside, as members of the Paris Commune of 1871 and the Chinese Communists of the 1920s discovered" (Goldstone 1994b: 11–12). Goldstone argues that the links between the urban and rural are the determining factor in whether or not a social revolution will emerge.

Although peasants are typically conservative in nature (in that they seek to reclaim or hold on to their land), they have had the effect of radicalizing revolutionary situations. This happens in two ways. Peasants can radicalize a revolutionary situation by speeding up the collapse of the old regime when they take part in efforts to control the land. These typically localized and limited revolts are aimed at gaining more land from repressive landlords. When the state is weakened and needs more support from the traditional aristocracy, however, they are not able to provide it, because they are dealing with local rebellions. The French and Russian revolutions both exemplify this process. When military discipline eroded during World War I and peasants defected from the military in droves, they returned home armed and angry. Peasant land seizures skyrocketed at the very time that the tsar needed more income and conscripts to support the failing war effort. The second way in which peasants can radicalize a revolutionary situation is after the collapse of the old regime when the new regime attempts to consolidate control. Peasants may support revolutionary movements aimed at getting rid of a repressive regime, but they rarely support a new regime in its place. As Markoff argues, "After the Mexican Revolution of 1910 the new claimants to national authority were doggedly defied for years of bloody struggle by land-seizing peasants in the state of Morelos, a situation that was a major source of instability in Mexico City until the government accepted the land claims" (1998: 393). In the Mexican case, the involvement of the peasantry and their continued involvement after the collapse of the old regime forced the new government to more radical positions on land reform.

The conclusions that the literature comes to about the role of peasants in revolutions are paradoxical. Peasants are unlikely revolutionaries because of their class background. For social revolutions to occur, however, the peasantry has historically been an integral part of the process. This is because urban rebellions can more easily be repressed by the government. If urban elites, typically intellectuals, are able to gain support of a middle peasantry, then there is a chance that the urban discontent can spread to the countryside and motivate much broader social changes. The literature on peasants also reflects many scholars' assumption that revolution is a part of the modernization process. As there are fewer agrarian societies today, even in the developing world, the role of the peasantry is likely to be increasingly less important in future revolutions.

Ethnic Groups

Love your country. Your country is the land where your parents sleep, where is spoken that language in which the chosen of your heart, blushing, whispered the first word of love; it is the home that God has given you that by striving to perfect yourselves therein you may prepare to ascend to him. —Giuseppe Mazzini

The previous categories of challengers have all been identified with a particular class in society. This is because much of the revolution literature borrows from or overtly utilizes Marxist analyses of conflict that focus on class.

The dominant conflict in society, Marxists argue, is along class lines. Ethnic lines have also been a significant division within societies, however, especially in the postcolonial era during which independent state borders often do not follow historically accurate tribal or other sociocultural boundaries. Ethnicity is the socially determined relevant attributes and institutions that make one group of people culturally different from others. The factors that can distinguish one group from another include language, religion, geography, customs, history, physical characteristics, occupation, and family. The relevance of any of these distinguishing factors is determined both by the group and others. Thus, language or religion may be the key difference between two groups in one area (for example, religion was the primary dividing line between Bozniaks and Serbs), whereas two other ethnic groups share the same language and religion (most of the population of northern Sudan is Muslim, but the Darfur conflict is often portrayed as an ethnic struggle between "black" and "Arab" Africans). As both of these examples illustrate, conflict lines are often drawn along ethnic cleavages. These can grow to include revolutionary struggles.

In most ways, ethnic groups are like any other group in a society. As Rothchild puts it, "the leaders of ethnic groups act as do other political interests, using influence, concessions, alliances, threats, and at times even force to attain the ends of collective action" (1998: 161). The crucial difference between ethnic groups and other political groups in a society, however, is that an ethnic group's key identifier is permanent. Individuals can change their political affiliation or their position on an issue; they cannot, however, change their ethnic identity. "Ironically, even though many ethnic groups are of relatively recent origins and lack homogeneity and cohesiveness, they gain a life of their own because they represent poles around which peoples can mobilize to compete for scarce resources and to ensure group security in an uncertain political environment" (Rothchild 1998: 161).

Ethnic cleavages are more likely to encourage revolution when there are significant differences between two or more ethnic groups within a state in terms of economic development. This is further exacerbated if the government is perceived as taking an active role in promoting an ethnic group's development at the expense of another. A history of conflict is also important. In countries with "negative memories and a history of collective disrespect and low status," ethnic conflict is much more likely (Rothchild 1998: 161). Finally, when all of these factors are present. and the state is governed or closely aligned to the interests of one ethnic group, ethnic-based challenges become much more likely to grow into revolutionary movements. These structural factors make ethnic-based revolutionary activity more likely, but the outcome of this form of group identification does not appear to be any different from that of other political party challenges.

Political Parties

A party is the vanguard of a class, and its duty is to lead the masses and not merely to reflect the average political level of the masses. —V. I. Lenin

Political parties are the associations of individuals with the specific purpose of achieving political goals, that is, goals that are typically the domain of governments. In liberal democracies, political parties are primarily organized to effect these changes by gaining office through elections. In communist regimes, there is only one political party allowed, and it is tasked with guiding the government by providing policies. Political parties as revolutionary challengers are found in all types of regimes and are typically the organizations that arise to challenge the government, attempt to seize power after the old regime collapses, or both. As a result, the composition of individuals who make up the party often determines the role it will have in revolutions. If it is primarily capitalists, then it will behave more like capitalists (described in the next section). Given that parties, by definition, reflect the interests of their members, there is less to say about political parties as challengers to the government's rule. It is important to note, however, that almost all revolutionary challengers have been led by a political party.

Capitalists

Democracy for an insignificant minority, democracy for the rich—that is the democracy of capitalist society. —V. I. Lenin

Capitalists, in traditional Marxist class analysis, are the owners of the means of production. That is, they control the capital or the assets associated with economic transactions. As noted in Chapter 5, the bourgeoisie is the capitalist class. The early connotations of urban dwellers are still relevant, though not required; there are rural capitalists (e.g., the owners of crop land). In more developed economies, however, wealth tends to be more concentrated in urban areas. Further, in many developing societies, legally recognized ownership of any property is low compared to the industrial world in which workers often own their own homes. Capitalists, then, are those who own a business or property that is used to generate income. This can be a self-employed plumber who works alone or a member of the Walton family (which owns Wal-Mart, the largest grocery store chain in the world). Although the distinction between workers and capitalists is blurry in contemporary developed countries because of the widespread ownership of stock in retirement funds, in the developing world and throughout most of history, the line between those who own property and those who work for the owners has been clearer.

Traditional Marxists view capitalist interests as synonymous with those of the government. In fact, they usually see the government as the unimportant structure that does the bidding of the dominant class. Capitalists have proven to be revolutionary in some situations, however, and to have interests that diverge significantly from that of the government. Parsa's investigation of three recent revolutions (Iran, Nicaragua, and the Philippines) provides some generalizations about capitalists and their interests.

Parsa argues that capitalists typically fear class conflict more than any government actions (2000). The relationship of developing societies has been that a small group of capitalists benefits a great deal from state actions in the form of subsidies, tax breaks, and access to loans and land. The majority of capitalists do not receive this treatment, however. As a result, there is potential for a lot of capitalists to push for more assistance from the government. If the major force behind this reform is driven by workers or others who are motivated by class conflict, however, capitalists, even those excluded by the state, are unlikely to join the movement. According to Parsa, those excluded from the ruling coalition have ideologically favored nationalism or some form of democracy. "When capitalists are under pressure from foreign capital and multilateral agencies, they are more likely to advocate nationalism. . . . When they are excluded from the polity and adversely affected by the state, capitalists demand greater democracy and expansion of the polity" (2000: 198). The capitalists' ideology reflects a very pragmatic self-interested approach. If the state is the key threat to their interests, they favor democracy that will allow them to have more of a say in the government. If the international market is the key threat to their interests, they favor more nationalist movements that are more likely to enact protectionist measures than the current regime is. In this effort to create these changes, capitalists will align with more radical groups, but they never adopt their radical ideologies. For example, a group of influential business elite joined with the FSLN in Nicaragua when it became more likely that the Marxist group could overthrow the Anastasio Somoza regime and that it was toning down its class-conflict rhetoric.

Capitalists are relatively immune from repression and have access to significant resources to challenge the government. They are immune from repression because of their privileged status; that is, they control the primary elements of a market economy. Widespread repression of this class would be economically disastrous. Because they have control of the production of goods and services in a society, they have the ability to withhold them. In this sense, they have immense power to force the government to respond to their demands by holding the economy captive. Again, however, they will be the first ones hurt by these actions, so they are unlikely to engage in challenging the government for minor issues.

Clergy

Anyone who will say that religion is separate from politics is a fool; he does not know Islam or politics. —Ayatollah Khomeini

Clergy are all of those who are employed by or administer a church, mosque, synagogue, temple, or other religious institution. They are the people who lead religions, and across religions they have typically played very similar roles. The clergy have historically been very conservative. The relationship between the state and clergy in most countries has been mutually supporting. The clergy often give legitimacy to the government, or at least encourage obedience, and the state either supports or at least does not infringe upon the clergy. In the West, since the Treaty of Westphalia, there has been a separation of power between the Roman Catholic Church and the states of Europe. In reality the church in each country has been an integral part of the government's power. For example, the origins of the French Revolution were in the refusal of the Third Estate (the commoners) to disband. The other two estates, the nobility and the church, were much more conservative supporters of the crown. The French model was the norm for church-state relations throughout most of Europe. This relationship was transplanted in the colonies throughout the globe. The colonization of most of the world was a two-pronged approach of opening up the country for trade and exploitation purposes as well as "saving" the uncivilized inhabitants through conversion to Christianity. Especially in Latin America, the relationship between the church and state thus continued even after independence. In most of the East, whether Orthodox Christian, Islamic, Hindu, or Confucian, the government and religion were historically the same thing. As a result, throughout much of the world, religious institutions have historically been very supportive of government institutions.

This relationship began to change in some countries after World War II. With Arab independence movements in the 1950s and 1960s, the Indian independence movement, and changes in the Catholic Church under the Second Vatican Council that spurred liberation theology, religious institutions became much more critical of existing government institutions.

The clergy have three tendencies that have made them relevant in revolutions during this time period. First, and most important, religious institutions are typically very well organized, with a vast array of resources. In many developing countries, a big part of the reason that the clergy and government were mutually supporting is that the resources of the two were very similar. The clergy often own significant land and control the dominant social institutions such as schools, media, hospitals and churches, and mosques, temples, or other religious meeting places. Further, they have a very captive audience who regularly come to those meeting places, so they can reach out to many parts of society relatively easily. Their control over schools can also give them access to the most active among the population; thus they are able to influence the direction in which radical activity can be channeled, as the Pakistani madrassas illustrate.

Second, because they are generally moderate or reformist in nature, clerics have been central figures in some revolutions for bringing together coalitions of other groups. Like students, the motives of clerics are usually assumed to be associated with their existing leadership in the spiritual realm. Thus, the social status of clergy in most societies is very high, especially compared to the political and business elite. Further, because they are this type of central figure, they are often less likely to advocate radical changes that would isolate and potentially harm part of their following. This is not a hard-and-fast rule, however, as the Iranian and Afghanistan cases illustrate (radical clerics came to power in each case).

Third, clergy are typically much more immune from repression by the government than other segments of society. This is explained by several factors. Because they are typically more moderate and reformist, they are less likely to be the focus of repression, as the government will target radicals first. Also, because of their status, repression of clerics is typically viewed as a taboo. The reaction to the assassination of Archbishop Oscar Romero in El Salvador is an example of how the public reacts to this kind of repression. In this case, there had been many deaths by the military and paramilitary forces; this high-profile assassination, however, led to increased mobilization of many in El Salvador. Romero's funeral mass was attended by more than 250,000 people, which was commonly viewed as a forum for reacting against the repressive regime.

Clergy are also more immune from government aggression because of their ties to others within their religion outside of their country. The Catholic Church has the strongest external organization, with the pope and a hierarchy of authorities outside of the country that operate over leaders within a country. This gives an otherwise small group tremendous external support. For example, the independence movement in East Timor was in many ways sustained by the support of the church there and its contacts and communication to the wider world through the Vatican. The pope's visit to East Timor in 1989 further pushed Indonesia to change its policies regarding the occupation of the half-island. Although less hierarchical, similar organizations and networks of clergy exist among most of the world's religions. These external connections raise the potential costs to the government if it chooses to repress, as other governments, pressured by these religious institutions, may exert pressure on the repressing government.

The role of clergy is somewhat limited by the fact that they oftentimes remain aloof from politics. Parsa argues that the clergy only really matter in revolutions when they become politicized or active in the political struggle (2000). Despite their vast resources and role as spiritual leaders, clergy are almost never the leaders of revolutionary movements, even when they become politicized, with Iran again being the exception. Typically the role that clergy play in revolutions is the provision of the means for other groups to mobilize. They provide a safe space, in the form of physical buildings where groups can meet and not be repressed by the government. They also provide networks for linking up disparate groups in society. Finally, they can provide the larger ideological framework that encourages participation. That is, they can legitimize the struggle against the government by framing it in terms of creating justice that is in line with divine law.

Summary of Challengers

Looking back at the list of potential challengers that have often emerged to challenge the state, one may be tempted to view this as a complete list of any group in society. There are many other groups, particularly groups within the state, that have not emerged to challenge the government in revolutionary movements. For example, when the military challenges the government, it typically takes the form of a coup. Police forces, bureaucrats, and other functionaries of the government rarely become active as a group in revolutionary activity. They are all in privileged positions and thus are likely to lose significantly should a revolutionary movement succeed. When individuals from each of these forces begin to defect to join the challengers or cease to carry out the government's orders, then a revolutionary situation progresses. Those marginalized in societies are also rarely a force in revolutionary movements, as they do not have the resources to lend much support. Those groups not covered in this chapter are largely the followers of the revolutionary leaders. These followers and their behavior in revolutions are the topic for the next chapter.

Questions for Discussion and Reflection

1. Who do you know who would qualify as an intellectual?

2. What would have to happen for you to participate in an antigovernment demonstration?

3. What similarities exist for the individual intellectuals described in this chapter?

4. What ideology might have been used to justify the breakup of the former Yugoslavia in the early 1990s?

5. Why does Parsa call workers "opportunistic revolutionaries"? Is this a derogatory term?

6. What role did peasants play in the Mexican revolution?

7

Mobilizing
the Masses

Avoid revolution or expect to get shot. Mother and I will grieve, but we will gladly buy a dinner for the National Guardsman who shot you.
—Paul Williamson on the Kent State massacre

The quote above indicates the stakes for participating in revolution—it is very often a life-or-death matter. With the stakes this high and the likelihood of success questionable, one must wonder why anyone would join a revolutionary movement. The point of this chapter will be to answer two related questions: Why do people participate in revolution? How do they participate in revolution? Although there has been a honing of our understanding of the structural causes of revolutionary situations and of the people who rise to lead revolutions, there is no such consensus as to why people join in revolutionary movements. The explanations that have been developed are almost as diverse as the populations of revolutionary movements themselves. Participants in revolutionary activity are motivated by a wide variety of goals, and the literature has tried to improve our understanding of what makes one group of people actively sacrifice their lives to overthrow a government while others sit out the movement on the sidelines. Most of the explanations are focused on the psychological and social-psychological aspects of participants. To answer *how* people participate in revolutions, there is also a wide spectrum of literature on the variety of strategies and tactics used to overthrow governments. These span from protests and noncooperation through guerrilla movements on to full-scale conventional military battles.

Psychological Explanations

Give people a convincing reason and they will lay down their very lives.
—Patrick Dixon

127

The fields of psychology and social psychology are often utilized to answer why people participate in revolutions. Ted Robert Gurr asked and answered the famous question: "Why do men rebel?" or participate in collective action. The fundamental answer to his question was what he termed "relative deprivation," which he defined as "the perceived discrepancy between men's value expectations and value capabilities" (1970: 13). That is, there is a difference between what people expect and what a society is likely to be able to provide. It is important to distinguish this from deprivation or poverty in general. Poverty does not make people want to rebel. In fact, it is a good deterrent. An impoverished individual does not have the means to address the sources of his or her poverty or any reason to see the situation as anything other than what is to be expected. It is only when a person thinks his or her life should be better that a rebellious attitude can arise. As Kimmel argues, it is the combination of despair and hope that fuels revolutions (1990). Despair is not enough; it "may make revolutionary activity necessary, but hope transforms a rebellion or revolt into a purposive and visionary movement" (1990: 12).

Gurr argues that there are actually two types of relative deprivation. The first is what he calls decremental deprivation, a state in which expectations are fixed and the capacity to meet them declines. This is what traditional Marxists view as happening with the growth of capitalism. Workers' conditions become worse as capitalist exploitation increases. Gurr points out that this has not historically been the force motivating revolutionary activity. In contrast, aspirational deprivation is the relevant form of deprivation. This is the state in which capabilities remain constant but expectations rise. Thus the spread of new ideas, contact with others who are much better off, government promises, or other factors can contribute to rising expectations. A recurring spark for revolutions since the end of the Cold War has been the calling of elections. When people think that they have a say in their government, but the election is rigged or not followed, people erupt in public opposition. Gurr states that when governments are not able to restructure their economy to meet these rising expectations, rebellions are much more likely.

The form that rebellion will take depends on who is affected by the relative deprivation. There are three potential types of rebellion. The first, turmoil, is often violent protests that repeatedly occur, involving spontaneous outbursts of antigovernment activity. This is likely when the relative deprivation is high among masses but low among elites. This distinction is critical because without elites also suffering from relative deprivation, there is no focal leadership. The result is that there are sporadic outbursts of violence that do not significantly challenge the government. In contrast, when there is high relative deprivation among elites and low relative deprivation among the masses, conspiracy, the second type, is likely. This is apt to result in coup attempts or other changes that are internal to the government. Without popular support for changes, because the motivating factor does not exist for the masses, there is less likely to be a revolution. Third, when both the masses and elites suffer from high relative deprivation, there is likely to be an internal war. When this happens, revolutions are much more likely, as there is popular participation to challenge the government that can be aligned with those most likely to restructure the government.

James Davies argues that

> revolutions are most likely to occur when a prolonged period of objective economic and social development is followed by a short period of sharp reversal. The all-important effect on the minds of people in a particular society is to produce, during the former period, an expectation of continued ability to satisfy needs—which continue to rise and then, during the latter, a mental state of anxiety and frustration when manifest reality breaks away from anticipated reality. (1962: 5)

The point, then, is that economic changes lead to changes in people's perceptions. The result is that revolutions attempt "to bring social realities into line with their expectations, motivated by the psychological discomfort which is the result of the disparity between such realities and potentialities" (Kimmel 1990: 73). Hoffer's analysis of "true believers" says that "a rising mass movement attracts and holds a following not by its doctrines and promises but by the refuge it offers from the anxieties, barrenness and meaninglessness of an individual existence" (Hoffer 1951). This suggests that for the true believer, someone so committed to a cause that he or she is willing to die for it, ideologies are interchangeable. For the true believer, the particular belief ironically is less relevant than having the belief. Again, the underlying dynamic is the psychological process that is important and activated by changing conditions.

A psychological study of those who participated in the American Revolution is a telling illustration of the role of psychological factors. Hull, Hoffer, and Allen compare loyalists, those who took some action that was recorded in history as favoring the continuation of British rule of the colony of New York, and patriots, those who took an action supporting independence. After analyzing the writings of thirty-nine colonists, they were able to conclude that the individual's psychological elements were as important as structural elements in determining their likelihood of supporting the British or independence. The psychological elements included aspects such as an individual's need for order, tolerance for dissonance and ambiguity, and submission to authority. This personality score was compared to structural factors that would encourage one to be either loyalist or rebel in this context. These included age, income, the holding of public office (in the colonial government), religion, and a number of family factors (such as how many generations the family had been in the colony). The latter are all nonpsychological factors that have been used to explain why people participated in the revolution. The authors find that both the structural and psychological factors explain an individual's participation in rebellious activity. From this they argue that "human action is *never* directly caused by situations; it is invariably mediated by psychological variables" (Hull, Hoffer, and Allen 1978: 344).

Rational Choice Theory

> *Madness is the exception in individuals but the rule in groups.*
> —Friedrich Nietzsche

Rational actor theories approach the same question of why people participate in revolutions but answer the question by building on economic or social-psychological theories rather than explicitly psychological ones. In this regard, the unit of analysis is still the individual, but the analysis conducted is rational choice. Before summarizing the rational choice literature's answer to this question, it would be useful to review rational choice theory.

Because of rational choice theory's origins in economic theories, there are different interpretations of what rational means. In its starkest terms, rationality is defined as "nothing more than an optimal correspondence between ends and means" (Tsebelis 1990: 18). Implied in this definition is the understanding that an actor will choose the best means to achieve her or his most desired ends. It is from basic assumptions about individuals that different situations can be analyzed. These situations are typically referred to as games in the rational choice literature. Different situations create different games, such as a prisoner's dilemma, chicken, assurance, and deadlock (Tsebelis 1990). The clarity of the assumptions about what constitutes rationality is crucial to rational choice theory. Stephen Walt identifies a number of basic assumptions of most rational choice models in political science:

1. Rational choice theory is individualistic: social and political outcomes are viewed as the collective product of individual choices.
2. Rational choice theory assumes that each actor seeks to maximize its "subjective expected utility." Given a particular set of preferences

and a fixed array of possible choices, actors will select the outcome that brings the greatest expected benefits.

3. The specification of actors' preferences is subject to certain constraints: (a) an actor's preferences must be complete (meaning we can rankorder their preference for different outcomes); and (b) preferences must be transitive (if A is preferred to B and B to C, then A is preferred to C).

4. Constructing a formal theory requires the analyst to specify the structure of the game. This typically means identifying a set of players, the likelihoods of each player's pattern of preferences, each player's information at every choice point, and how they see their moves as connected to the possible outcomes. (1999: 10–11)

The growing body of revolution literature that explicitly utilizes a rational choice approach has tended to focus on one overriding concern: explaining why individuals engage in the seemingly irrational action of revolution (Lichbach 1994). In Mancur Olson's *The Logic of Collective Action,* he lays out what has become know as the "free-rider" problem stemming from his distinction between "collective goods" and "selective incentives" (1965). Collective goods are those that, if enjoyed by any one person in a group, no other person in the group can be kept from enjoying. Clean air is a classic example. No one in a neighborhood can be denied the benefits of a factory cleaning its smokestack, thus reducing its toxic emissions in a neighborhood. In contrast, selective incentives are goods that can be withheld from those who do not help to produce them. Only those who work at a factory will be paid wages; they are not distributed evenly regardless of whether a person works. Given this distinction, Olson argues that it is irrational for people in large groups to contribute to public goods because they will contribute more than they will benefit. No one would work at the factory if everyone is paid regardless of whether they work. In a similar argument, no one individual in the factory neighborhood will pay to clean up the smokestack when he or she could not do so and still get the benefits of clean air should others clean it. Those who do not contribute, but receive the benefits, are referred to as free riders. Will Moore shows how the free-rider problem exactly matches the situation of revolution: the replacement of a disliked government with one that is potentially more just is clearly a collective good, and thus many rational choice theorists try to explain why people participate in this irrational action (1995).

The paradox that scholars utilizing the rational choice approach must reconcile is why rational individuals participate in irrational activities, such as revolution. There are three types of solutions to this paradox that have emerged: the selective incentive, the contracts and conventions, and the tipping model.

What Moore (1995) terms the "selective incentive solution" entails organizations' creating selective incentives to potential members to get them to mobilize for collective action. One of the earliest versions of this solution is by Gordon Tullock, who argues that "revolutions are carried out by people who hope for private gain" (1971: 99). That is, there are some who see the potential benefits as sufficiently great to risk death and likely failure in order to "have a good position in the new state which is to be established by the revolution" (98). These individuals are motivated by the potential selective incentive of becoming the new rulers in society. Intellectuals such as Vladimir Lenin, Leon Trotsky, Ayatollah Ruhollah Khomeini, and Vaclav Havel were isolated from their respective power structures. They were often jailed or exiled to be silenced, the most extreme version of being shut out of the government (other than death). Thus, they would be much better off if they were successful in leading a revolutionary movement.

An alternative to this self-interest theory is one put forth by Muller and Opp (1986), which suggests that leaders of revolutionary movements may adopt a "martyr syndrome," in which fears of death and the free-rider problem no longer inhibit individual action. For those true believers, the prospect of death is not an inhibiting factor in promoting their cause. These "altruistic political entrepreneurs" are likely to encourage group participation through their leadership, despite the fact that they pay significant potential costs with little likelihood of real gain (Taylor 1987). In this type of analysis, the belief system of the individual is crucial in setting his or her preferences so that fidelity to beliefs is more important than material well-being (Hoffer 1951; Meier 1970). Whether self-interested or true believers, individuals have incentives to participate in collective action.

Will Moore (1995) calls the second solution to the free-rider problem the "contracts and conventions" approach. Scholars who adopt this approach build on the notions of social contract developed by Enlightenment thinkers. The fundamental proposition of these scholars is "all-or-none (i.e. not one person contributes unless everyone who would be needed to provide the good contributes)" (Moore 1995: 436). The focus of these scholars necessarily shifts from explaining the apparent irrationality of individuals to analyzing group behavior. For example, Muller and Opp argue that "in regard to an average citizen's choice of whether or not to rebel, considerations of what is collectively rational can override the individually rational logic of the private interest theory" (1986: 485). This may be done by employing previously existing social structures to enforce group norms, as James Scott found in some peasant villages (1976). Groups of individuals can avoid the free-rider problem caused by collective goods by utilizing existing social networks. James Coleman argues that when there are significant social connections, individuals can influence each other to participate—eliminating the free-rider problem (1990). This explanation of why groups engage in revolution is important because it brings in the discussion of group behavior.

Group behavior can lead to irrational behavior (including participating in revolutionary movements) for a variety of reasons. Crowd psychology builds on the social-psychological work of Sigmund Freud and others who argue that people behave differently in groups than they would as individuals. In the context of crises faced by a group, individuals typically become more activist, enthusiastic, and prone to taking risks they might not take if they were not in the group. This outcome of crowd psychology is what has been described as the risky-shift phenomenon: "People deciding in groups are reluctant to appear overly cautious or, worse, fearful. . . . For psychological reasons, they reach shift-to-risk decisions under peer group pressure. Thus, it has been argued, groups are usually dominated by their most reckless (and neurotic) member. People will sacrifice themselves for and take chances on behalf of others that they would not normally take when acting for themselves alone" (Wittkopf and Jones 2008: 284). One of the explanations for this difference in group behavior is groupthink, "a mode of thinking that people engage in when they are deeply involved in a cohesive in-group, when the members' strivings for unanimity override their motivation to realistically appraise alternative courses of action" (Janis 1982: 9). This is more likely when members of a group are very similar in background and share similar beliefs. This can lead to "the danger that independent critical thinking will be replaced by groupthink, which is likely to result in irrational and dehumanizing actions directed against out-groups" (1982: 13). The focus on group behavior helps to explain how normal people can take part in some of the most horrendous atrocities that can accompany revolutions and civil wars.

The third type of solution to the free-rider problem integrates the roles, perceptions, and actions of individuals into the group-oriented second solution in what has been broadly referred to as "tipping models" (Moore 1995). A tipping model explains how small actions can lead to widespread change. Utilizing this form of rational choice modeling, Timur Kuran shows how significant actions by individuals can bring about revolutionary changes in public perceptions (1991). If an individual acts out against the government, reflecting a widely held dislike of the government, that individual can spark "revolutionary bandwagoning," a situation in which, as more individuals challenge the government, they attract more support, spiraling into a rapidly growing, broad-based movement. This slight shift in perception can topple a disliked government but is dependent upon the initial public action and the privately held perceptions of individuals.

Kuran's theoretical development of his tipping model is the clearest expression of how revolutionary bandwagoning occurs. Reflecting the practice of rational choice economic theories, Kuran creates a model for explaining this process. He begins with a hypothetical ten-person society and the assumption that "the government commands almost unanimous public support," though "individuals with different private preferences and psychological constitutions will have different revolutionary thresholds" (1991: 17). This means that people will choose to participate in challenging the government if enough other people also participate, but that level is different for different people. The ten people in the society might range from someone who opposes the government regardless of whether any one else does (a radical activist) to someone who would always support the government even if no one else did (a loyal patriot). The other eight people would fall in between, with a number assigned that indicates their general opposition to or support of the government. The number signifies the percentage of the population (how many others) that would have to oppose the government before that person would join in. For example, in Table 7.1, Persons 2 and 3 in Society A would join the opposition when 20 percent of the population opposed the government, but for Person 9, fully 80 percent of the population would need to oppose the government before he or she would participate in revolutionary activity.

Given this hypothetical population, Kuran suggests, let us assume that the opposition consists initially of a single person, or 10 percent of the population. Because the other nine individuals have thresholds above 10, this situation is self-sustaining; it constitutes an equilibrium. This equilibrium is sensitive to very slight changes, however, given the distribution of this hypothetical country. Suppose that Person 2 has an unpleasant encounter at some government ministry that raises her alienation from the regime and lowers her threshold from 20 to 10. This means that she will participate in an activity that challenges the government, raising the percent of the population in opposition to 20. When Person 2 participates, she has broken the

Table 7.1 Opposition Support Threshold in Two Hypothetical Societies

Percentage of Population in Opposition Required Before People Will Participate in Revolutionary Activity	Person									
	1	2	3	4	5	6	7	8	9	10
In Society A	0	20	20	30	40	50	60	70	80	100
In Society B	0	20	80	80	90	90	90	100	100	100

equilibrium and set off a rapidly spiraling shift of support. Her participation now allows Person 3 to defect to the opposition, and so on down the line, so that 90 percent of the population quickly defects from supporting to opposing the government.

Initial participation in opposing the government could be as simple as "tossing an egg at the country's long-standing leader during a government-organized rally" (Kuran 1991: 19). This expressive form of opposition can trigger others in the society to lower their threshold and join the movement in what Susanne Lohmann terms "information cascades" (1994). New information can change public perception about the likelihood that a person's actions will be effective. This could include the egg-throwing incident, the apparent success of revolutionaries in a neighboring country (a major factor in Eastern European revolutions), or loss in war (a key component in Skocpol's theory). As individuals engage in successful acts challenging the state, others' perceptions of their ability to effectively challenge the state will change, and they may be more likely to participate. With the addition of each individual, the costs of joining become lower, encouraging more of those with lower thresholds to join. Kuran concludes that "a slight shift in one individual's threshold has generated a *revolutionary bandwagon,* an explosive growth in public opposition" (1991: 20).

Returning to Table 7.1, bandwagoning will not occur in Society B and thus a revolution there is extremely unlikely. The acts required for revolutionary bandwagoning to occur would need to convince half of the population to reduce their revolutionary threshold by half (that is, move from 80 or 90 to 40 or 45). This kind of radical shift in opinion is not likely to happen quickly.

The utility of this type of rational choice analysis is that it supplements structural explanations of when revolution is likely. Structural explanations give us a laundry list of preconditions, each of which makes revolution increasingly likely. Having all of the factors on the list does not mean, however, that revolution will happen. This only occurs when an individual chooses to act out against the government, publicly expressing what others may feel but are too afraid to express. Once someone has stepped forward, then revolutionary bandwagoning begins. The important dynamic that determines whether such revolutionary bandwagoning will occur is individual preferences as they are expressed publicly. In this sense, the individual's personal preferences, as might be analyzed with psychology, are less important than the preferences they are willing to publicly acknowledge. Thus, in the hypothetical case, everyone may privately oppose the existing government, but for various reasons, they are not willing to engage in public opposition until a critical mass also participates. The context of when people will choose to participate moves us back to the discussion of structures, away from the psychological explanations. Rational choice explanations thus provide a bridge from the individual analysis to the structural analysis.

These diverse answers to why people participate in revolutions reveal much about our understanding of individual and group psychology. They help us understand why individuals participate in revolutions but also why they so often choose not to. As covered in Chapter 2, the importance of participation is widely recognized as a fundamental element in revolutions; it is the mobilization process that leads to coalitions powerful enough to overthrow the government. I now turn to the strategies utilized in revolution.

Strategies for Creating Revolution

> *To affirm that men and women are persons and as persons should be free, and yet to do nothing tangible to make this affirmation a reality, is a farce.*
> —Paulo Freire

In Chapter 2 I discussed the general process of revolutions and the importance of mobilizing people to participate. I now turn toward the specific strategies that are utilized to mobilize people to overthrow the government in order to create revolutionary change. A strategy is the larger or higher-level plan for doing something. With processes as complex as revolutions, the strategy can be subdivided into tactics. The spectrum of strategies ranges from relatively low-intensity (likelihood of casualties) to higher intensity. All of these involve force, because governments with power do not want to give up that power, but the level of violence that the opposition intends toward the government or population varies significantly. We can arrange these strategies into two poles according to the intensity of the strategy: those characterized by nonviolence and those that advocate violence (dominated by the strategy of guerrilla warfare). There are common elements to both sides of this spectrum, and the defining line between the two can be hazy in several revolutions. It is important to note that this is a categorization of the opposition's strategies; the government may also employ a wide range of responses that shape the opposition's tactics. I will begin on the low-intensity end of the spectrum with nonviolent tactics.

Nonviolence: Protest and Noncooperation

> *The practice of violence, like all action, changes the world. But the most probable change is to a more violent world.* —Hannah Arendt

Mohandas Gandhi's refinement of various tactics to force the British to "quit India" is probably the earliest, most comprehensive, and best known use of nonviolent action in history. He embodies many of the ideals of nonviolent action, given his principled and pragmatic stance that the British could no longer rule India and that the creation of an independent state that was qualitatively better than the colony could not be created with violence. Rather, he argued that the most effective and principled way to earn India's freedom was through a concerted campaign of noncooperation. Gandhi built on a rich philosophical legacy, and since World War II, a number of revolutions have adopted nonviolent tactics to successfully overthrow the old regime. The theory explaining the underlying dynamics of nonviolent action has grown in light of further successes as more recent revolutionary movements have been planned based on the scholarship of those studying nonviolence. For example, Gene Sharp has cataloged an extensive array of nonviolent social movements in history to develop a theory of nonviolent action. His work has been used to train activists in creating revolutionary change in Serbia and in designing a strategy for nonviolent defense in Estonia, following independence.

Sharp has argued eloquently about the fundamental nature of power within a society, distinguishing between monolithic and pluralist notions of power (1984). The monolithic view of power sees power as constantly controlled by a large and potentially repressive apparatus. The state is viewed as so dominating, with such extensive methods of coercion, that it is inconceivable to challenge its authority, and any challenge must be of significant strength to smash the monolith. Sharp states that, although this is how people have historically viewed the state, a more accurate conception of power is the pluralist notion. This perspective views power as dependent upon relationships. The head of a government cannot force anyone to do anything. Rather, a coercive state depends upon many individuals to participate in that coercion, whether bureaucrats, information gatherers, police, the military, prison guards, and so on. The leader depends upon the cooperation of all of them. Thus, for groups to challenge the authority of the state, they must gain support of those who have traditionally supported the state. In this way, even in nondemocratic regimes, individuals can "vote with their feet" by supporting opposition groups. This second notion of power provides the opportunity for nonviolent action to be much more effective than mobilizing troops for battle. It is this second notion of power that sets the framework for the strategy of nonviolent action.

Nonviolent action is action that does not use physical force to intentionally damage or destroy opponents or their property and is directed at creating political change that is motivated by conflicts of such significance that compromise is not possible within existing structures (Sharp 1984). Because this definition has many components, it is useful to take each in turn. Nonviolence is, above all else, action. The pragmatic school of nonviolence argues that nonviolence is relatively limited: it is a strategy or category of tactics to be used, similar to guerrilla warfare, terrorism, or conventional warfare (Sharp 1984; Burrowes 1996; and Ackerman and Kruegler 1994). Each of these categories represents a kind of action within struggle that encompasses many actual tactics. Terrorism, for example, can be carried out through bombing, hijacking, kidnapping, and assassination. Sharp has similarly classified 198 nonviolent actions, including demonstrations, marches, sit-ins, and noncooperation (1984). All of these methods entail doing something. This is an important distinction because nonviolent action is not the same as pacifism. Pacifism is the belief that violence is never an acceptable way of dealing with conflict. It does not require any action but is a belief. In contrast, nonviolent action is a tactic that is detached from any belief system. Again, in comparison with terrorism, there have been nationalist terrorists, communist terrorists, and Islamic terrorists. The terrorism does not depend upon the belief system. Nonviolent action similarly does not depend upon a particular belief system, though pacifists are obviously much more likely to advocate nonviolent action.

Nonviolent action does not use physical force to intentionally damage or destroy an opponent or her or his property. One individual cannot try to kill or injure another individual or conduct acts of sabotage against another's property. Although there must be an absence of physical force aimed at destruction or death, force is a key aspect of nonviolence. Action is aimed at getting opponents to do that which they do not want to do (Fisher and Ury 1991; Keohane and Nye 2001). Because physical destruction of the opponent disqualifies an action from the category of nonviolence, alternative power sources are required (as opposed to the violent power of guns, bombs, and tanks). The source of power that nonviolence depends on is the withdrawal of consent or, as it is more commonly referred to, noncooperation and civil disobedience. A lack of physical force does not mean that nonviolence is never physical. Sit-ins, blockades, marches, and human chains are all often very physically intensive. Physically intensive nonviolence is distinguished from violence because it is not aimed at the destruction of life or property (Zunes 1999: 138). The point of these actions is to make an opponent change without threatening bodily injury.

Nonviolence is action aimed at creating political change of such significance that compromise is not possible within existing institutional structures. This distinction is included to limit the scope of analysis. Without this clause, almost all human activities are nonviolent. Eating, sleeping, and working are usually absent of violence. Including all of these activities would make the term *nonviolence* meaningless. Sharp argues that nonviolence must involve "conflicts [that] do not yield to compromise and can be resolved only through struggle. Conflicts which, in one way or another, involve the fundamental principles of a society, of independence, of self-respect, or of people's capacity to determine their own future" (1984: 3). Critical conflicts arise when society's needs are not met by the government. The easiest way to discern whether an issue fits this criterion is to see if popular groups exist that advocate the use of violence to address the issue or if the situation is similar to historical cases where violence was typically used. As Tarrow argues, "people do not want to risk their skins . . . unless they have good reason to do so" (1998: 6). When people "risk their skins," it is likely that the issue is very significant. For example, in a liberal democracy, the restriction of a particular form of speech by the state is not something that individuals typically respond to with violence, primarily because the judicial system exists to safeguard this civil liberty. In contrast, in a patrimonial society a similar restriction of speech might be combated by violence—taking to the streets, assassinating individuals, or forming guerrilla groups—primarily because the system does not have adequate outlets for popular expression. Under these circumstances, because institutional compromises are not available or incomplete, noninstitutional force is required either in the form of violence or nonviolent action. Further, nonviolent action takes place outside of the normal institutional structures of government. Kurt Schock argues that "nonviolent action is not composed of regular or institutionalized techniques of political action such as litigation, letter writing, lobbying, voting or the passage of laws . . . nonviolent action occurs outside the bounds of institutional political channels" (2003: 705). This is because it is confined to these substantive conflicts in which compromise is not possible.

There are several reasons why nonviolence can be an effective strategy. First, almost anyone can participate in the opposition movement. The very old, young, and infirm can all participate. Sitting in the street or not paying taxes is very easy, though suffering the consequences may not be. This leads to a second reason for the attractiveness of nonviolence, what Smithey and Kurtz have called the "paradox of repression" (1999). Jailing, beating, or otherwise repressing seniors or children makes a government look unjust. Zunes and Kurtz argue that nonviolence encourages regime splits because "few regimes are as prepared to deal with unarmed revolts than armed ones" (1999: 311). Soldiers who had been involved in a long counterinsurgency campaign against guerrillas in the Philippines defected en masse when they were ordered to shoot nuns and priests who were blocking streets by kneeling and praying. The same soldiers had no problem killing guerrillas (and civilians in the hunt for guerrillas), and the death of those guerrilla fighters did not arouse unanimous public outcry. That is because military forces are expected to fight and kill those who try to fight and kill them. Building on Max Weber's definition of government as the legitimate controller of violence, governments are expected to have repressive capabilities to protect their citizens (1958). This includes police and military forces. Those forces are given the power to kill those who would kill civilians and government workers. But nonviolent action promises to not kill or harm civilians or government workers. In this way, many of the tactics of nonviolence use the strengths of the government against it. A government has a military and police, which the opposition can use to help demonstrate the lack of popular support—when a government represses peaceful demonstrators who are demonstrating because the government is repressive, it proves their point in a very clear way to the rest of society.

My own study of velvet revolutions builds on the concepts of Sharp's notion of power and nonviolence to explain when this type of revolution is likely to be successful (Van Inwegen 2006). The key factor in determining the success of a velvet revolution is the interaction of dissidents, the government, and the mass public. For a velvet revolution to occur, the interaction must go in a certain direction. First, the dissidents must be ideologically committed to nonviolence. The stronger the commitment to nonviolence, the more likely they are to maintain it as a primary tactic in challenging the government. Second, those dissidents committed to nonviolent action must be organized to successfully provoke the state into insufficiently repressing dissidents or inadequately reforming the government. Building off of Parsa's work on coalition formation, to be effective at provoking the government, an opposition needs to be organized. Further, to be successful at maintaining nonviolence, a high level of organization is required. This organization allows the mass public to continue to participate in antigovernment activities that continually undermine the government's power. Finally, the government must be ineffective in repressing these provocations. The mass public ultimately decides whether or not the government is effective by whether they continue to participate in provocations or not. As pointed out in Chapter 2, although in Czechoslovakia the repression of tear gas and billy clubs was not sufficient to end the protests, in China the military crackdown in response to the Tiananmen Square prodemocracy movement of 1989 was sufficient. In Czechoslovakia, the mass public continued to react, whereas in China they did not.

Although nonviolence is in many ways the exact opposite of warfare (in that it condemns violence while warfare depends upon it), we will see that there are also many similarities.

Guerrilla Warfare

The conventional army loses if it does not win. The guerrilla wins if he does not lose. —Henry Kissinger

Violence that is done in isolation rarely plays any role in revolutions. Despite the mythical appeal in Russian history of the "lone wolf" anarchist who assassinates government leaders, unless violence is organized, it is no more effective than an isolated individual practicing nonviolence. Because the consequences of violence against the government are more immediately obvious than many forms of noncooperation, however, collective or organized violence usually begins at the small scale and, with success, becomes more organized and larger until it mirrors the government's military forces. Most revolutionary movements that adopt violent strategies begin with guerrilla tactics.

The term *guerrilla,* meaning "the little war," was coined during the Spanish War of Independence (1808–1813) to denote the actions of small bands of peasants who operated outside of effective political control in resistance to the French-imposed monarch (Napoleon replaced the Bourbon ruler with his brother Joseph).

As Timothy Wickham-Crowley's exhaustive account of Latin American guerrilla movements begins:

> Guerrilla warfare is nothing new, and most certainly not a twentieth-century invention found first in the writings of Vladimir Lenin, Mao Zedong, or Che Guevara. "Barbarian" leaders of many different peoples . . . all employed guerrilla warfare against the Roman imperial forces in ancient Europe. Francis Marion ("The Swamp Fox") waged guerrilla-style warfare against the British army in the British-American colonies, as did other American armed forces; later the United States' armed forces would suffer similar tactics in their attempts to conquer the various American Indian peoples in the following century. . . . Guerrilla warfare, in fact, is almost surely the most ancient form of warfare, and is best defined in strictly military terms, not in social or political terms. (Wickham-Crowley 1992: 3)

Guerrilla warfare is distinguished by (1) a small group of fighters who (2) rely on surprise, (3) elusiveness, and (4) popular support. Because they are small initially, this tactic requires avoiding a direct confrontation with a powerful military and thus (5) utilizes an opponent's strengths against them, (6) relies on local knowledge, and (7) can eventually build up to larger military battles.

To more fully understand the use of guerrilla tactics in the context of revolution, we will investigate more fully each of the seven defining characteristics. First, guerrilla tactics are adopted because the opposition group is at a significant power disadvantage. Guerrilla warfare was historically the tactic of a people who had been invaded (such as ancient Romans, neighboring French, or colonial North Americans). If the conquered or occupied people were militarily strong enough to effectively fight the aggressors, they would not be occupied. In the past hundred years, this has grown to include domestic groups utilizing guerrilla tactics to overthrow the government, based on the same power dynamic—they could not militarily defeat the government's standing army. Thus, they are forced to rely on alternative means of resistance. "The almost natural military response is to (re-)invent guerrilla warfare: to avoid direct, massed engagements with the enemy and instead to concentrate on slowly sapping the enemy's strength and morale through ambushes, minor skirmishes, lightning raids and withdrawals, cutting of communication and supply lines, and similar techniques" (Wickham-Crowley 1992: 3). Second, all of these techniques rely on the element of surprise. The point of the guerrilla attack is to hit when the opponent is least expecting it and to hit at its weakest points. In this way, the guerrilla force is never in a position to directly fight the superior military power. The successful guerrilla always chooses the time and location of any fight: when and where the opponent is most vulnerable. In contrast, the military usually is engaged in a defensive fight. They must occupy and protect towns, government buildings, and military barracks. The guerrilla has no such fortifications to defend, and as such does not worry about defensive battles (Taber 1970: 21).

One caveat to the notion of surprise attacks must be mentioned. Although there is often a blurring of what is acceptable in the heat of battle, guerrilla warfare almost never targets civilians. The ambushes, surprise attacks, raids, and so on always target military personnel and equipment. "General George Grivas, founder and head of the Cyprito EOKA, asserted in his memoirs: 'We did not strike, like a bomber, at random. We shot only British servicemen who would have killed us if they could have fired first, and civilians who were traitors or intelligence agents'" (Combs 2006: 13). Thus, often brutal and public assassinations are acceptable, but not of innocents. This is one of the key distinguishing features between guerrilla and terror tactics.

To avoid a direct fight, guerrilla attacks must be followed by rapid retreat, the third characteristic of guerrilla warfare. Guerrillas are elusive; their quick attacks are followed by quick retreats so that they never stay to fight a pitched battle. Again, this is for an entirely pragmatic reason: a guerrilla force cannot militarily compete with the government or occupying force. The point of this pattern of quick and small attacks followed by rapid retreats, Robert Taber argues, is to wear the enemy down, by chipping away at the morale of the government troops and by inducing the maximum expenditure of funds, material, and manpower in the effort to suppress him. At the same time he will endeavor to build his own forces through the capture of government arms and by recruitment from an increasingly alienated populace, avoiding a military confrontation until the day—and it will come late—when an equalization of forces has been obtained. . . .

Analogically, the guerrilla fights the war of the flea, and his military enemy suffers the dog's disadvantages: too much to defend; too small, ubiquitous, and agile an enemy to come to grips with. If the war continues long enough—this is the theory—the dog succumbs to exhaustion and anemia without ever having found anything on which to close his jaws or to rake with his claws.

But this may be to oversimplify for the sake of analogy. In practice, the dog does not die of anemia. He merely becomes too weakened—in military terms, over-extended; in political terms, too unpopular; in economic terms, too expensive—to defend himself. At this point, the flea, having multiplied to a veritable plague of fleas through a long series of small victories, each drawing its drop of blood, each claiming the reward of a few more captured weapons to arm yet a few more partisans, concentrates his forces for a decisive series of powerful blows. (Taber 1970: 28–29)

The fourth characteristic of guerrilla warfare is that guerrilla groups require a base of support. The reason for this is that to be elusive, the guerrillas have to have somewhere to go. Despite the mystique of vanishing into the jungle, in reality, an ambush party must retreat to somewhere to find shelter. In this jungle scenario, that somewhere is usually a peasant village. If the peasants in that village do not support the ambush party, it will be quickly given up to the military forces and the guerrilla group will be exterminated or imprisoned. The same holds true in almost any location—whether it is a pastoral countryside, a mountainous region, an urban area, or a plantation. Mao Zedong understood this when he argued that "guerrillas are the fish, and the population is the sea in which they swim." Without the sea, the fish are dead. It is the hallmark of the successful guerrilla to one minute be a normal villager, the next an assassin or thief, and the next a normal villager again. Finding and capturing this type of combatant is extremely difficult for a military when the individual has the support of those around him or her.

Fifth, guerrillas utilize an opponent's strengths against them in a variety of ways. First, and foremost, they physically utilize their opponent's strengths against them by capturing arms and using them. The reason that guerrillas cannot compete with the military is that they do not have access to weapons. The first attacks of guerrilla groups are almost always to capture weapons for future attacks. On its own, this form of thievery does not present a real danger to the ruling regime. The problem is when they began to utilize the weapons against the regime by attacking military or government targets, often securing more weapons. The second, and related way, that guerrillas capitalize on their opponent's strength is in the evasion of the military. The successful guerrilla alluded to in the previous paragraph is very hard to capture. The easiest way for a military to capture this guerrilla is to detain anyone who could be the guerrilla, which has the effect of revealing a repressive apparatus for maintaining power. As more innocent people are jailed, tortured for information, or killed, the government appears increasingly repressive, encouraging more people to join the guerrilla movement (very similar to the participation of individuals in nonviolent protests).

Building on the local support, guerrilla groups typically include a significant contingent of locals, the sixth characteristic. This gives guerrillas another edge over military forces that often comprise individuals from another area (e.g., a foreign country or other part of the country). This element also highlights how quickly a small group without local knowledge or support can be eliminated, as was the case with Che Guevara's attempt to train guerrillas in Bolivia, where they were unable to gain significant support.

The seventh characteristic of guerrilla warfare is "scalable attacks": the ability to begin small initially, leading to larger confrontations, eventually to conventional war. Taber discusses three categories of guerrilla campaigns that illustrate this element (1970: 45–47). First, a guerrilla revolutionary victory can come about when the guerrilla attacks inspire a popular uprising that undermines the regime. The uprising includes massive noncooperation such that the old regime crumbles without a major military confrontation. Cuba is the model of this type of transition. Second, in the context of a colonial regime, the guerrilla attacks are aimed at sapping the benefits of retaining a colony, encouraging the colonizer to leave. "In the case of actual colonies, it will not be a matter of discrediting the colonial power or its government, but simply of taking the profit and prestige out of colonialism" (1970: 47). Cyprus is a good example, where guerrilla groups targeted British government workers to the extent that they no longer felt safe and could not conduct business in the country. This serves the same function as an economic boycott, though it is achieved through violence and intimidation. The third type of revolutionary success is achieved through wars won on the battlefield. This is the ultimate progression of guerrilla warfare. It begins with small attacks to gain arms, which become increasingly larger, so that eventually the guerrillas control means similar to the government's and then engage in conventional warfare against the old regime, typically utilizing heavy weaponry and direct confrontation. The Chinese Civil War from 1911 to 1949 demonstrates this progression, as the communist party grew from a small defeated group escaping to the countryside (the Long March), then eventually returning as a large conventional military.

Summary of Popular Participation

The literature that helps to explain why people participate in revolution has not come to a strong consensus; there are many reasons why people participate in revolution. These explanations help us understand why individuals participate in revolutions but also why they so often choose not to. Just as there are many reasons for participation, there are many ways to participate. The two cases of the Rwandan revolution of 1994 and the South African revolution of 1994 demonstrate this variety. Both of them effectively mobilized significant parts of the population in opposition to the government; they obviously differ, however, in the way that they mobilized people. Rwanda's mobilization looked much more like the later stages of guerrilla warfare moving into conventional warfare to end a genocide, whereas South Africa's struggle achieved victory primarily because of the nonviolent actions taken.

Questions for Discussion and Reflection

1. How might radical reforms implemented by a government in an attempt to appease opposition or discourage rebellious action actually encourage a revolt or revolution?

2. Compare Gurr's ideas of relative deprivation with Huntington's modernization theory (Chapter 3).

3. How can understanding group behavior help explain some of the atrocities of Rwanda?

4. Do you think revolutionary leaders are motivated more by the selective incentives explanation or the true believer explanation of why they choose to participate?

5. Given the variety of actions that states have taken that end up providing more opportunities for mobilization, what can a government do to stop mobilization?

6. Compare the role of the United States in encouraging revolutions in Nicaragua, Iran, and the Philippines. What lessons would you draw from this?

7. In what ways are nonviolence and guerrilla warfare similar? In what ways are they different?

8. The Tiananmen Square democracy movement was not a revolution, but it clearly illustrates a revolutionary situation as well as how revolutionary situations do not always lead to revolutions. Another contemporary Asian case, that of Nepal, illustrates the shifting strategies employed as a case moves from a revolutionary situation to a full revolution. Contrast the strategies employed in each case. Do you think this affected the outcome of each case?

8

The Outcomes
of Revolution

In a revolution, as in a novel, the most difficult part to invent is the end.
—Alexis de Tocqueville

As I discussed in the first chapter, the normal flow of revolutions follows a basic story line of introduction, climax, and resolution. The resolution of revolutions involves the process of normalization as political, social, and economic interactions become more regularized. How long this takes and what constitutes normal after a revolution has varied greatly across history. The focus of this chapter is: What is the outcome of revolution?

Institutionalization and Consolidation

Every revolution ends by becoming either an oppressor or a heretic.
—Albert Camus

The status quo of modern governments is that a government holds legitimate power to coerce citizens into following the laws it establishes. Revolutions break that status quo and in the process create a new government that tries to create a new status quo. Much of this book has focused on the part of revolution prior to the overthrow of the government and the process involved in overthrowing the government. For the status quo to return, however, the new government must create legitimate power to coerce citizens into following the laws it establishes. Eric Selbin's work on Latin American revolutions sheds light on this process. He argues that in the final phase of revolution, revolutionary leaders are faced with two essential and completely intertwined tasks: institutionalization and consolidation.

147

Institutionalization is the "establishment of some sort of at least minimal government that can gain international and domestic acceptance . . . it entails the simultaneous dismantling of whatever institutions remain from the old regime and their replacement or reconfiguration" (Selbin 1993: 14). Institutions, Selbin points out, "can be crudely lumped into two broad categories. The first serves the immediate institutional needs of the nascent government" (1993: 15). This typically involves quickly establishing some sort of a justice system: the military, police, and judges who capture and try individuals according to the law. In the aftermath of revolution, the military and police have usually been dismantled or destroyed. The new forces are typically some combination of "the victorious revolutionary army and/or former members of the military or police who were sympathetic to the revolutionary process" (1993: 15). Once a force is able to capture wrongdoers, someone must judge whether or not they are guilty of the alleged crimes. "The judiciary—often after having served as the legal bulwark in the old regime's repression of the population—must dispense justice in a society in transition, where the very notion of what is just and legal is being hotly contested, sometimes formulated and reformulated on the spot" (1993: 15). As a result, typically judges are also quickly replaced by important political figures. Maximilien Robespierre's position on the Committee of Public Safety during the French Revolution and Che Guevara's postrevolutionary position during the Cuban Revolution as director of La Cabana fortress prison (where those convicted of being counterrevolutionaries were held) both indicate the important roles that judicial powers can have in eliminating the opposition to secure power.

The power that the judicial system has, however, stems from someone or something that creates laws, which is why other institutions are also quickly created. The legislative and administrative branches of government are also part of the initial institution-building process. The point of these institutions is at least twofold: to first create laws, which will in turn create legitimacy. As Selbin puts it, when investigating many Latin American revolutions, "the legislature, previously a largely irrelevant, privileged arena of the powerful, reflects the whole population, and a large number of laws are passed. Commonly these statutes are aimed at dismantling the vestiges of the old regime and legalizing the new" (1993: 15).

The FSLN's creation of new legislative and administrative institutions in Nicaragua following the ouster of Anastasio Somoza demonstrates its ability to create legitimacy. To make sure that the leftist ideas of the revolution advocated by the FSLN were not lost to the late unification with bourgeois interests, the FSLN National Directorate walked a fine line between creating a stronger opposition and pressing for reforms. It did this by first setting up a government of national reconstruction that included what were perceived as some bourgeoisie, some moderates, and only one leftist. The moderates sided with the leftist, however, and were able to create leftist reforms. Important businessmen were initially appointed to key ministries such as Economic Planning, Industry, and Agriculture (Gorman 1981). This shielded the new regime from counterrevolutionary forces supported by the United States. When it was clear that the FSLN was going to implement its leftist policies, many of these more conservative government officials resigned and were replaced with more left-leaning ones. The short term-result was that

> at the end of its first year, the revolutionary process in Nicaragua must be considered a success from several different perspectives. The war-torn economy has been stabilized, a progressive agrarian reform program initiated, a large state sector formed on the basis of expropriated Somocista property, an independent foreign policy adopted, and a massive literacy campaign launched throughout the country. Most important, however, has been the imposition of a high degree of political stability coupled with, and partially growing out of, the consolidation of power in the hands of a cohesive revolutionary vanguard. (Gorman 1981: 133)

The most important aspect of creating legitimacy, Selbin argues, is dealing with the transfer of power. This involves setting the limits on personal power as well as outlining how new people will be brought into the government. The institutionalization of power has the drawback of being bureaucratic and lacking the passion of the revolution. As a result, several leaders have sought to recapture the revolutionary zeal, most famously in Mao Zedong's Cultural Revolution from 1966 to 1969 (and in many ways until Mao's death in 1976). A less famous, but similar attempt was Castro's "rectification" campaign of 1986, which was "in part an attempt to de-institutionalize the social revolution and regain the vibrancy, creativity, egalitarianism, and nonexclusivity that were once distinguishing characteristics of the revolution" (Selbin 1993: 18). Establishing new institutions is not sufficient to create stability: "societies require institutions to deal with the issues inherent to collective existence, but those institutions function only if the population breathes life into them" (1993: 19). Institutions must become adopted and accepted by key segments of society.

The second key task of revolutionary leaders is consolidation, which "involves convincing the people that political victory in itself does not signify the success of the revolution" (Selbin 1993: 14). Success in consolidation "is measured by the degree to which the population adopts the core of the social revolutionary project not simply in words but in deeds . . . the factors central to consolidation are trust, opportunity, and vision of the future, which are bound together by an underlying sense of empowerment" (1993: 22). Trust is "manifested, in part, by a general acceptance of the new institutions and 'rules of the game'" (1993: 22). The reason people trust their government is that new opportunities exist, "access to what had been the exclusive province of the powerful—education, housing, and the ability to get things done—in other words, efficacy and efficiency" (1993: 22). This, in turn, feeds into people's creating a new vision for the future, "often rooted in intergenerational justice, that is, the belief that things may be bad now, but with greater opportunity, they will be better for one's children. This notion is critical; people accept present suffering in exchange for a better future. What holds these factors together is the sense of empowerment, that is, people's belief that they can make a difference" (1993: 22). The point of consolidation is that it focuses on the extent to which the masses internalize the program of the revolution. The greater this internalization, the more likely the revolution will be maintained in its social program.

Selbin acknowledges that it is difficult both to quantify consolidation and to clearly demonstrate when it has been achieved. Debate about the future of Russia is an indication of how difficult it is to determine when consolidation has occurred. In a review of scholarship on Russia after the fall of communism, Henry Hale and Rein Taagepera show that there is a complete lack of consensus as to whether Russia is likely to dissolve into many states or consolidate power (2002). The fact that this article was written eleven years after the fall of the Soviet Union is an indication of how difficult and potentially long the consolidation phase can be after a revolution.

Domestic Implications

The ultimate end of all revolutionary social change is to establish the sanctity of human life, the dignity of man, the right of every human being to liberty and well-being. —Emma Goldman

Before turning to the domestic and international outcomes of revolutions, it is worthwhile to frame the extent of the following discussion. As Theda Skocpol has argued, the outcome of a particular revolution is a function of the revolution itself. The revolution has a structural context that makes revolution likely, which is activated by a revolutionary process. If we want to know the outcome of revolution, we must know the preconditions and the processes that occurred in the revolution. This will, in large part, dictate what is likely to be the outcome. Her comparison of China and Russia nicely illustrates this point.

Russia's postrevolutionary economic development was based on "absolute national political priority for investments in heavy industry," whereas China's was focused on the peasants' domination of an agrarian society (Skocpol 1994b: 250). Skocpol sought to answer the question: How do we explain the difference between outcomes of China and Russia, despite the fact that they were both ostensibly communist revolutions? "Stalin's strategy called for huge, sustained investments in heavy industries, coupled with administrative mechanisms (collectivization from above) to force the peasantry to grow crops, surrender surpluses, and release manpower for the sudden urban-industrial expansion" (1994b: 250). He could do this, Skocpol argues, because Russia was already relatively industrialized; 16 percent of the national income in tsarist Russia derived from heavy industry and one in twenty workers was employed in the industrial sector (1994b: 244). By comparison, after reconstructing the industrial areas of Manchuria, China

> began to come up against the limits of an economy very different from that which the Russians had to deal with from the 1920s. For one thing, there was a well-developed heavy industrial base only in Manchuria. In other centers, overall industrial development was much less, and light industries and commercial enterprises were often more predominant. Even more decisive, the rural economy of China had problems and possibilities diametrically opposite to those of Russian agriculture. Chinese agriculture became, between 1400 and 1900, maximally productive within the limits of the traditional technology, social structure, and available land area, and the Chinese population expanded steadily from 1700, until it virtually saturated the expansive capacity of the agrarian sector (roughly 1850 on). . . . The total output of all modern industries never (before 1949, let alone 1911) exceeded 3.5 percent of the national income of China, and the industrial workers remained substantially fewer than 1 percent of the labor force. (1994b: 251, 244)

Skocpol concludes that "even the most brutal Stalin-style methods of appropriating agricultural surpluses and channeling them into heavy industry could not have worked" in China because there simply was not the "inherited industrial base. . . . The point is not that no fundamental changes occurred, but that those which did occur recapitulated certain structural patterns of the old regimes" (1994b: 251). The key insight here is that revolutionary outcomes are part of the process of the revolution that builds on the prerevolutionary conditions. Revolutions represent some of the most extensive and rapid changes that societies, economies, and political entities can encounter; the limits of the change are bounded, however, by the structural realities that exist leading up to the revolution as well as by the process of revolution itself.

Revolutions set out to change the government, which is the bare minimum required for a social movement to be considered a revolution. Most revolutions also set out to change more than just those in power; they seek to change the structures of government, to change political behavior by requiring a change in political beliefs, to change the economy by eliminating or lowering economic inequality, and to change society more generally. I will review the literature that has assessed the scope of these changes in a variety of revolutions and has noted the implications for the ability of revolution in general to effect these changes.

Political Behavior and Beliefs

> *During times of universal deceit, telling the truth becomes a revolutionary act.* —George Orwell

There is a long-standing scholarly debate over the lasting changes revolution makes in political attitudes and behaviors. Although some scholars and most revolutionary leaders regard revolution as transformative, research on revolution's behavioral and cultural legacies after transfers of state power suggests a mixed picture. Booth and Richard investigated the residual impact on electoral participation, civil society engagement, and social capital by comparing postrevolutionary Nicaragua to its Central American neighbors (2006). Their findings were mixed. In some ways Nicaragua was unique among its neighbors, which is likely to be attributed to its successful revolutionary history. There was higher electoral engagement in Nicaragua than in the other nations in the region as well as greater support for civil disobedience, greater school and union activism, and more frequent leftist political identification (controlling also for unsuccessful insurgencies). This indicates at least some legacy of change.

The most surprising finding was that "despite the extensive mobilization and countermobilization during the Sandinista period, Nicaraguans were less engaged overall in civil society than citizens in the other Central American countries" (Booth and Richard 2006: 128). The reason the authors give for this difference is the way the FSLN created and managed its community organizations. These became increasingly authoritarian in the late 1980s, and the war and economic situation prevented the government from delivering on much of its promises, thus undercutting the effectiveness of these organizations. As a result, many people abandoned the organizations and became less active in civil society. The authors conclude, "once the struggle over the regime ends, as it did in Nicaragua in 1990, many citizens may disengage from the groups through which they once pressed for their interests. They may do so whether defeated or victorious, disillusioned or validated, and, in any case, probably exhausted from the protracted political conflict and tension of organizational life in a polarized society" (Booth and Richard 2006: 132).

In many ways, the residual effects of revolution in Nicaragua appeared to have decayed rapidly. This is not unexpected; as Booth and Richard note, a variety of works have indicated that "even in long-term great social revolutions, the effects of revolutionary public policy decay over time, leaving the post-revolutionary society with problems and politics that resemble those that preceded the revolution" (2006: 118). There are many reasons to think that the Nicaraguan Revolution would not be as encompassing as some others, given that the program was relatively limited, control of the media was not complete, opposition parties were allowed (and even won seats), and the economy was only partially nationalized. Thus, the reforms were not as drastic as in some other cases. It is important to note that, because of the unique choice of implementing a competitive electoral system, Nicaragua differs from most social revolutions that involve "revolutionary war and governance by victorious revolutionaries [that] inevitably lead toward authoritarianism and corruption" (2006: 118). In contrast to the norm, "the Nicaraguan revolution's main institutional legacy is a more democratic electoral system and lessened institutional authoritarianism" (2006: 132).

An indication of the lasting effects of revolution on political beliefs is found in Seymour Martin Lipset's classic comparative study of Canada and the United States. He argues that even though the two countries are very similar, there are differences in the collective values of each country that can be attributed, in part, to their differing political origins (Lipset 1970: 39). Canada, Lipset argues, was born in part in reaction to the American Revolution. Loyalists who lost in America fled to Canada, swamping some of the otherwise neutral areas. "The Loyalist émigrés from the American Revolution and Canada's subsequent repeatedly aroused fears of United States encroachment fostered the institutionalization of a counterrevolutionary or conservative ethos" (Lipset 1970: 55). This led to more of an emphasis on hierarchy as opposed to egalitarianism, because of longer and more sustained links with the British monarchy and Anglican Church. The result, for Canada, was that the

> unification of British North American colonies into a federal union was procured by Empire-oriented Canadian Conservatives who feared United

States expansion across the border, and the growth in influence within Canada of reform-minded "pro-American" frontier settlers who favored local autonomy. The decision to provide Canada with a strong central government, which unlike that of the United States would be able to veto or "disallow" provincial laws, was designed to resist the democratic threat within and across the border. . . .

In contrast to Canada, the United States is the result of a successful revolution and prolonged war of independence organized around the ideology embodied in the Declaration of Independence, which proclaimed the validity of egalitarian and universalistic social relations. Out of a sort of Utopian conception of men's egalitarian and universalistic relations with one another a national consciousness arose which infused men with a new awareness and new confidence in what they were. (Lipset 1970: 58–59)

The results of this differing origin, despite the vast similarities in the two countries, account for much of the value differences that exist in contemporary North America. The revolutionary origins are thus still present in the United States, more than 200 years later.

In addition to this long-lasting change in political beliefs, more recent work has demonstrated that there can be significant short-term changes in political beliefs. Anna Fournier's study of Kyiv high school students before and after the Orange Revolution in Ukraine at the end of 2004 indicates that the revolution had a profound effect on their political beliefs. Patriotism in the Ukraine was historically defined as "tame, predictable, and obedient to authority" (2007: 116). Because of the mass participation in opposition to the fraudulent elections, "high school pupils' experience of new forms of community and solidarity during the revolution led to the emergence of novel articulations of national identity" (2007: 116). In the immediate aftermath of the revolutionary situation, the meaning of patriotism had changed to include those who stood up to the government to demand accountability.

This short-term change can also be reflected in external measures of political and civil liberties. Figure 8.1 shows the levels of civil and political liberties for states that have had a revolution since 1972, as evaluated by Freedom House (2010). Of those cases where there was a significant change, the vast majority (nineteen of the twenty-three cases with more than a three-point change) have greater civil and political liberties than under the old regime. The change toward more freedom, furthermore, was much more extreme than those few cases that became less free. The greatest change in a state becoming less free was a movement of seven points in Lebanon (from 1975 to 1991, a span of sixteen years). In contrast, the changes toward more freedom were often sudden and significant—most of the Eastern European countries saw a significant change from being some of the least free countries to being in the free category (Freedom House categorizes countries as free, partly free, and not free). The scope and speed of the change are again an indication of the change that is possible in revolutions. Although there is a change in the civil and political liberties of postrevolutionary countries, in many countries that change is not very large (there were twenty cases with data that had a change of less than three points higher or lower). A move of 0–2 points on the Freedom House score is not uncommon in reform-oriented regimes over several years. That is, the change that can take place in some reforming countries is as great as many of the postrevolutionary regimes listed in Figure 8.1. Those with this type of minor change were evenly divided between more and less freedom (eight cases with less, three cases with no change, and nine cases with more freedom).[1]

**Figure 8.1 Civil and Political Liberties
in Postrevolutionary States, 1972–2006**

Countries with less freedom
7-point decline: Lebanon (1975–1991).
5-point decline: Tajikistan (1991).
4-point decline: Uganda (1981–1986).
3-point decline: Grenada (1979).

*Countries with minimal change in levels of civil and political freedoms
(less than 3 points higher or lower)*
Azerbaijan (1991), Afghanistan (1978–1996), Philippines (2000–2001), Nepal (1996–2008), Congo-Brazzaville (1997–1999), Liberia (1989–1996), Belarus (1990–1991), Rwanda (1990–1994), Georgia (2003), Armenia (1991), Nicaragua (1977–1979), Croatia (1991–1992), Chad (1979–1996), Iran (1977–1979), Thailand (1973), Congo-Kinshasa (1996–1997), Philippines (1985–1986), Russia (1991), Bosnia and Herzegovina (1992–1995), Kyrgyzstan (2005).

Countries with greater freedom
3-point increase: Georgia (1989–1991).
4-point increase: South Korea (1987), Thailand (1992), Moldova (1989–1991), Ukraine (1990–1991), Haiti (1986–1991).
5-point increase: Serbia (2000), Mali (1991–1992), Indonesia (1998–1999).
6-point increase: Hungary (1988–1990).
7-point increase: Poland (1988–1990), Romania (1989).
8-point increase: South Africa (1990–1994).
9-point increase: Czechoslovakia (1988–1990), Latvia (1988–1990).
10-point increase: Estonia (1988–1991), East Germany (1989–1990),[a] Lithuania (1988–1991), Bulgaria (1989–1990).

Source: Freedom House, "Freedom in the World 2010," www.freedomhouse.org.
Note: a. Postrevolutionary freedom score is newly combined Germany.

Government

There is the moral of all human tales; 'Tis but the same rehearsal of the past, First Freedom, and then Glory—when that fails, Wealth, vice, corruption—barbarism at last. —Lord Byron

A consistent theme of revolution literature since Karl Marx and Max Weber has been that revolutions are part of the process of modernization. But does revolution modernize governments? Theda Skocpol has argued convincingly that revolutions have in fact modernized countries in several very specific ways. After investigating China, Russia, and France, she concludes that revolutions produce stronger, more bureaucratic, and more mass-mobilizing states (1979). John Foran and Jeff Goodwin have replicated her analysis on more recent revolutions and come to the same conclusion (2003). Because state strength and the extent of mass mobilization are difficult to measure, there has been much more focus on comparing bureaucracies.

An example of this type of comparison is found in the 1917 Russian Revolution. In 1722, Peter the Great had introduced a Table of Ranks to classify the different positions of prestige within the civil service. The extensive table was designed to create a hierarchy based on merit and years of service, but the traditional nobility continued to dominate the civil service for a variety of reasons. When the Bolsheviks came to power in 1917, one of their first acts was to eliminate the table of ranks. As Alf Edeen argues, "the aim was to build up a completely new social order with no roots in the past, and the heritage from the overthrown Tsarist regime was formally severed by means of a series of governmental decrees. . . . With the stroke of a pen, Peter's Table of Ranks, which for nearly two centuries had formed the cornerstone of Russian administrative structure, disappeared" (Edeen 1994: 207). For the next decade, the bureaucratic system embodied the ideals of communist rhetoric, with leveling of salaries and collapsing of all officers' ranks into the single term of commander. Over time, however, the complexity of the bureaucracy grew so that by World War II, Peter the Great's rejected Table of Ranks had effectively been "re-established with its ostentatious titles, rank distinctions, and uniforms, displaying the social status of the civil servant before the general public" (Edeen 1994: 210). To a certain extent, this may be an indication of the nature of bureaucracies; regardless of the revolutionary ideology behind their creation, they eventually come to resemble each other.

How this process of de- and reconstruction of the bureaucracy occurs is illustrated in the Iranian Revolution. In the early stages of the revolution and consolidation, during the provisional government and turbulent radicalization, "a debureaucratization of society and a democratization of the administrative system was begun" (Farazmand 1987: 337). The bureaucracy was targeted because it was widely viewed as a major part of the shah's coercive apparatus; it was an instrument of his power. During the first few years of consolidation, "more and more activities of public administration were taken over by the non-bureaucratic, independent grass-roots organizations that sprang up during and after the revolution" (1987: 337). After 1982, however, a "policy of consolidation, centralization, control and system-maintenance was pursued by the Mousavi administration" (1987: 337). In this later phase, many of the revolutionary changes in the bureaucracy faded, and "patronage and many pathological behaviors, including corruption, of the bureaucracy [became] pervasive again" (1987: 337). In societies that already have established bureaucracies, it is clear that revolutions typically eliminate them but quickly replace them with very similar bureaucracies run by new people and that they typically become mired in the same problems that exemplified the old regime.

Socioeconomic Impacts

Revolutions have never lightened the burden of tyranny: they have only shifted it to another shoulder. —George Bernard Shaw

In Chapters 4 and 5 I discussed the ideologies created to justify revolutions. As should be clear from those chapters, all ideologies point to a better life under new guiding principles. The question arises: Does revolution make life better for people? One of the simplest indicators of the economic impact of revolutions is gross domestic product (GDP). Comparable economic data are relatively nonexistent and unreliable for older revolutions; for more recent revolutions, however, data are available that give an indication of the overall economic effects of revolution. The change in GDP per capita from the year after the revolution to five years after the revolution indicates whether the revolution established a framework for economic growth. Of the forty-two cases with economic data, eighteen countries experienced a decline in GDP in the five years following the revolution. The biggest declines were in already extremely poor countries, such as Uganda (1981–1986), Tajikistan (1991), and Zimbabwe (1965). But other countries such as Ukraine (1990–1991), South Africa (1990–1994), and Thailand (1992) also had negative growth. Twenty-four of the cases with data grew after their revolutions and did so much more than the global average of 2–3 percent for much of the post–World War II era. Many of the East European and post-Soviet states saw a doubling of their GDP in the five years after the revolution.[2]

The complexity of attributing economic growth or decline to a revolution, however, is illustrated by the case of Iran. This is a country for which relatively good data were available both before and after the revolution, but untangling the causation is still very difficult. Homa Katouzian argues that there are three interrelated factors "most responsible for economic change in Iran: the revolution, the Iran-Iraq war, and the fall in oil prices" (1989: 55). Should all of these be considered caused by the revolution? The Iranian Revolution created a situation in which war between Iran and Iraq was increasingly likely. Further, the short-term rise and subsequent decline in oil prices were caused by the events of the Iranian Revolution. The spike in oil prices occurred when anti-Western forces took control and made clear their intention to not sell oil to the United States. Oil prices declined, in part when it was clear that Iran would nonetheless sell oil on the global market at a rate consistent with past volume, thus not disrupting the global market. Even though the Iranian Revolution had an impact on these other two events (war and changes in oil prices), both could have happened without the revolution. Thus, it is difficult to say that the revolution was the primary reason for economic change in Iran.

Another way to look at the economic impact of revolutions is to investigate the issue of economic inequality. Jonathan Kelly and Herbert Klein argue that in the short run, revolutions reduce inequalities, but that inequalities inevitably reemerge (2003). The short-term gains are due to the nature of revolutions. They destroy the existing system, which usually means bringing down those at the top; but this also provides new opportunities in administration, management, and small business (if there is private property). Thus, initially there is a leveling of income and assets associated with inequality. In each of those new areas of opportunity, people with more education and skills advance, however, and typically these people are wealthier. Over time, then, the inequalities reemerge. Kelly and Klein also point out that, because most revolutions modernize societies, there is a similar trend toward more industrialization, which encourages technical, academic, and managerial skills. These also require greater education, which again is typically associated with wealth.

Martin King Whyte's study of inequality in China illustrates this. He found very little change, despite the fact that it was a communist revolution: "There is no question that the revolution did sweep away the most glaring inequalities in income of pre-1949 China, and in the fortunes of a privileged few. But important differentials remain" (Whyte 1994: 214). In fact, there is little difference in terms of income inequality prior to the communists taking power in 1949 and in the following decades up to Mao's death in 1976. For example, in 1936, peasants earned 46.9 percent of what wage-laborers earned. In 1956, seven years after the revolution, that figure was nearly unchanged at 45.1 percent (1994: 216). Whyte argues that "China can at least be credited with preventing the sort of sharp increases in inequality which often seem to accompany early industrialization in other societies" (1994: 231).

Figure 8.2 shows changes in Gini index scores for countries that have undergone revolutions, where data were available. Of the 32 cases with data, most of them either saw no change in inequality, or there was greater inequality after the revolution.[3] The Gini index is a measure of a country's inequality where 0 = perfect equality (everyone owns exactly the same amount) and 100 = perfect inequality (one person owns everything and everyone else owns nothing). Of the 32 cases with data, 13 cases had an increase of 5 percent or more in their inequality, 14 cases had a 4 percent change, either higher or lower, and only 5 cases had more than a 5 percent change decrease in inequality. This trend toward inequality is likely explained by the fact that most of the cases are recent, and most recent revolutions have resulted in more liberal democratic regimes that have free-market economies, which have tended to have higher inequality compared to the communist countries.

Another way to investigate whether life is better for most people in a postrevolutionary society is to look at their health and social welfare. Several studies that compared revolutions with reforms in nonrevolutionary countries concluded that there were limited gains in health services. Susan Eckstein compares postrevolutionary Mexico, Cuba, Bolivia, and Peru with

---

Figure 8.2 Changes in Gini Index Scores of Countries That Have Undergone Revolutions

Countries with an increase in inequality of more than 5 percent

Mali (1991–1992), Russia (1991), Moldova (1989–1991), South Africa (1990–1994), Lithuania (1988–1991), Belarus (1990–1991), Serbia (2000), Estonia (1988–1991), Armenia (1991), Bangladesh (1971), Georgia (1989–1991), Hungary (1988–1990), Czechoslovakia (1988–1990).

Countries with a decrease in inequality of more than 5 percent

Georgia (2003), Israel (1946–1948), Bosnia and Herzegovina (1992–1995), Thailand (1973), Cuba (1956–1959).

Source: UNU-WIDER, World Income Inequality Database, Version 2.0c, May 2008.

reforms in Brazil, Dominican Republic, Colombia, and Ecuador (2003). Confirming Skocpol's work on the limits of revolutionary change, Eckstein's primary conclusion is that development of any kind depends significantly on external realities. Creating a broader social safety net depends upon revenue, which in Latin America typically involves exports. Revolution does not change a country's position in the global capitalist system (unless it removes itself completely from the system). Thus, the scope of change is relatively limited: poor societies will continue to be poor, and middle-income countries will likely continue to be middle-income countries.

Socialist revolutions allow some options not available in reforming countries, however. The example of Cuba is particularly illuminating. Because of Cuba's position in the global capitalist system, Eckstein argues, its economic growth is horrible, but its preventative health system is better than that of most Latin American nations. The reason for this could be that the system is not based on private interests, which may tend to go toward expensive options and nonpreventative health care. This change, Eckstein argues, is due to the socialist orientation of the Cuban regime. A similar comparison between Chile's and Cuba's health care systems confirms this finding (Waitzkin 1983). Cuba's more radical health care changes were made possible by the more complete consolidation of power that occurred after the revolution, when compared with the less radical change in the left-leaning Salvador Allende government of Chile, a democratically elected government.

In a final approach to the issue that confirms much of the previous work on the trajectory of postrevolutionary regimes, Eckstein finds that the initial gains in social welfare typically erode over time (2003). This is most relevant for peasants. Eckstein argues that consolidation keeps most new governments busy, which benefits peasants—they are not taxed, mobilized, or tasked with doing anything other than what they typically want (to work the land for themselves). Once the new government has consolidated power, however, it typically turns toward industrialization, which usually hurts peasants, as the Russian case under Stalin clearly illustrates.

A minimalist indication of health is whether many people are killed during a revolution. The more people die as a result of revolution, the less people benefit from the revolution. Most revolutions involve casualties, and, as will be shown below, they often trigger international wars that lead to further casualties. There are several ways to look at the scope of casualties in revolutions. The easiest, though still difficult to track, is the raw number of people killed. Table 8.1 gives an indication of some of the casualties in revolutions. When looking at sixty-eight cases with data, eighteen had

Table 8.1 Casualties in Revolutions (includes civil wars, but not related international wars)

Country/Case	Approximate Casualties
Turkey (1908), Pakistan (1942–1947), Ghana (1946–1957), Congo-Kinshasa (1959–1960), Congo-Brazzaville (1960), Grenada (1979), Haiti (1986–1990), South Korea (1987), Poland (1988–1990), Czechoslovakia (1988–1990), Hungary (1988–1990), Germany (East) (1989–1990), Bulgaria (1989–1990), Russia (1991), Mali (1991–1992), Thailand (1992), Kyrgyzstan (2005)	Fewer than 50
Bolivia (1952), Thailand (1973), Ireland (1919–1921), Romania (1989)	600–1,000
Costa Rica (1948), Nepal (1996–2008), Cuba (1956–1959), Indonesia (1945–1949), Iran (1977–1979)	1,000–5,000
Croatia (1991–1992), Congo-Brazzaville (1997–1999), Malaysia (1948–1957), Kenya (1946–1963), South Africa (1990–1994)	5,000–15,000
Guinea-Bissau (1963–1974), Rwanda (1959–1962), China (1911–1992)	15,000–20,000
Zimbabwe (1965–1980), Bangladesh (1971), Chad (1979–1996), Tajikistan (1991)	20,000–50,000
Nicaragua (1977–1979), Philippines (1985–1996), United States (1775–1783), Congo-Kinshasa (1960–1965)	60,000–100,000
France (1789–1794), Lebanon (1975–1991), Colombia (1956–1958), East Timor (1975–1999), Liberia (1989–1996)	100,000–200,000
Bosnia and Herzegovina (1992–1995), Laos (1950–1975), Turkey (1919–1923), Haiti (1791–1804), Spain (1931–1939), Vietnam (1945–1954), Eritrea (1981–1991)	200,000–400,000
Mexico (1810–1821), India (1942–1947), Algeria (1954–1962), Uganda (1981–1986), Angola (1961–1975)	400,000–725,000
Rwanda (1990–1994)	937,000
Mexico (1910–1920)	1,000,000
Mozambique (1964–1975)	1,000,000
Yugoslavia (1941–1945)	1,500,000
Afghanistan (1978–1996)	1,800,000
Cambodia (1970–1975)	2,500,000
China (1947–1949)	2,500,000
Congo-Kinshasa (1996–1997)[a]	3,800,000
Russia (1917–1922)	9,000,000

Source: Meredith Reid Sarkees, "The Correlates of War Data on War: An Update to 1997," *Conflict Management and Peace Science* 18, no. 1 (2000): 123–144.

Note: a. Figures include international war, as civil war spread internationally.

extremely low casualties (fewer than fifty people died as a direct result of the revolution). Eight of the countries had estimated casualties of more than 1 million (Sarkees 2000).

Another indication of the scope of casualties in revolutions is to look at the casualties in terms of the percentage of the population killed. Of the sixty-one revolutions with casualties and population data, an average of 4.7 percent of the prerevolutionary population died as a result of the revolution (Sarkees 2000). As Table 8.2 shows, there is significant variability in terms of the percentage of the population killed. Smaller countries tend to have much high percentages of the population killed. The fact that ten of the revolutions had more than 10 percent of their prerevolutionary population killed in the revolution is a reminder of the ferocity with which people will fight to govern themselves.

An investigation of gender relations gives us an insight into the depth of social change that occurs in revolution. Valentine Moghadam has argued

Table 8.2 Countries with More Than 1 Percent of Their Prerevolutionary Population Killed

Country	Approximate Percentage
Rwanda (1959–1962), Congo-Kinshasa (1960–1965), Tajikistan (1991)	1
Colombia (1956–1958), Spain (1931–1939), Vietnam (1945–1954), Turkey (1919–1923)	2
Nicaragua (1977–1979), Guinea-Bissau (1963–1974)	3
United States (1775–1783), Uganda (1981–1986), Lebanon (1975–1991)	5
Bosnia and Herzegovina (1992–1995)	6
Mexico (1910–1920)	7
Mexico (1810–1821), Liberia (1989–1996), Chad (1979–1996)	8
Russia (1917–1922)	10
Rwanda (1990–1994)	14
Afghanistan (1978–1996), Mozambique (1964–1975), Laos (1950–1975)	15
Angola (1961–1975), Eritrea (1981–1991)	16
Congo-Kinshasa (1996–1997)	28
East Timor (1975–1999)	30
Algeria (1954–1962)	57

Source: UNU-WIDER, World Income Inequality Database, Version 2.0c, 2008, http://www.wider.unu.edu/; and Meredith Reid Sarkees, "The Correlates of War Data on War: An Update to 1997," *Conflict Management and Peace Science* 18, no. 1 (2000): 123–144.

that in regard to gender, there are two basic outcomes of revolutions. These are what she terms the "woman-in-the-family model" and the "woman's emancipation model" (Moghadam 2003: 98). The relevant aspect of these ideas is less about the outcome for women than about how each of these models and thus notions of gender itself are entirely embedded in the revolution. The woman-in-the-family model "excludes or marginalizes women from definitions and constructions of independence, liberation, and liberty. . . . It assigns women the role of wife and mother, and associates women not only with family but also with tradition, culture, and religion" (2003: 98). An example of this type of view is expressed by Andri Amar, a Jacobin deputy (the Jacobins were radical revolutionaries in France): "Morality and nature itself have assigned her functions to her: to begin the education of men, to prepare the minds and hearts of children for the exercise of public virtues, to direct them early in life towards the good, to elevate their souls, to educate them in the cult of liberty——such are the functions after household cares" (quoted in Moghadam 2003: 99). It is no surprise, then, that women did not fare better after the revolution in France until changes in the twentieth century. Women were "excluded from modern political institutions like labor organizations, political parties, militias, and legislatures"; women were not allowed to vote until after World War II (2003: 99). This model was common among revolutions, including the Mexican, Algerian, Iranian, and Russian (1991) and the Eastern European revolutions of 1989. Despite the significant social changes that occurred in some of these revolutions, changes in gender roles were absent, or in the case of more modern regimes, reactionary.

Conversely, the woman's emancipation model of gender in revolution "holds that the emancipation of women is an essential part of the revolution or project of social transformation. It constructs Woman as part of the productive forces and citizenry, to be mobilized for economic and political purposes; she is to be liberated from patriarchal controls expressly for that purpose" (Moghadam 2003: 102). In contrast to the quote above by Andri Amar, Vladimir Lenin expressed his views "on the subject of women, revolution, and equality" as intermixed:

> Woman continues to be a domestic slave, because petty housework crushes, strangles, stultifies and degrades her, chains her to the kitchen and to the nursery, and wastes her labor on barbarously unproductive, petty, nerve-racking, stultifying and crushing drudgery. Enlightenment, culture, civilization, liberty—in all capitalist, bourgeois republics of the world all these fine words are combined with extremely infamous, disgustingly filthy and brutally coarse laws in which woman is treated as an inferior being, laws dealing with marriage rights and divorce, with the inferior status of a child

born out of wedlock as compared with that of a "legitimate" child, laws granting privileges to men, laws that are humiliating and insulting to women. (quoted in Moghadam 2003: 102)

Again, it is not surprising that initially the plight of women appears to be much better in revolutions that embody the emancipation model. As Moghadam shows, the gains are often reversed, even in ideal cases. The 1917 Russian Revolution is a perfect example of this. The Bolsheviks took emancipation to the extreme, including, as Lenin's quote suggests, the liberation of women from the slavery of their social position. Throughout the 1920s, various programs were aimed at ensuring that this change occurred, including the "land code and the family code, with their emphasis on individual rights and freedoms—including women's rights to land and for maintenance," which had the intended consequence of undermining the "collective principle of the household, the very basis of peasant production" (Moghadam 2003: 103). Then, in the 1930s, as Stalin consolidated power, the state became much more conservative in orientation and advocated "'the socialist family' as the proper model of gender relations" in which each gender had its traditional role to play (2003: 103).

International Implications

Those who make peaceful revolution impossible will make violent revolution inevitable. —John Fitzgerald Kennedy

Revolutions have profound international implications that often dwarf the social, political, and economic domestic changes. The end of the Cold War is the best example of the global significance of revolutions. Although the change from an authoritarian communist regime to a democratic capitalist system was surely a profound change for those who lived in the former Soviet Union, the impact was no less relevant to the rest of the world that had been divided between two superpowers. The literature suggests that revolutions have two primary effects internationally: they encourage war or aggressive behavior, and they encourage the spread of revolution to other countries. I will address each of these in turn.

War

Every revolution has its counterrevolution—that is a sign the revolution is for real. —C. Wright Mills

In *Revolution and War,* Stephen Walt (1996) makes a compelling argument for why revolutions lead to war or at least aggressive behavior. To make the argument, he develops realist theory, which argues that states are generally self-interested, seeking to promote their own national security in a zero-sum game of power in an anarchical international system. Walt argues that war is affected by perceptions of threat. A war is likely when one country perceives that another country poses a threat to its existence. The simplest example of this would be when one country invades another; the aggressor clearly poses a threat to the invaded country. The invaded country then retaliates and that is war. Realists argue that it is in a nation's best interests to wait until your country is invaded to confirm that a threat exists; thus, threat perception is vital.

The perception of threat is shaped by three key factors: changes in power, changes in perception of intent, and changes in the offense-defense balance. In simple terms, power is the state's total resources: "population, industrial and military capability, raw material endowment, etc."; the more power a country has, the greater the perception of threat to others (Walt 1996: 19). Usually countries rise and fall in power rather slowly. For example, although China's economic growth is rapid, it has been occurring since the 1980s, a thirty-year period. That kind of change in power encourages states to shift alliances or alter their relationships over time, in effect avoiding war. In contrast, revolutions are often viewed as unlocking pent-up energy or tapping unused resources. The explosion of France's military might after the revolution is one indication of the change in power of a country brought about by revolution. As Walt notes, however, revolutions almost always initially weaken the state. "The demise of the old regime hinders any efforts to mobilize resources for war (at least until the new regime acquires the institutional capacity to tax and allocate resources), and the armed forces will be severely disrupted if they have not collapsed completely" (1996: 21). The combination of the long-term prospect of a more powerful state with a short-term weaker state encourages foreign powers to try to act early in gaining an advantage rather than waiting. In this way, revolutions encourage war.

To pose a threat, a state must be viewed as likely to invade. "If a state is believed to be unusually aggressive, potential victims will be more willing to use force to reduce its power, to moderate its aggressive aims, or to eliminate it entirely" (Walt 1996: 19). Revolutions call into question the intent of all states because there is a change in government; to foreign governments, "the old regime's reputation for credibility, restraint, prudence, and so on is of little or no use" (1996: 30). In the aftermath of revolutions,

Walt argues, ideologies become increasingly important indicators of a regime's intent. This is true for foreign governments attempting to figure out the likely foreign policies of the new regime as well as for the new regime as it tries to figure out the likely foreign policies of foreign governments. Neither group can reliably know the intent of the other; thus ideology fills the void. After the 1917 Russian Revolution, foreign powers took the Bolsheviks at their word and responded as if they would try to unite the workers of the world (an aggressive foreign policy). The Bolsheviks similarly viewed foreign powers through Marxist ideology as imperialist powers bent on exploiting the masses.

Simply because of the change in regime, a further result is that the people conducting foreign policy are very likely to be inexperienced and prone to blunders. This is exacerbated by the fact that the information that foreign powers receive about the revolutionary regime is most likely from exiles, many of whom "are members of the old regime, and therefore hostile to the revolutionary government and eager to return to power" (Walt 1996: 31). Revolutions also often "damage the normal channels of communication between states at precisely the time when the need for accurate information is greatest, hindering even more the ability of both sides to understand the information they do have" (1996: 32). Diplomats are often recalled or sent into exile; damage to communication facilities and inexperienced technicians all encourage this process. Thus revolutions, by changing the perception of intent, increase the perception of threat and thereby encourage interstate war.

The third factor, the *offense-defense balance,* is the term Walt uses to describe the calculation that states make when looking at their own capabilities compared to those of a potential rival.

> States will be less secure when it is easy for them to harm one another and when the means for doing so are easy for them to acquire. Furthermore, incentives to use force increase when the offense has the advantage, because the expected cost to the attacker will decline and the expected benefits of aggression will increase. Offensive power is usually defined in terms of specific military capabilities (that is, whether the present state of military technology favors attacking or defending), but political factors can be equally important. In particular, the ability to undermine a foreign government through propaganda or subversion can be an especially potent form of offensive power, because it allows one state to "conquer" others at little or no cost to itself. In general, the greater a state's offensive power is, the greater the threat it will pose to others and the greater their incentive to try to contain or reduce the danger. (Walt 1996: 19)

Revolutions change the offense-defense balance because they change the absolute power of the revolutionary state. The short-term weakening and long-term strengthening create a "window of opportunity" for foreign powers to seize territory or demand concessions (1996: 32). This is further fueled by international competition. If one country does not take advantage of the window of opportunity, another potential rival might, which encourages the quick action toward aggression of all foreign powers. In this way, for foreign states, the offense-defense balance is tipped toward offensive behavior, which makes war very likely.

The offense-defense balance is also tipped toward offense for the new revolutionary regime. Having succeeded in overthrowing the old regime, revolutionaries see vindication in their ideology, which typically has a more universal appeal. Thus, they often seek to export the revolution to others, believing that their success will be replicated. Foreign sympathizers with the new regime may also encourage this misperception, which can feed into their fears of counterrevolution. "Unless opposing states are swiftly overthrown, the argument runs, they will eventually join forces with domestic counterrevolutionaries in order to crush the revolutionary state" (Walt 1996: 39). For all of these reasons, revolutions tip the offense-defense balance toward offense, encouraging war. The aftermath of the Iranian Revolution demonstrates how all of these occurred.

Iraq invaded Iran on September 22, 1980. This meant that Ayatollah Ruhollah Khomeini was actively consolidating power at the same time he was repelling an invasion. The two worked well together in that he was able to associate political opponents with the military forces of Saddam Hussein. As outlined above, based on Walt's work, the war between Iran and Iraq so soon after the revolution was spurred by a typical postrevolutionary pattern.

There were obvious changes in power in Iran. Most important was that the repressive military forces were largely purged of their specialists (including the dismantling of the entire SAVAK, the Iranian secret police). Iraq thus perceived Iran as significantly weaker and more vulnerable to attack. Further, Iraq saw an opportunity to access the vast oil fields just over the Iranian border, an area historically occupied by Arabs (as opposed to Persians, the ethnic majority of Iran).

The revolution also created changes in the perception of intent for both regimes. Even though Hussein and the shah had similar ideological beliefs, both saw themselves as secular modernizers; Khomeini and Hussein had diametrically opposed beliefs. Add to this the fact that Khomeini was in exile in Iraq until Hussein bowed to the shah's pressure and forced him to leave. For Khomeini, Hussein was in the same category as the shah and the United States. Hussein, in contrast, was particularly concerned about Khomeini's encouraging the building of a second Islamic republic in Iraq, whose majority population was Shia Muslims (like Iran), whereas Hussein's Baathist party was dominated by Sunni Muslims.

These factors combined to shift the offense-defense balance so that Iraq had an advantage in invading Iran during its window of opportunity. If he waited, Hussein reasoned, he would face a stronger Iran that would then make good on its claim to export the revolution. The sad result was that the war was fought for eight years with no changes in the borders, no exporting of the revolution, and more than a million casualties.

Walt shows that the French, Russian, Iranian, American, Mexican, Turkish, and Chinese revolutions all led to war or a significant increase in tensions that made war very likely (1996). Of the 105 revolutions analyzed in Table 8.3, thirty-two countries went to war within ten years of having a revolution. War is a relatively uncommon phenomenon, so when one-third of the countries with revolution go to war, it is likely that there is a strong correlation. These wars often increased the casualties of revolution far beyond the civil conflicts. In France, 1.3 million of a total population of 26 million died between 1789 and 1815 in the civil and Napoleonic wars, and as many as 1.5 million were killed in the Iran-Iraq war following the Iranian Revolution (Goldstone 2003).

Confirming and developing much of Walt's theory on revolution and war, Fred Halliday has analyzed the ways in which foreign governments have been involved in counterrevolutionary movements. Counterrevolution is the attempt to reverse a successful revolution, and the term is often also used to describe policies intended to prevent "revolutionary movements that have already gained some momentum from coming to power" (Halliday 2003: 136). In his analysis of cases from 1789 to 1989, Halliday finds that foreign interventions are usually half-hearted and bungled. Only two revolutionary regimes have been overthrown by external forces: France at Waterloo in 1815 and Grenada in 1983 (both of which involved significant military force). The more numerous failed counterrevolutionary interventions include United States (1776–1812), Russia (1917), Vietnam (1970s), Nicaragua (1979), and Iran (1979).

The failures of counterrevolutionary intervention are driven by a number of factors. First, although people in a revolutionary state may be combat weary, foreign aggression almost always spurs patriotism, which tends to support the revolutionary regime. The case of Iraq's invasion of Iran discussed above illustrates this process. Support for Khomeini's new Islamic Republic increased significantly when it was viewed as the source of resistance to the unjust invasion by Iraq. Second, even though there are many governments who may want to undo the revolution, there are also many who stand to gain from the revolution's success. Thus, foreign aid to counterrevolutionaries is often matched by foreign aid to the revolutionary government. The United States sought to support Cuban exiles in retaking

Table 8.3 Countries That Went to War Within Ten Years of Revolution

Country	Years of Revolution	Opponent
Afghanistan	1978, 1996	United States invades in 2001
Algeria	1954, 1962	Morocco (Sand War border disputes)
Argentina	1816, 1816	Peru and Bolivia
Armenia	1991, 1991	Azerbaijan (continuation of preexisting conflict)
Azerbaijan	1991, 1991	Armenia (continuation of preexisting conflict)
Bolivia	1952, 1952	Chile and Argentina
Britain	1688, 1689	France
Cambodia	1970, 1975	Vietnam invades in 1978
Chile	1818, 1826	Peru and Bolivia
China	1911, 1912	Participated in World War I against Germany
China	1947, 1949	United States (through Korea)
Congo-Kinshasa	1996, 1997	Second war, with most of central Africa involved
Cuba	1956, 1959	United States invades in 1961
Eritrea	1981, 1991	Ethiopia border war 1998–1992
France	1789, 1794	Various European nations in Bonaparte conquests
Georgia	2003, 2003	Russia invades in 2008
Grenada	1979, 1979	United States invades in 1983 to remove leftist coup leaders
Haiti	1986, 1991	Coalition of international peacekeepers (UN)
India	1942, 1947	Pakistan and India fight for Jammu and Kashmir; treaty signed in 1948
Iran	1977, 1979	Iraq invades in 1980
Israel	1946, 1948	Israel invades Sinai in 1956
Kenya	1946, 1963	Somalia
Malaysia	1948, 1957	Thailand (continuation) and Indonesia
Netherlands	1795, 1798	England and France (1801)
Pakistan	1942, 1947	India and Pakistan fight for Jammu and Kashmir; treaty signed in 1948
Peru	1821, 1824	Chile and Argentina
Rwanda	1959, 1962	Tutsi guerrillas from Burundi invade Rwanda
Rwanda	1990, 1994	Rwanda invades Congo-Kinshasa (now Democratic Republic of Congo)
Thailand	1932, 1932	Thailand invades French Indochina in 1941
Thailand	1973, 1973	Vietnamese forces cross borders to attack Khmer bases
Turkey	1908, 1908	World War I
Vietnam	1945, 1954	Vietnam war to unify North and South Vietnam

Source: Meredith Reid Sarkees, "The Correlates of War Data on War: An Update to 1997," *Conflict Management and Peace Science* 18, no. 1 (2000): 123–144.

power, whereas the Soviet Union supported the new Cuban regime to ensure that socialism prevailed. Finally, Halliday argues that the conflict context is crucial to appreciating the failures of counterrevolutionary activity from abroad. Intervention takes place in revolutionary countries where there are undoubtedly more people to mobilize, who can mobilize longer, and who need not defeat their opponents but just frustrate them. This helps to explain the failure of the United States in Vietnam. As Ho Chi Minh famously warned the French, "You can kill 10 of my men for every one I kill of yours, yet even at those odds, you will lose and I will win" (quoted in Karnow 1998).

The Spread of Revolution

> *One revolution is just like one cocktail, it just gets you organized for the next.* —Will Rogers

The fear that drives both international war following revolution and counterrevolutionary intervention is that the revolutionary leaders are right— that their ideals are universal and that the revolution will spread to other countries. Although this is rare, there are enough cases where revolutions have spread that the potential exists for a revolution to encourage uprisings in neighboring or similarly positioned states. The dominoes of Eastern European communist regimes collapsing or the democratic trend of post-Soviet republics toppling quasi-democratic leaders indicate the fears of governments are not unfounded. The spread of revolutions has been called a revolutionary wave by Mark Katz. As Katz has argued (1997), these waves typically involve a group of revolutions with similar objectives, the most important element of which is the spread of the ideas associated with the revolution. According to Katz, there are two basic types of waves: anti- and pro-. In antirevolutions, the point of revolution is to get rid of an existing regime. This includes the anticolonial, antimonarchical, antidictatorial, and anticommunist. The first two, Katz argues, are waves that have become the norm; that is, they seem to have been successful at spreading to all regions of the world. In contrast, the prorevolutions are aimed at getting rid of an existing regime to bring in a specific new type of regime. These include democracy, communism, Arab nationalism, and Islamic fundamentalism. Again, Katz reminds us, democracy is the one pro revolution that seems to have global appeal.

Revolutions necessarily depend upon domestic factors, and thus, even though there are similarities in the objectives of the revolutions, there is also significant variance within revolutionary waves. Katz says that there are two types of revolutions within a revolutionary wave. First, and most important, is the central revolution. This revolution articulates a vision of altering the existing international system by inspiring a series of revolutions similar to its own. To have this kind of impact, the revolution must occur in either a regional or global great power. The American, French, Russian (1917), and Iranian revolutions are examples of a central revolution. Next are what Katz calls aspiring revolutions, which include smaller powers that seek to emulate a central revolution and often seek assistance to do so. Most neighbors and foreign governments fear that revolutionaries in their country will successfully tap into the new vision articulated by a neighbor or similarly positioned country and replicate its success domestically. Anticolonial, democratic, and communist revolutions throughout much of the world after the central revolutions in the United States, France, and Russia, respectively, would be examples of this second category. An aspiring revolution has the real potential of altering international relations. It does this in two primary ways, Katz argues: "first, revolutions can magnify the importance of the countries experiencing them, even if the countries are relatively small and weak. . . . Second, revolution can upset existing alliance patterns" (Katz 2001, 1).

The dramatic events of 1989 in Eastern Europe demonstrate the power of revolutionary waves. In June 1989, elections were held in Poland that allowed the noncommunist party Solidarity to run. Solidarity won almost all of the seats it ran for, and equally important, the Soviet Union did nothing to reverse the election (as it had in Hungary in 1956 and Czechoslovakia in 1968). In September, the newly elected Solidarity formed the first noncommunist party government, again without reprimand from the Soviet Union. On September 10, Hungary opened its border to Austria to help East German refugees flee to West Germany. This spurred a mass exodus of East Germans traveling through Czechoslovakia to Hungary. Up to this point, travel within the Soviet bloc was allowed, but not beyond. On October 5 through 7, the Hungarian parliament dissolved itself, forcing new elections. After a month of East German exodus, East Germany stopped the free passage into Czechoslovakia, spurring widespread protests that culminated on November 9, when the Berlin Wall was toppled, allowing passage to the west. The next day, November 10, Bulgaria instituted reforms to keep some power, but the president resigned in protest. From November 17 to 22, massive demonstrations and strikes took place in Czechoslovakia, forcing negotiations between the opposition and the Communist party. Soon after, the negotiations broke down, and on December 10, the Czechoslovak president resigned and a new government took power. This was followed by a week of demonstrations and riots in Romania (from December 15 to 25) that ended when President Nicolae Ceausescu and his wife were killed. A similar, but slightly more drawn out process, occurred in the Soviet republics as the wave spread throughout the Soviet Union in 1990 and 1991.

Summary of Outcomes

This chapter has shown that the outcome of revolutions, like that of most complex sociopolitical processes, is mixed. In some cases, when all of the requisite elements exist, the grand ideologies of revolutions actually come close to fruition. The remarkable transitions of most of the Eastern European countries in 1989 exemplifies this ideal. In almost every quantifiable way, domestically and internationally, life is better for the vast majority of people living in those countries. These cases demonstrate that it is possible for revolutions to have a profoundly positive impact with few relatively minor drawbacks (such as the increase in inequality most former communist states experienced). These revolutions also demonstrate the wave effect of spreading revolutions. Other cases suggest, however, that revolutions make no difference for most people living in those countries or, worse, encourage deadly wars and more severe repression. Although we would like to have a clear and concise answer to what is the likely outcome of revolution, the literature clearly suggests that such is not possible. This reminds us that revolutions are incredibly complex processes that are shaped by structural realities and the people and groups that act within them. That fact also reminds us of the relevance of the study of revolutions—they are not detached romantic episodes of high ideals but a fundamental part of the social and political fabric of the world around us. Understanding revolutions is a way of understanding that complex world.

Questions for Discussion and Reflection

1. What are some of the effects that a revolution might have on neighboring countries divided between government supporters and dissatisfied citizens demanding structural change?

2. How does consolidation differ from the routine functioning of government?

3. One of Selbin's arguments is that consolidation requires the citizens to internalize the ideology of the revolution. Go back to the chapter on ideologies and consider how internalization would be evident for the various ideologies.

4. Weighing the costs and consequences, investigate several revolutions to determine whether they were "worth it."

5. Given that more recent revolutions have tended to create more liberties for their population, would you think that more revolutions in the future would likely be a positive development?

Notes

1. The data came from the Freedom House ranking of civil and political freedom of countries (2010). The scores for the year prior to the beginning of the revolution and five years following the end of the revolution were used to compute the change in liberties. Five years after was chosen to allow for an end of the consolidation phase. The cases were selected from regime changes that fit the definition of revolution in Chapter 1.

2. Given the variability in the length of the revolutions, comparing pre- and postrevolution is not as appropriate. Five years after the revolution was chosen because of the likelihood that the revolution itself would cause short-term disruptions but that once the new system was implemented a recovery would occur. Due to the limitations of when economic data are collected, however, most cases are not exactly five years after the revolution, and the majority are closer to ten years after. In these cases, the nearest approximate is given. Data collected from the World Research Institute (2010).

3. The GINI indexes for the year prior to the beginning of the revolution and one year following the end of the revolution were used to compute the change in inequality. The cases were selected from regime changes that fit the definition of revolution in Chapter 1.

9

The Study of
Revolution

History doesn't repeat itself—at best it rhymes. —Mark Twain

In this book I have sought to bring together the learning that has taken place in the vast revolution literature on one of the most complex social phenomena possible. At the end of this series of questions about revolution, it is useful to answer one final question: What have we learned from the study of revolution? This chapter summarizes the areas of consensus and debate that still exist in the revolution literature.

Areas of Consensus

Every generation needs a new revolution. —Thomas Jefferson

The first area of consensus within the revolution literature is that there is a general process that most revolutions go through. The story line depicted in Chapter 2 covered much of this material that is assumed by most scholars. There is a revolutionary situation that emerges when something threatens the government, there is a crisis that topples the government, and then a new group takes control of the government and implements reforms. Within this very general outline, there is much room for variety. What threatens the government, how that happens, when it leads to a crisis, what topples the government, who takes control and how, what reforms they implement, and how successful they are at implementation all shape the flow of various historical revolutions. They all have these basic components, however.

The second area of agreement, and the one that has dominated most of the revolution literature, is that structural preconditions determine most of what happens in revolutions. This does not mean that there is agreement about the structures or how they shape revolutions, but the fact that structures are extremely important is widely agreed upon. There is further consensus about the types of societies that are likely to have revolutions and those that are very unlikely to have them. Governments that are patrimonial, repressive, exclusive, and relatively weak are very susceptible to revolution. This has become so accepted that instruments such as the Failed State Index have used these structural theories to indicate which regimes are most likely to succumb to revolutions in the near future.

Building on the strength of the structurally oriented literature is a consensus that structures shape who is likely to lead and support revolutions. There will always be those who would like to get rid of their government and take power, but usually revolutionary leaders come from a very narrow band of society. These intellectuals are most often the leaders of revolutions because of their position in society. It is not who they are (as individuals) but what they are (as structural entities). In addition, who is likely to follow revolutionaries is also largely determined by structural realities. Relative deprivation and rational choice theories all depend on some element of a structural reality. The debate exists in terms of how important that structural reality is compared to other factors, as I discuss in the next section.

Areas of Debate

Political convulsions, like geological upheavings, usher in new epochs of the world's progress. —Wendell Phillips

Although there is consensus on these aspects of the study of revolution, there are a number of continuing contentious debates in the field. The first area of debate that continues within the revolution literature is probably the most fundamental: How is revolution defined and how is that definition applied? In this book, I have defined revolution fairly broadly as a forcible, irregular, popularly supported change in the governing regime. This has allowed us to look at more cases but to narrow the field of social movements more generally. This differs from much of the literature that has focused more on social revolutions, the most extreme versions of revolution. Almost every study of revolution begins with a definition that justifies the cases that it will analyze or the concepts that are going to be relevant. Tied to this debate about definitions is a related debate about how much revolutions really change a society or government.

Revolutions, especially social revolutions, seek to redefine much of society in terms of all social relations. For example, in the Iranian Revolution, power centered around the monarchy was replaced by power centered around a small group of clerics. That radical change in which social groups controlled the government led to a similar control of power, however. For example, the new government disbanded SAVAK, the secret police force that was loyal to the shah and replaced it with the Revolutionary Guard, a similar institution with loyalties to the clergy. These two institutions served the same function but had different loyalties and would have viewed themselves as radically different. Class changes are also an important part of revolutionary change in history. For example, in the French Revolution, the power of the landed aristocracy was replaced by the business elite in the cities. Gender relations can also be reconfigured in revolutions. Building on the notion of exploitation, Chinese communists sought to liberate women from the oppressive traditional family structures of the dynasties. There can also be seemingly unrelated changes that come out of revolutionary movements, such as the measurement of a bottle of wine or the temperature of the human body. This recalibration of weights and measures is what Eric Hobsbawm calls the French Revolution's "most lasting and universal consequence," the metric system (quoted in Kimmel 1990). In their restructuring of everything possible, the newly formed convention set out to refashion humanity's entire understanding of its relationship with the world. They also created a new calendar that took away the Christian-tainted names of months and years, replacing it with one beginning in October 1793.

One of the most important changes that takes place in revolutions is a change in ideas. The conceptions of role of government, of morality, of rights and responsibilities have all changed in some revolutions. The ideas of "no taxation without representation," that "all men are created equal," and the rights to "life, liberty and the pursuit of happiness" all were important in the American Revolution. The idea of exploited classes seizing power from their oppressors was radical when the Bolsheviks seized power in October 1917, no less so than when the Mexican constitution instituted the right to land and a redistribution scheme to ensure peasant access to land earlier that year. The idea of sovereignty, although not new, can radically change a group's perception of its relation to others, driving much of the ethnic conflict in Central Europe and Africa following the Cold War. It is these changes in ideas, and less so the reconstitution of governments and societies, that have fueled the passions of revolutionaries throughout history.

But we must also be careful not to assign too much to revolutions and the changes they create. Although France stands out as the hallmark of revolutionary change, George Lawson points out that France was "overturned by the restoration of the Bourbons in 1815; many of the families who enjoyed positions of influence under the *ancient regime* retained their privileges during the first half of the nineteenth-century" (2005: 6). Alexis de

Tocqueville, a founding scholar in studying revolutionary change and a participant in the French Revolution, commented that the revolution "stirred up society rather than changed it" and wrote in 1852 that "nothing, or almost nothing has changed since 1780" (1998: 8). Although the American Revolution began as a battle for life, liberty, and the pursuit of happiness, it was only for land-owning white males, and there is no indication that the education, wealth, or other demographic background factors were much different between the colonial governors and the state legislators who replaced them in the United States.

Another perennial debate in the literature, and one that has reflected a larger debate in the social sciences, is the relative importance of agents versus structures. A significant part of this debate is the role of ideology. On the one hand, people do not rise up to overthrow their government for no good reason. On the other hand, ideas do not make revolutions. The idea of liberty existed throughout the rule of the Soviet Union; the idea only took root and became revolutionary in Eastern Europe, however, when the conditions were ripe. These conditions, many argue, are the structures that make revolutions possible. The debate thus continues because there is much to be learned from both sides. It is true that revolutions do not spring out of ideas alone, but it is also true that people do not rise up without good cause. As the discussion on rational choice in Chapter 7 indicated, revolutions are not actions that result from normal rational choice calculus. They need the ideas of hope and change that revolutionary ideologies provide to help move people toward action. The debate over agents versus structures in playing a more prominent role in revolutions has continued, though more recent research has attempted to meld the two together. Much of the more recent work on the process of revolution pulls together structures that shape individual actions while integrating the role of individuals in actually taking those actions.

The last area of contentious debate revolves around the predictive power of theories about revolution. The likelihood of future revolutions is hotly debated in many conclusions and closing paragraphs. The ideal of much of the social scientific literature is to be able to detect trends that not only suggest the way things have happened in the past but also project them into the future. Predicting an individual revolution is exceptionally difficult. The fall of the Soviet Union is just one very clear example of the difficulty in forecasting how the dance between opposition and government will unfold. Elections in Iran during the summer of 2009 and Mexico in 2007 exploded into protests that no one predicted. The progression to a full revolution beyond that is even more difficult to predict. Many researchers have sought to increase the validity of their theories by suggesting whether revolution is more or less likely in the future. Although we may have a vested interest (as scholars of these phenomena) to suggest that they are still likely to occur and thus are relevant topics of study, there are those who argue that the age of revolution has passed.

Because revolutions are a product of the relationship between social forces and governments, changes in society and government over time have affected and are likely to continue to affect the future of revolution. Given that governments control the state, most discussion of trends in revolution start with the birth of what we conceive as states, after 1648 and the Treaty of Westphalia. States and societies have changed a great deal over the more than three centuries that have passed, so it is not surprising that revolutions have changed as well. Charles Tilly argues that three larger trends that occurred in Europe, through its colonies, and eventually the world have shaped the development of states and thus revolutions (1995). First, the population of countries has grown significantly since 1750 (though this growth has slowed and in some European countries has even reversed into decline). Second, this change led to the growth of landlords, who were able to control land and get more out of it, and merchants, who took excess workers and turned them into wage labor. The excess labor contributed to industrialization. This began with small-scale manufacturing of goods in the countryside, then in the 1800s and 1900s led toward factories and segmenting the population into rural agricultural and urban industrial. In the 1900s the labor force expanded into services (government, transportation, banking, education, health, etc.). As industrialization progressed, the increase in wage labor and decrease in control over production also spread. With these changes in population and work came the third trend toward urbanization, as population centers moved from the coutryside to growing cities.

These changes in societies and states led to changes in revolution. Early in the development of states, most revolutionary movements involved the nobility revolting against monarchs (usually for independence). These rebellions tended to be patron-client in orientation; the nobility revolted because the monarch could not keep his end of the bargain. Throughout this time, between 1600 and the 1800s, revolutions usually tended to be communal and typically involved peasant revolts against regional landlords. As European states expanded their powers, revolutions typically took the form of resisting the expansionist state, though successful revolutions tended to modernize and thus continue to expand state power. Beginning in the 1800s, class distinctions began to become increasingly relevant to revolutionary movements. This included most of the classic Marxist struggles during the twentieth century. With the decline of the colonial era, there has also been a trend toward a more nationalist orientation. These are similar to communal revolts that sought independence, but at a higher level in which national affiliations replaced patron-client ties. The list of revolutions in Figure 9.1 clearly shows that the twentieth century was an explosive age of revolution. This list was created by starting with the Political Instability Task Force's "Historical State Conflicts, Crises, and Transitions, 1955–2004," which tracks regime change in history. I then supplemented it with independence movements in history as well as information from news sources for more recent regime changes (Goldstone 1994; DeFronzo 2006).

Just as revolutions have changed along with the context in which they exist, so too has the study of revolutions. George Lawson notes that

> in Europe, revolution—derived from the Latin verb revolvere—traditionally evoked a return to a previous order, for example the restoration of constitutional monarchy witnessed by the Glorious Revolution in England in 1688. It was only during the eighteenth-century that the classical concept of a return to a previous order was replaced by a notion of volcanic ruptures, quasi-astronomical alignments, sharp breaks with the past from which societies could not turn back, ideas that were harnessed and exemplified by revolutionaries in France and America. (2005: 4)

Due to the work of Enlightenment thinkers such as Charles-Louis Montesquieu, François-Marie Voltaire, and Jean-Jacques Rousseau, the concept of revolution has become more narrowly focused on the element of rapid and radical change. This has involved not only labeling current events, but returning to history to reinterpret events as revolutions, including the eighteenth-century reinterpretation of the English civil war of the 1640s, the revolt of Netherlands, and the American War of Independence. After the French Revolution, the concept of revolution took on an entirely new meaning. It was associated with not just a break from the past but also a change of historical epochs. After the French Revolution, revolution became equated with modernization, liberty, equality, and all of the progress associated with the ideals of that revolution.

A similar change occurred, though more gradually, during the Cold War. Whereas the French Revolution made the concept of revolution an enormously positive, even romantic idea, the experiences of many citizens in Marxist states who espoused revolution soured them to the concept. The failure of communist governments to bring to fruition the ideas of their revolution fomented a distrust of grand political ideas. Many dissidents in these countries eschewed revolution in favor of "living in truth" as Vaclav Havel, the leading Czech dissident, termed it. Toward the end of the Cold War, revolution had a distinctly negative connotation. Those living in revolutionary regimes, such as the Eastern bloc, witnessed the hypocrisy of the regimes. Capitalist democracies feared revolutions as likely to bring about the spread

Figure 9.1 Revolutions in History

Up to 1800

Great Britain (1688–1689), United States (1775–1783), France (1789–1794), Haiti (1791–1804), Netherlands (1795–1798).

1800–1900

Bolivia (1809–1825), Ecuador (1809–1825), Paraguay (1810–1811), Mexico (1810–1821), Venezuela (1810–1823), Colombia (1810–1830), Uruguay (1816–1828), Argentina (1816), Peru (1821–1824), Brazil (1821–1825), Chile (1818–1826), Greece (1821–1832), Belgium (1830).

1900–1950

Iran (1905–1909), Turkey (1908), Mexico (1910–1920), China (1911–1912), Russia (1917–1922), Germany (1918–1920), Ireland (1919–1921), Turkey (1919–1923), Spain (1931–1939), Thailand (1932), Burma (1933–1948), Yugoslavia (1941–1945), India (1942–1947), Pakistan (1942–1947), Guatemala (1944), Indonesia (1945–1949), Vietnam (1945–1954), Ghana (1946–1957), Israel (1946–1948), Kenya (1946–1963), China (1947–1949), Costa Rica (1948), Malaysia (1948–1957).

1950–2000

Laos (1950–1975), Bolivia (1952), Algeria (1954–1962), Colombia (1956–1958), Cuba (1956–1959), Guinea (1958), Congo-Kinshasa (1959–1960), Rwanda (1959–1962), Congo-Brazzaville (1960), Congo-Kinshasa (1960–1965), Angola (1961–1975), Guinea-Bissau (1963–1974), South Yemen (1963–1967), Zanzibar (1963–1964), Mozambique (1964–1975), Zimbabwe (1965–1980), Cambodia (1970–1975), Bangladesh (1971), Thailand (1973), East Timor (1975–1999), Lebanon (1975–1991), Nicaragua (1977–1979), Iran (1977–1979), Afghanistan (1978–1996), Chad (1979–1996), Grenada (1979), Uganda (1981–1986), Eritrea (1981–1991), Philippines (1985–1986), Haiti (1986–1991), South Korea (1987), Czechoslovakia (1988–1990), Hungary (1988–1990), Latvia (1988–1990), Poland (1988–1990), Lithuania (1988–1991), Estonia (1988–1991), Romania (1989), East Germany (1989–1990), Bulgaria (1989–1990), Georgia (1989–1991), Moldova (1989–1991), Liberia (1989–1996), Belarus (1990–1991), Ukraine (1990–1991), Rwanda (1990–1994), South Africa (1990–1994), Russia (1991), Tajikistan (1991), Armenia (1991), Azerbaijan (1991), Croatia (1991–1992), Mali (1991–1992), Thailand (1992), Bosnia and Herzegovina (1992–1995), Congo-Kinshasa (1996–1997), Kosovo (1996–2008), Nepal (1996–2008), Congo-Brazzaville (1997–1999), Indonesia (1998–1999).

2000–2005

Philippines (2000–2001), Serbia (2000), Georgia (2003), Kyrgyzstan (2005).

Source: Political Instability Task Force, "Historical State Conflicts, Crises, and Transitions, 1955–2004," Center for Global Policy, School of Public Policy, George Mason University, 2009, http://globalpolicy.gmu.edu; Jack A. Goldstone, ed., *The Encyclopedia of Political Revolutions* (Washington, DC: Congressional Quarterly, 1994); and James V. DeFronzo, ed., *Revolutionary Movements in World History From 1750 to the Present* (Santa Barbara, CA: ABC-CLIO Inc., 2006).

of communism and thus funneled massive amounts of aid to weak states open to capitalism if not democracy. With the end of the Cold War, many scholars assumed that the golden age of revolutions had ended. As the more recent types of revolutions (democratic, negotiated, and velvet) suggest, however, the way in which revolutions occur has changed, but not the fact that they occur.

The occurrence of revolution, if history and the structural theories that explain revolutionary success of the past remain useful guides, will be shaped by the types of regimes that exist. As more countries move to embrace liberal democratic structures, the likelihood of revolution will diminish. There are a great many regimes in existence today that are far from strong, inclusive, and bureaucratic regimes. Given the outcomes discussed in Chapter 8, it might be wise for policymakers and those who lobby them to push for more subtle changes that do not involve the rapid transition of revolution. As a brief glance at the revolutions in history also suggests, the likelihood that the future of revolution will look the way it has in the past is very low. As governments and societies continue to change owing to pressures of globalization and technology, the future of revolution will likely look very different from the anticolonial movements from the 1800s through the Cold War and the nationalist, communist, and democratic movements of the twentieth century.

APPENDIX

Case Studies

Fifteen revolutions that have been used as examples to highlight concepts in the text are summarized below in chronological order. For each case there is also a short time line of events, a description of some of the key characters, and recommendations for further reading. The revolutions that follow are:

The American Revolution (1776–1789)
The French Revolution (1789–1799)
The Mexican Revolution (1910–1920)
The Russian Revolution (1917)
The Chinese Revolution (1949)
The Cuban Revolution (1959)
The Nicaraguan Revolution (1979)
The Iranian Revolution (1979)
The Philippine Revolution (1986)
The Tiananmen Square Prodemocracy Movement (1989)
The South African Revolution (1994)
The Rwandan Revolution (1994)
The Serbian Revolution (2001)
East Timorese Independence (1974–2002)
The Nepalese Revolution (1996–2008)

The American Revolution (1776–1788)

Following wars with France and its Spanish allies, the British Empire was in desperate need of revenue to maintain its growing colonies in North America. At the same time, it sought to rein in control over increasingly autonomous colonies. In 1764 and 1765, Parliament passed a number of acts to tax the colonists in new ways, including the Sugar Act, Currency Act, Stamp Act, and Quartering Act. There was significant resistance to complying with the acts in some areas, Boston and New York in particular. In response, Parliament repealed the Stamp Act in March 1766 but passed the Declaratory Act, stating that the British government had total power to legislate any laws governing the American colonies in all cases whatsoever.

In this atmosphere of heightened tension, an increasing number of British troops were sent to ensure compliance with the acts and maintain order. On March 5, 1770, a mob harassed British soldiers, who fired their muskets pointblank into the crowd, killing three people instantly, mortally wounding two others, and injuring six, in what colonists referred to as the Boston Massacre. Soon after, all of the new taxes (except for tea) were eliminated, as was the Quartering Act (which required colonists to house British troops and provide them with food). To resist the tax on tea, colonial activists disguised themselves as Mohawk Indians and dumped all 342 containers of tea into the harbor: the Boston Tea Party. In response, Parliament enacted the Coercive Acts that targeted Massachusetts and also reinstated the Quartering Act throughout the colonies. Included in the Coercive Acts were the Boston Port Bill, which effectively shut down all commercial shipping in Boston harbor until Massachusetts paid the taxes owed on the tea dumped in the harbor and reimbursed the East India Company for the loss of the tea; the Administration of Justice Act, which allowed murder trials of British officers against colonists to be held in England; and the Massachusetts Government Act, which greatly curtailed the colony's autonomy.

To create a stronger organization to resist British control, leaders of opposition groups formed the First Continental Congress, declared its opposition to the Coercive Acts, and promoted the formation of local militia units. Soon afterwards, the English Parliament declared Massachusetts to be in a state of rebellion. On April 19, 1775, 700 British soldiers en route to Concord, Massachusetts, to destroy a weapons depot that a colonist militia had created were met by about 70 armed Massachusetts militiamen at Lexington. The British destroyed the depot and returned to Boston but lost 250 men in the fighting with militiamen. The Provincial Congress in Massachusetts ordered 13,600 American soldiers to be mobilized, and colonists flocked to siege British-controlled Boston as the struggle for autonomy shifted to war.

On May 10, 1775, the Second Continental Congress convened in Philadelphia and placed the colonies in a state of defense; it later appointed George Washington commander-in-chief of the new Continental Army. The first major fight between British and American troops occurred at Boston in the Battle of Bunker Hill on June 17, 1775, where 1,000 British soldiers were killed as well as 400 Americans.

To cut off support to the colonists, King George III issued a royal proclamation closing the American colonies to all commerce and trade, to take effect in March 1776. King Louis XVI of France shortly thereafter committed one million dollars in arms and munitions to the colonists, and Spain also promised support.

On July 4, 1776, the Continental Congress approved the United States Declaration of Independence. It outlined the reasons why the colonists should no longer be subjects of the English crown as well as cataloged the harms that England had done. Thomas Jefferson, the key author of the document, argued that the purpose of the declaration was "not to find out new principles, or new arguments, never before thought of . . . but to place before mankind the common sense of the subject, in terms so plain and firm as to command their assent, and to justify ourselves in the independent stand we are compelled to take" (Jefferson 2010). As such, it was imbued with Enlightenment philosophy of natural rights and self-determination.

During the winter of 1776, George Washington battled the British throughout New York and New Jersey, and it was not until October 1777 at the Battle of Saratoga that the Americans won their first major victory of the war. As the war continued, the Continental Congress adopted the Articles of Confederation, which created a loose association of the colonies into a new country. The articles reflected the colonists' fears created by their existence under a strong but distant parliament and as a result lacked a strong central government and granted most powers to the individual colonies. Soon after, in February 1778, France officially recognized the United States and became an increasingly important supplier of money, munitions, and leadership. This, along with Dutch trading with the French and Americans, widened the war to Europe, Africa, India, and the high seas.

After major battles in the southern colonies, the British began to lose several key garrisons, leading to a House of Commons vote against further war in the United States in 1782. In March of that year, Lord North, the British prime minister, resigned, and his successor, Lord Rockingham, began negotiations with the Americans. Near the end of 1782, a preliminary peace treaty was signed in Paris, and early in 1783, England officially declared an end to the Revolutionary War. George Washington disbanded the Continental Army soon after, in June. In September the Treaty of Paris was signed by the United States and Great Britain acknowledging the independence of the thirteen colonies and defining the boundaries of the new country. Soon after, George Washington voluntarily resigned his commission.

Not long after the war, Congress authorized Secretary of War Henry Knox to raise an army to put down a rebellion in Massachusetts (Shays' Rebellion). In 1787, partly in response to Shays' Rebellion, Congress endorsed a resolution calling for a constitutional convention to reassess the structure of the confederation. Between May and September, 1787, delegates from each of the states met to radically restructure the country into a federal republic with a bicameral legislative branch, an elected president, and an independent judicial branch. On July 2, 1788, the new Constitution of the United States took effect. Three years later, the first ten amendments to the Constitution were ratified as the Bill of Rights.

Time Line

1764   The Sugar Act and Currency Acts are created by Parliament to tax the colonists to repay war debts (mainly from the French-Indian wars). In response Boston merchants begin a boycott of British luxury goods.

1765   The Stamp Act and Quartering Acts are passed by Parliament. The Sons of Liberty is formed. There is widespread noncooperation with the act and some rioting and looting in New York.

1766   *March:* Repeal of the Stamp Act; passage of the Declaratory Act stating that the British government has total power to legislate any laws governing the American colonies in all cases whatsoever.

1767   *June:* Townshend Revenue Acts passed; Bostonians decide to reinstate a boycott of English luxury items.

1770   *March 5:* The Boston Massacre occurs as a mob harasses British soldiers, who then fire their muskets into the crowd, kill three instantly, mortally wound two others, and injure six.

April: All taxes (except for tea) are eliminated as is the Quartering Act.

1773   *December 16:* Boston Tea Party occurs as colonial activists board ships and dump all 342 containers of tea into the harbor rather than pay taxes on the tea.

1774   *March:* the Boston Port Bill effectively shuts down all commercial shipping in Boston harbor until Massachusetts pays the taxes owed on the tea dumped in the harbor and also reimburses the East India Company for the loss of the tea. Bostonians at a town meeting call for a boycott of British imports.

    October: The First Continental Congress declares its opposition to the Coercive Acts and promotes the formation of local militia units.

1775   *April 18:* Seven hundred British soldiers are sent to Concord to destroy the colonists' weapons depot.

    April 19: About 70 armed Massachusetts militiamen fight with the British who take the depot.

    April 23: The Provincial Congress in Massachusetts orders 13,600 American soldiers to be mobilized.

    May 10: The Second Continental Congress convenes in Philadelphia, places the colonies in a state of defense, and appoints George Washington commander-in-chief of the new Continental Army.

    June 17: The first major fight between British and American troops occurs at Boston in the Battle of Bunker Hill.

    December 23: King George III issues a royal proclamation closing the American colonies to all commerce and trade.

1776   *January 5:* The assembly of New Hampshire adopts the first American state constitution.

    May 2: King Louis XVI of France commits one million dollars in arms and munitions. Spain also promises support.

    July 4: United States declares independence.

    August–December: British soldiers take control of New York City.

    December 25–26: George Washington halts British advance south at Trenton, New Jersey.

1777   *October 7:* The Battle of Saratoga results in the first major American victory of the Revolutionary War.

November 15: Congress adopts the Articles of Confederation as the government of the new United States of America.

1778   *July 10:* France declares war against Britain.

December 29: The British begin a major southern campaign with the capture of Savannah, Georgia, followed a month later with the capture of Augusta.

1781   *September 28:* Washington begins the siege of Yorktown with the support of French ships.

October 19: Cornwallis surrenders Yorktown.

1782   *February 27:* British House of Commons votes against further war in the United States.

November 30: A preliminary peace treaty is signed in Paris.

1783   *September 3:* The Treaty of Paris is signed by the United States and Great Britain.

1786   *October 20:* Congress authorizes Secretary of War Henry Knox to raise an army of 1,340 to put down Shays' Rebellion.

1787   *May 25–September 17:* Drafting of new Constitution.

Cast of Characters

Samuel Adams (1722–1803): organized the revolutionary Sons of Liberty to oppose British; guiding force behind Boston Tea Party

John Hancock (1737–1793): organized the revolutionary Sons of Liberty; president of Continental Congress

George Washington (1732–1799): commander in chief of Continental Army; first president of United States

Thomas Jefferson (1743–1826): author of Declaration of Independence; led revolutionary movement in Virginia

Benjamin Franklin (1706–1790): key negotiator with French and eventually British for end of war

Further Reading

Countryman, Edward. 2003. *The American Revolution: Revised Edition.* New York: Hill and Wang.

Fischer, David Hackett. 2004. *Washington's Crossing: Pivotal Moments in American History.* New York: Oxford University Press.

Maier, Pauline. 1991. *From Resistance to Revolution: Colonial Radicals and the Development of American Opposition to Britain, 1765–1776.* New York: W. W. Norton.

Nash, Gary B. 2005. *The Unknown American Revolution: The Unruly Birth of Democracy and the Struggle to Create America.* London: Viking Penguin.

Raphael, Ray. 2002. *A People's History of the American Revolution: How Common People Shaped the Fight for Independence.* New York: New Press.

Richards, Leonard L. 2002. *Shays's Rebellion: The American Revolution's Final Battle.* Philadelphia: University of Pennsylvania Press.

Wood, Gordon S. 1992. *The Radicalism of the American Revolution.* New York: A. A. Knopf.

The French Revolution (1789–1799)

In the late 1780s, King Louis XVI of France was deep in debt after financing mid-century wars and supporting the American War of Independence in hope of destroying Great Britain's power. Due to the continued financial paralysis and general unrest, Louis XVI was forced to convoke the Estates-General in 1789, the first meeting of the general assembly since 1614.

The Estates-General was a general assembly of representatives from various sections of the French citizenry. It was composed of three houses representing the orders of clergy (100,000), nobility (400,000), and everyone else in the kingdom (25 million). Each house had an equal vote, thus the First and Second Estates could outvote the Third Estate even though the latter represented a vast majority of the population. The Third Estate demanded double representation, and with a massive publicity campaign they gained it by the elections of spring 1789. When the Estates met on May 5, it appeared as though the double representation that the Third Estate had gained was a sham. This underrepresentation produced a groundswell of hostility toward the clergy and nobility.

On June 17, 1789, with the support of a few renegade clergy, the Third Estate declared itself the National Assembly (later renamed the National Constituent Assembly) with full sovereign powers residing in the people of the nation. The king and certain nobles tried to resist the Third Estate's claim and even threatened the use of military force, which subsequently resulted in public alarm. On June 20 the king closed the Salle des États, the hall where the National Assembly met. The assembly then moved its deliberations to the king's tennis court, where they affirmed the Tennis Court Oath, a pledge not to separate until they had created a constitution for France.

The king dismissed his finance minister, Jacques Necker, on July 11, blaming him for the troubles. French citizens, responding to Necker's dismissal and fear that a royal coup was in the making, stormed the Bastille prison on July 14 with the help of military mutineers. The people of Paris were terrified of intervention by foreign regiments that surrounded the city and stormed the prison in order to arm themselves (the prison served as an arms depot). The storming of the Bastille forced Louis XVI to abandon his resistance to the National Constituent Assembly.

Largely as a response to peasant unrest during the period known as the Great Fear, the National Constituent Assembly issued the August Decrees, abolishing the feudal system. The assembly also desired a constitution that would call for the regular election of public officials, separation of power, and decentralization of authority. Thus, Marquis de Lafayette drafted the Declaration of the Rights of Man and of the Citizen, which was adopted by the Assembly on August 26, 1789. The declaration's seventeen points included freedom from arbitrary arrest, civil equality before the law, freedom of thought and speech, the inviolability of property, and the sovereignty of the nation. The declaration was intended to usher in a transition from an absolute to a constitutional monarchy.

King Louis XVI attempted to resist the August Decrees and limitations on his legislative power. A group of Parisian women marched to Versailles on October 5–6 in what became known as the October Days, forcing the king, his family, and the assembly to relocate to Paris where they would be under constant public scrutiny.

The next summer, the assembly passed the Civil Constitution of the Clergy on July 12, 1790 (although not signed by the king until December 26), requiring all clergy to take an oath of loyalty to the state. Louis XVI, uneasy with the proceedings of the revolution, fled to Varennes, where he was captured and returned to Paris. The king's capture unleashed a wave of republicanism and declining support for a constitutional monarchy. This alarmed the National Assembly (which favored a constitutional monarchy), and it sought to reinstate the king and appease him with conservative amendments to the nearly completed constitution. Republican petitioners protesting the reinstatement of the King were massacred at the Champ de Mars on July 17, 1791.

On September 13, 1791, the king formally accepted the constitution, which called for the replacement of the National Constituent Assembly with the Legislative Assembly and officially declared France a constitutional monarchy. The Legislative Assembly, with which the king was forced to share power, consisted of 330 Girondists (liberal republicans) and Jacobins (radical revolutionaries headed by Jean-Paul Marat and Maximilien Robespierre), 165 constitutional monarchists, and about 250 deputies from other parties.

The king and the constitutional monarchists felt that war would increase the king's popularity, and the Girondists wanted to export France's revolution throughout Europe. So, on April 20, 1792, France declared war on Austria and Prussia, marking the beginning of the French revolutionary wars. France offered assistance to anyone who desired liberty and declared "peace to the cottages, war on the castles." The French revolutionary wars would include conflicts with the Austrian Empire, Prussia, Great Britain, Spain, the Russian Empire, and Sardinia.

On August 10, 1792, an insurgent mob assailed the Tuileries, and the king and his family were arrested and taken into custody. The Paris Commune demanded the abolishment of the constitutional monarchy. The Legislative Assembly declared that a National Convention should be created to govern the nation and draw up a new constitution. The convention first met on September 22 and with a unanimous vote abolished the monarchy and declared France a republic. The convention then found the king guilty for betraying the nation, and on January 21, 1793, he was executed. Later that year, on October 16, his queen, Marie Antoinette, was also beheaded.

In the summer of 1793, the Jacobins seized power in a parliamentary coup, and ensuing national policy became very radical. Under Maximilien Robespierre, the Reign of Terror was unleashed from 1793 to 1794 in which anyone accused of counterrevolutionary activities was executed. The terror was ended on July 27, 1794, when Robespierre was arrested and executed. Girondists who survived the terror took control of the government and persecuted Jacobins and former members of their own party in what was known as the White Terror.

The convention approved a new constitution that took effect on September 26, 1795. The new constitution installed a five-person Directory as the governing body and created a bicameral legislature. During the Directory era, the final stage of the French Revolution, General Napoleon Bonaparte's army gained power by suppressing riots and counterrevolutionary activities. By 1799, the Directory proved unable to protect property rights without political upheaval, and it was ousted by Napoleon in the coup of 18 Brumaire on November 9.

In the years that followed, Napoleon installed the Consulate and became dictator and eventually emperor of France. From 1799 to 1815, the Napoleonic wars were fought throughout Europe; in these wars Napoleon expanded the French empire and destroyed the order of ancien régime throughout most of Europe. French power rose quickly but declined with the disastrous invasion of Russia in 1812. By 1815 Napoleon's army was defeated, and monarchy was restored in France as Louis XVIII (Louis XVI's younger brother) was declared king.

Time Line

1740   War of Austrian Succession; French monarchy falls into debt.

1776   American War of Independence; French support to the colonists worsens debt but heightens revolutionary ambitions.

1787   *February 22:* Assembly of Notables refuses a new tax on property of nobles and clergy.

1788   *November 6:* Second Assembly of Notables convenes, refusing to consider doubling representation of the Third Estate.

1789   *May 5:* Estates-General convenes in Versailles.

June 17: The Third Estate declares itself the National Assembly.

June 20: Tennis Court Oath: The National Assembly swears to not dissolve until France has a constitution.

June 22: Majority of clergy join National Assembly.

June 24: Forty-eight nobles join National Assembly.

June 27: Louis XVI orders the First and Second Estates to join the Third.

July 9: National Assembly becomes National Constituent Assembly.

July 11: Food shortages cause riots, leading to the Great Fear when peasants confiscate aristocratic lands.

July 14: Parisians capture Bastille fortress.

August 4: National Constituent Assembly abolishes feudalism.

August 26: Declaration of the Rights of Man and of the Citizen.

October 5: Women's march on Versailles, demanding that Louis XVI move to Paris as sign of good faith.

October 6: Louis XVI relocates to Paris.

1790   *February 13:* Monastic vows abolished.

July 12: Civil Constitution of the Clergy makes priests take an oath of loyalty to the state.

1791   *June 20:* Royal family flees disguised as servants.

June 21: Louis XVI is recognized; taken back to Paris.

July 10: Leopold II (holy Roman emperor) calls on other European powers to be ready to intervene in France.

September 14: Louis XVI formally accepts the constitution.

October 1: Legislative Assembly replaces National Constituent Assembly.

1792   *April 20:* France declares war on Austria.

July 25: Brunswick Manifesto: Austrian threat that if the French royal family is not harmed, the French citizens will not be harmed.

July 30: Austria and Prussia invade France.

August 10: Tuileries stormed; Louis XVI and family arrested.

September 20: National Convention replaces Legislative Assembly.

September 21: National Convention abolishes monarchy; declares First French Republic.

December 3: Louis XVI goes on trial for treason.

1793   *January 21:* King Louis XVI executed.

July 17: Robespierre elected to Committee of Public Safety; begins Reign of Terror.

October 16: Marie-Antoinette executed.

October 21: Anticlerical law makes priests subject to death penalty.

1794   *June 7:* Robespierre recommends that the National Convention acknowledge existence of God.

July 27: Robespierre executed; Reign of Terror ends.

1795   *August 22:* National Convention ratifies new constitution.

October 26: National Convention dissolved.

November 2: Directory, created by the constitution, takes on executive power.

1799   *November 9:* Bonaparte, general of the army, stages coup d'état on 18 Brumaire (in the revolutionary calendar), ending the Directory.

Cast of Characters

Louis XVI (1754–1793): Last King of France

Jacques Necker (1732–1804): French finance minister who was popular with Parisians; his dismissal in 1789 led to Bastille riots.

Charles Maurice de Talleyrand-Périgord (1754–1838): Served as deputy for the Church in the meeting of the Estates General, where he supported reforms, including the Civil Constitution of the Clergy

Georges Danton (1759–1794): Chief force in the movement to overthrow the monarchy and establish the first French Republic; first president of the Committee for Public Safety; his opposition to the Reign of Terror and his moderate policies led to his death by guillotine.

Maximilien Robespierre (1758–1794): Elected to the Estates-General and served as an influential member of the Jacobin Club. Rose to prominence as the key leader of the Terror, which effectively ended when he was arrested and guillotined.

Napoleon Bonaparte (1769–1821): French general who became emperor of France in 1799; the beginning of his reign marked the end of the revolutionary period.

Further Reading

Hibbert, Christopher. 1999. *The Days of the French Revolution.* New York: Harper Perennial.

Lefebvre, Georges. 2005. *The Coming of the French Revolution.* Princeton, NJ: Princeton University Press.

Rudé, George F.E. 1959. *The Crowd in the French Revolution.* Oxford, United Kingdom: Clarendon Press.

Skocpol, Theda. 1979. *States and Social Revolutions: A Comparative Analysis of France, Russia, and China.* Cambridge: Cambridge University Press.

Sutherland, Donald M.G. 1986. *France 1789–1815. Revolution and Counterrevolution.* New York: Oxford University Press.

Tocqueville, Alexis de. 1955. *The Old Regime and the French Revolution.* Garden City, NY: Doubleday.

The Mexican Revolution (1910–1920)

Mexican independence from Spain was declared in 1810, followed by almost fifty years of civil conflict and power struggles. When General Porfirio Diaz restored the republic, he ruled Mexico from 1876 to 1910, when the revolution began. Under Diaz's rule, Mexico was a textbook case of what Foran terms "dependent development" (2005). There was rapid development within the confines of domination by European and especially US businesses. Foreign capital controlled "90 percent of Mexico's eighty largest capitalized business concerns" (Foran 2005: 36). US investments in 1910 represented "80 percent of foreign investments and more than the entire Mexican bourgeoisie. American companies and individuals controlled about 80 percent of mining, owned over 100 million acres of land, and provided 57 percent of imports, while taking 75.6 percent of exports in 1910" (2005: 36). One of the effects of this type of development was skyrocketing inequality as peasants were increasingly squeezed off the land in favor of larger landowners. To maintain support, Diaz became increasingly repressive, with the slogan "*pan y palo*" ("bread and the stick") indicating the combination of patronage and repression that provided his support. There was an economic downturn around the 1907–1909 period that shocked the system, setting the stage for revolution.

Francisco Madero, a wealthy landowner who was educated in France and the United States, advocated a liberal revolutionary ideology that included some populist and nationalist elements (the right to unionize, some land reforms, and restrictions on foreign capital). In 1910, Diaz publicly stated that Mexico was ready for democracy and held elections in which Madero was viewed as the key opposition leader. But in the run-up, Madero and thousands of his supporters were jailed, and Diaz was named president in elections that were widely viewed as manipulated by his supporters. In October 1910, Madero escaped into Texas and became a more vocal advocate for the overthrow of Diaz. He encouraged others to rise up and militarily challenge Diaz's forces. Some of the key local leaders who responded to Madero's call included Emiliano Zapata south of Mexico City and Pascual Orozco and Francisco ("Pancho") Villa in the north and numerous others throughout Mexico.

In the spring of 1911, the uprisings throughout the country proved too much for Diaz's military, and on May 25, he resigned, turning power over to Madero in an agreement that maintained the military and much of the government structure. Madero was elected president on October 1, 1911, but his administration was plagued by the competing interests that had propelled him to victory: business elites tired of Diaz's exclusionary rule and lower classes looking for more significant labor and land reforms. Several uprisings, including ones led by Zapata and Orozco, posed significant challenges to the new government. In February 1913, one of Madero's generals, Victoriano Huerta, took control of the capital when the ex-dictator's nephew led a rebellion there. In just over a week, Huerta had secured US support for a military coup, taken control of the government, and had Madero executed.

Despite initial support of Huerta's regime by all of the forces that had supported Diaz, they quickly turned to oppose Huerta. In addition, the United States and various European powers competed for influence in groups opposing or supporting Huerta, including a US military intervention in Veracruz in 1914 to block arms shipments from Germany to the Huerta government. Later that year, Huerta stepped down, and the country descended into civil war. Villa and Zapata each pushed separately for more radical reforms, though they did not have a national program. Venustiano Carranza and Alvaro Obregon both advocated more moderate reforms but were initially confined to northern Mexico. By the end of 1915, Carranza and Obregon had largely pushed Villa out of Mexico City (though they had not defeated him by any means). In 1916, while the fighting continued, elites met to draft a new constitution that embodied a moderate liberal ideology but included labor standards, state ownership of oil and other natural resources, and agrarian reforms—all as constitutionally protected rights. On March 11, 1917, Carranza was elected president under the new constitution. Carranza's rule was marked by minimal gains in land reforms, continued urban strikes, a lack of support from the United States, and continued peasant guerrilla warfare (though Zapata, the preeminent peasant leader, had been killed in April 1919).

When Carranza threw his support for someone other than Obregon, his forces retaliated, and Carranza tried to flee the country, but was killed. Obregon seized power and six months later won election as president. He served until 1924, when he was succeeded by Plutarco Elias Calles, a revolutionary general, governor, and then key member of Obregon's government. Calles later created the National Revolutionary Party (Partido Nacional Revolucionario; PNR) that eventually became the Institutional Revolutionary Party (PRI) that consolidated power and ruled Mexico for the next seventy years. The promises of the 1917 constitution never became fully realized, though by the 1940s there had been significant attempts at nationalization of oil and land redistribution.

The Mexican Revolution was undoubtedly dominated by traditional elites, but unlike any previous revolution, peasants also played a significant role in the conflict. Because Villa and Zapata had a peasant base of support, the peasants' interests were brought into the revolutionary governments. Further, the peasants constituted such a significant class that the revolution could not be secured without their cooperation. In many ways, as Foran argues, the Mexican was both the last bourgeois revolution and the first peasant revolution of the twentieth century. It represents a bridge from the liberal revolutions of the United States and France to the communist revolutions of Russia, China, and Cuba.

Time Line

1876   Porfirio Diaz seizes power and is reelected president until 1910.

1907–   Economic downturn.
1909

1908   Diaz states that Mexico is ready for democracy and schedules elections.

1910   *June 26:* On election day, Madero and thousands of his supporters are jailed, and Diaz is named president.
          October 4: Madero escapes into Texas and calls for revolution.

1911   Spring uprisings throughout the country.
          May 25: Diaz resigns, turning power over to Madero.
          October 1: Madero elected president.

1912   Uprisings continue, including ones led by Zapata and Orozco.

1913   *February 9–23:* General Victoriano Huerta leads coup.
          February 22: Madero executed.

1914   *April:* US military intervention in Veracruz to block shipment of weapons for Huerta.
          July: Huerta steps down, replaced by Carranza, but the country descends into civil war.
          Winter: Pancho Villa takes control of Mexico City, installs Eulalio Gutierrez as president.

1915   *April 6–15:* Battle of Celaya where Obregon defeats Villa and captures Mexico City; Carranza installed as president.

1916   Draft of new liberal constitution begun.

1917   *March 11:* Carranza elected president under the new constitution.

1919   *April 10:* Zapata killed.

1920   *May 21:* Carranza supports someone other than Obregon for president; Carranza tries to flee the country, but is killed.

        June 1: Adolfo de la Huerta serves as interim president while elections take place.

        December 1: Obregon elected president.

        Obregon signs peace agreement with Villa.

1923   Villa assassinated.

1924   Plutarco Elias Calles succeeds Obregon as president and founds the precursor to the PRI.

1926–   Cristero War fought in reaction to changes Calles makes to church-
1929   state relations.

1934   Calles's hand-picked successor, Lazaro Cardenas, is elected president, then turns on Calles and, over the next six years, implements major land reforms, strengthens labor unions, and nationalizes Mexican oil.

Cast of Characters

Porfirio Diaz (1830–1915): A general in the Mexican military, Diaz ran for president and lost. Later he orchestrated a coup and named himself president, amending the constitution so that he could be reelected.

Francisco Madero (1873–1913): A liberal politician, ran against Diaz for president, but was jailed. Became the central figure around which a wide variety of anti-Diaz activists could coalesce. Served as president from 1911 to 1913 when he was overthrown in a coup.

Emiliano Zapata (1879–1919): Pragmatic revolutionary military leader who championed the plight of the peasants. He created the Plan de Ayala for land redistribution following the successful overthrow of Diaz. He then fought Madero, Huerta, and Carranza as too moderate.

Francisco "Pancho" Villa (1878–1923): A rebel from the province that bordered the United States, Villa was instrumental in the overthrow of Diaz, but pushed for more radical land reforms than Madero advocated. Initially supported Huerta's coup, then turned against him. He was eventually sidelined by Carranza.

General Victoriano Huerta (1850–1916): A general in the Diaz regime who was kept on when Madero came to power. Orchestrated a battle in Mexico City that he used as a reason for seizing power in 1913. Was defeated by an alliance of Carranza, Obregon, Villa, and Zapata.

Venustiano Carranza (1859–1920): Supported Madero in overthrow of Diaz; when Huerta overthrew Madero in a coup, led opposition against Huerta and eventually became president and ushered in the new constitution. Was killed by Obregon.

Alvaro Obregon (1780–1928): Military leader who allied with Carranza to initially fight Huerta and then against Villa and Zapata for a more moderate liberal democracy. When Carranza was viewed as too moderate, Obregon advocated more land reforms. Forced Carranza from power and was elected president.

Plutarco Elias Calles (1877–1945): A general who supported Obregon and succeeded him as president.

Further Reading

Joseph, Gilbert, and Daniel Nugent, eds. 1994. *Everyday Forms of State Formation: Revolution and the Negotiation of Rule in Modern Mexico.* Durham, NC: Duke University Press.

Katz, Friedrich. 1981. *The Secret War in Mexico: Europe, the United States, and the Mexican Revolution.* Chicago: University of Chicago Press.

Tutino, John. 1986. *From Insurrection to Revolution in Mexico: Social Bases of Agrarian Violence, 1750–1940.* Princeton, NJ: Princeton University Press.

Womack, John, Jr. 1968. *Zapata and the Mexican Revolution.* New York: Alfred A. Knopf.

The Russian Revolution (1917)

When revolutionary situations arose at the end of the nineteenth and beginning of the twentieth centuries in Russia, it was by no means the type of country that Marx had envisioned leading a communist revolution. The Russian Empire was controlled by the tsar, a monarch with a vast empire that was economically backward compared to its European neighbors. "At the time of the revolution, only about 15% of the population lived in cities" (DeFronzo 2007: 34). Up to 1861, much of the Russian population were serfs and thus were legally bound to live on and work the plot of land owned by a landlord. As part of a modernization campaign, the tsar abolished serfdom and encouraged industrial development. To create a more modernized workforce required creating an education system. The exposure to education and technology from western Europe spread new ideas that clashed with the old system of society and government controlled by the tsar.

As a result, a number of opposition groups began to emerge, challenging the tsarist regime. One of the more popular was an anarchist philosophy that advocated communal living that would not require a central state (and thus no tsar). The philosophy built on Russian traditional social structures, including the *mir,* a rural collective ownership of land that is worked by peasants. "The *mir* assigned individual parcels of land to be worked by particular peasants and established taxation rates for individual households" (DeFronzo 2007: 36). The ideal society, the anarchist/populist philosophy argued, was one where the *mirs* governed all life uninhibited by a central government. The country would be composed of thousands of small collectives. The tactic that the anarchists were most successful at utilizing was guerrilla-style assassinations, most prominently of Tsar Alexander II in 1881. The Social Democratic Party adopted much of this ideology and blended it with Marxist ideology from western Europe.

By the turn of the century, discontent with the tsar had risen significantly, and there were a variety of groups pressing for reform and revolution in a variety of ways (strikes, riots, assassination attempts, etc.). In 1905, the tsar sought to gain popular support by declaring war on Japan. He thought that Russia would easily win the war, and that would rally the population around his rule. Instead, the war was a disaster for Russia, as Japan won repeated military victories, and the Russian population rose up in opposition. "Hardships caused by the war intensified worker discontent. In January 1905 a peaceful procession of thousands of workers, led by an activist priest named George Gapon, attempted to present the Tsar a petition listing grievances and calling upon him for assistance. But soldiers fired on the demonstrators, killing scores of people. Following the massacre, known as Bloody Sunday, strikes and peasant uprisings spread through many areas of Russia" (DeFronzo 2007: 40–41). The revolutionary situation ended when the tsar granted civil reforms, including the creation of a parliament called the Duma, and then ended the war with Japan so that military forces could be brought back for domestic stability in the west.

A new revolutionary situation emerged shortly after Russia's entrance into World War I. The same basic conditions existed as in the 1905–1906 revolt, only this time in more extreme forms. Thousands of residents of Petrograd (then the capital city) demonstrated on the anniversary of Bloody Sunday in January 1917. In late February, thousands of marchers took to the streets of St. Petersburg. They were met with thousands standing in bread lines (the drafting of 15 million peasants to serve in the military had caused drastic food shortages). The tsar responded to the masses' taking to the streets by closing several factories, which led to more discontented workers in the streets. When they challenged the government, military forces did not follow orders and allowed the protests to continue. In a panic, the tsar abdicated, leaving the newly recalled Duma in power, which quickly called for elections to a new Constituent Assembly.

The provisional government was split along class interests—the Duma reflected aristocrats' and wealthy business's interests, whereas the Petrograd Soviet reflected the workers' interests. Soviets had emerged during the revolutionary situation as local associations of workers and activists advocating their interests. Initially the Petrograd Soviet supported the Duma when opposing the tsar, but with the abdication, the alliance broke down. The Petrograd Soviet was dominated by Mensheviks and Bolsheviks, the two groups that had emerged from the Social Democratic Party. The Mensheviks advocated a more reformist approach that would allow capitalism to create the conditions for the movement toward socialism. The Socialist Revolutionaries, or Bolsheviks, advocated a more rapid transition under the leadership of the vanguard of the proletariat. Paralyzed by the class divide, the provisional government opted to continue fighting with Germany and delayed economic reforms; both of these decisions undermined public support for the new government. Throughout the summer, the situation continued to worsen.

Bolsheviks became more popular in the soviets in Petrograd and Moscow, and September elections propelled them to a majority in those soviets. The Bolsheviks had campaigned on ending the war, "all land to the peasants," and "all power to the soviets" (DeFronzo 2007: 44). On November 7, Leon Trotsky led soldiers and armed workers to take control of government buildings and of communication and transportation centers. The provisional government crumbled, and the Bolsheviks instructed local soviets to seize large estates and church-owned land. They also announced intentions to end the war with Germany. The Bolshevik party moved quickly to consolidate power over the soviets. A day after the new Constituent Assembly (which reflected the variety of interests and parties that existed in the empire) met, the Bolsheviks disbanded it, claiming that the soviets retained the true will of the people (despite the fact that they were a primarily urban phenomenon).

By 1918, the Bolshevik party had become more important than the soviets, even crushing revolts by soviets that wanted to retain autonomy. Vladimir Lenin gained significant peasant support by confiscating large estates and redistributing them to the peasants, including church property, and by building on the *mir* structure to create peasant communes that mimicked the collective organization of the urban areas. The Bolsheviks did not gain immediate control over all of Russia. There were a wide variety of opposition groups, ranging from reactionaries who sought to reinstitute the tsar to anarchists; some of these groups were supported by foreign troops from Britain, the United States, and Japan. In response, the Bolsheviks raised a Red Army to consolidate power. The civil war between the Red Army and the various anti-Bolshevik forces lasted until 1923, when most opposition was eliminated.

Lenin died in 1924 and the leadership of the party passed to Joseph Stalin, who shaped the collectivization of the peasantry and the industrialization of the Soviet Union into a nuclear superpower.

Time Line

1905   *January 9:* Father George Gapon leads workers in St. Petersburg in a demonstration against the tsar because of rising food prices. The tsar's soldiers open fire, killing many on what becomes known as Bloody Sunday.

        Russian defeat in war with Japan and mass demonstrations lead to the tsar's creating the Duma.

1917   *January 9:* A demonstration by 140,000 residents in Petrograd commemorates Bloody Sunday.

        February: Strike by 100,000 in Petrograd; Duma reconvenes and attacks the government over food shortages.

        March 11: The tsar orders soldiers to break the strike, but most mutiny and join the workers. The tsar also disbands the Duma.

March 12: The Petrograd garrison mutinies, joins the protesters, and seizes arsenals. The Duma refuses to disband, instead forming a Provisional Committee to govern. The Petrograd Soviet of Workers' Deputies is created.

March 14: The Duma and Soviets elect members; the Petrograd Soviet claims authority over the army.

March 15: The tsar abdicates.

March–April: The revolution spreads across Russia, with mini Dumas (public committees) taking control of official, government, and police matters while workers and soldiers create parallel soviets.

April 16: Lenin returns to Russia, where he soon dominates the Bolshevik party.

April 17: Lenin gives a speech known as the April Thesis, which asks for power to all the soviets and promises bread, land, worker control, and an end to the war.

May 3–4: First Provisional Government falls when it is viewed as continuing the war policies of the tsar.

May 17: Trotsky returns to Russia from exile.

May 18: Coalition government forms from provisional government and Petrograd Soviet.

June 29–July 15: The provisional government plans a major attack on Germany to restore Russian morale, which fails, killing more than 400,000 Russians.

July 16–17: The July Days, an armed insurrection by soldiers and workers in Petrograd against both the provisional government and the Petrograd Soviet for their failures. Troops break up the protest and arrest high-ranking Bolsheviks.

July 20: The first coalition government collapses.

September 8–12: The Kornilov affair. Believing Russia to be at the mercy of the Soviet, right-wing hero General Lavr Kornilov marches to Petrograd to restore "strong" government and crush the socialists.

September: Strikes are continual, and there is massive defection from the military.

October 23: Having gained a majority in the Petrograd and Moscow soviets, the Bolshevik Central Committee decides to seize power.

November 7: Trotsky leads military forces to take control of key government and communication posts. Lenin outlines his plans for a new Soviet government. Provisional government leaders flee.

November: Soviet power spreads across Russia, with Bolshevik and other socialist groups seizing control.

November 16: Bolsheviks take control of Moscow and the Kremlin.

November 25: Elections to the Constituent Assembly. Lenin disbands the assembly the day after its first meeting.

Note: a. Dates are from the Gregorian calendar used by most of the Western world today. But, at the time, Russia used the Julian calendar that was several days off from the Gregorian calendar, which is why the March and November revolutionary events are often referred to as the February and October revolutions.

Cast of Characters

Tsar Nicholas II (1868–1918): The last crowned emperor of Russia. Nicholas was crowned tsar in 1894 and was forced to abdicate the throne during the revolution. Nicholas and his family were executed by the Bolsheviks.

Vladimir Ilyich Lenin (1870–1924): Bolshevik leader, author of the April Theses, October Revolution instigator, and governmental leader.

Leon Trotsky (1879–1940): Bolshevik revolutionary and Marxist theorist. Trotsky was the founder and commander of the Red Army.

Joseph Stalin (1878–1953): Bolshevik revolutionary, instigator of the October Revolution, Commissar of Nationalities, and governmental leader.

Further Reading

Bonnell, Victoria E. 1983. *Roots of Rebellion: Workers' Politics and Organizations in St. Petersburg and Moscow, 1900–1914.* Berkeley: University of California Press.

Galili, Ziva. 1989. *The Menshevik Leaders in the Russian Revolution: Social Realities and Political Strategies.* Princeton, NJ: Princeton University Press.

Kaiser, Daniel H., ed. 1987. *The Workers' Revolution in Russia, 1917: The View from Below.* Cambridge: Cambridge University Press.

Owen, Launcelot A. 1963. *The Russian Peasant Movement 1906–1917*. New York: Russell and Russell.

Pipes, Richard, ed. 1968. *Revolutionary Russia*. Cambridge, MA: Harvard University Press.

Rabinowitch, Alexander. 1968. *Prelude to Revolution: The Petrograd Bolsheviks and the July 1917 Uprising*. Bloomington: Indiana University Press.

Sablinsky, Walter. 1976. *The Road to Bloody Sunday: Father Gapon and the St. Petersburg Massacre of 1905*. Princeton, NJ: Princeton University Press.

The Chinese Revolution (1949)

The idea of China becoming "modernized" only has relevance from a certain perspective. For most of its very long history, China was the leader in technology and civilization and viewed all others as less civilized. This changed with the rapid economic and technological developments of western Europe during the Enlightenment. Over several centuries, China changed little while Europe underwent explosive changes, including the important development of more destructive implements of war. In the 1800s, when Europeans began to have more extensive contacts with Asia, the disparity between China and European countries was significant. European powers sought to establish trading posts and colonial ports to access the products as well as potential market of the Chinese, with an estimated population of 400 million. When Britain realized the amount of money that China was earning on its exports to Britain, because of tea, spices, silk, porcelain, and other goods, it sought to correct the trade imbalance by encouraging the importation of opium produced in Britain's colonies in India and Burma. China resisted the sale and Britain invaded, forcing open the markets as well as demanding possession of several trade ports (including Shanghai and Hong Kong). The failure of the emperor to defend China and retain its place as a civilizational leader led to increasing domestic rebellions, including the Taiping Rebellion (1851–1864), which resulted in more than 20 million deaths. The collapse of the Qing dynasty was precipitated with the death of the Empress Dowager Ci Xi and her nephew in 1908, which meant that the next in line of succession was three-year-old Emperor Fu Yi.

In 1911, amid widespread riots, military officers began to mutiny and declare independence from the emperor. Sun Yat-sen, a republican activist, had organized a vast underground opposition group that quickly linked the mutinous military officers. General Yuan Shikai was called on by the emperor to restore order. The general convinced the royal family that the only way to escape execution was to abdicate the throne and let him take control. In February 1912, the emperor abdicated, and in March Yuan, in collusion with Sun, became president of the republic. Two years later, Yuan disbanded the new parliament and a year later declared himself emperor. In 1916, he died, leaving the country largely divided into domains controlled by local warlords. In the meantime, Sun had organized opposition to the new emperor under the Goumindang (Nationalist Party; GMD) that sought to bring about a democratic republic in China.

During this period of warlordism and instability, a variety of new ideologies flourished, spawning new groups who advocated different forms of government. In 1921, the Chinese Communist Party (CCP) was formed in Shanghai, coordinating several smaller Marxist groups, including one led by Mao Zedong. The Soviet Union encouraged the Chinese Communist Party to work with the GMD to unify the country and rid itself of imperialist domination. To further this agenda, the Union of Soviet Socialist Republics (USSR) worked with the GMD to defeat several warlords. In 1925, Sun died and Chiang Kai-shek assumed control of the GMD. Soon after, he launched another military campaign to reunify the country. Chiang then turned against the communists, launching an attack on the urban areas, killing or imprisoning and then executing many of the leadership in 1927. Up to that point, most of the Chinese Communist Party had advocated a Leninist, urban-centered strategy of bringing about socialism. Mao advocated a peasant-oriented strategy, however, that replaced the workers with the peasantry (90 percent of China's population was rural).

From 1927 to 1936, Chiang sought to consolidate power over a mostly unified China while also trying to eliminate the Communist Party. The base of communist support remained in Jiangxi province, in south-central China. Chiang waged five separate campaigns to crush the communist stronghold, and in 1934, 700,000 GMD troops surrounded the province. It is estimated that 100,000 communists were in the province and were forced to flee the surrounding army in what is referred to as the Long March. The group moved west and then north, continually battling and trying to evade the pursuing GMD forces as well as warlords along the way for more than a year. When they finally arrived in Yan'an in Shaanxi province in 1935, fewer than 20,000 had survived the nearly 4,000-mile march. There Mao, now in charge of the Communist Party, refined the peasant-based strategy that would govern China under his rule.

During the 1930s, Japan became increasingly aggressive in controlling the northern and coastal areas of China. In 1936, the communists kidnapped Chiang Kai-shek and forced him to form a second united front against the Japanese. Mao reasoned that only with the help of the GMD could the Communist Party get rid of Japanese imperialism. The alliance lasted until 1941, when they fought Japanese occupation separately. The Japanese, targeting the urban areas, decimated the GMD, whereas the Communist Party, with its base in rural areas, was strengthened by the war. After the Japanese surrender in 1945, the communists, with the help of the Soviets, seized Japanese weapons and in the spring of 1946 pushed south in battles against the demoralized and war-weary GMD. Despite US support for the GMD, the communists captured more and more urban areas. In January 1949, the communists captured Beijing, then quickly advanced south throughout the country. On October 1, 1949, Mao Zedong declared the People's Republic of China; the nationalist forces retreated to Taiwan along with 2 million refugees, mostly comprising the republican government and business community.

Although the revolution effectively ended with the end of the civil war, Mao utilized revolutionary fervor to ensure that the spirit of the revolution continued. He did this in a variety of campaigns, including the Great Leap Forward and the Cultural Revolution, both of which had devastating effects on the people of China.

Time Line

1839– Opium War with Britain.
1842

1851– Taiping Rebellion.
1864

1910   *October 10:* Rebellion by followers of the Nationalist leader Sun Yat-sen leads to collapse of the Qing dynasty.

1912   Yuan Shikai becomes president and then emperor; dies in 1916.

1914   Japan occupies Shandong Province.

1919   *May 4:* World War I ends and Sun's Nationalist Party, the GMD is reorganized.

1921   CCP is established; Mao Zedong is one of the party organizers.

1923   Soviets broker a union between the CCP and GMD (First United Front).

1925   Sun Yat-sen, leader of the GMD, dies.

1926   Chiang Kai-shek, commander-in-chief of the National Revolutionary Army, emerges as the new leader of the GMD. In July he launches the Northern Expedition, an effort to conquer the northern warlords and thus unite the country under GMD rule.

1927   The CCP and left wing of the GMD break away from the First United Front, declaring their own capital in Wuhan.

April 12: Chiang responds by arresting and executing hundreds of communists in Shanghai. He then declares his own rival government in Nanjing, representing the right-wing faction of the GMD.

Mao Zedong leads the Autumn Harvest Uprising in Hunan province.

In the subsequent White Terror, Chiang virtually wipes out the urban-based CCP.

1928   *June:* GMD captures Beijing from northern warlords, effectively uniting eastern China under GMD rule, giving Chiang legitimate claims at leadership of the country.

Communist groups organize, and Nationalists are unable to prevent them from taking control of regions of southern China.

1931   Japan occupies Manchuria.

1932   Japan attacks Shanghai.

1933   After four unsuccessful attempts to destroy the communists, Chiang launches a fifth aimed at encircling the communists in the Jiangxi region.

October: Escaping the tightening circle created by the Nationalists, the Communists begin the Long March.

1934–   Long March, a 4,000-mile exodus to the interior region of Shaanxi
1935   province. Mao becomes primary leader of the CCP and creates the foundations for revolution in northwestern China.

1936   *December 12:* The Xi'an Incident renegade GMD generals Zhang Xueliang and Yang Hucheng kidnap Chiang and force him to form the Second United Front with the CCP to fight the Japanese.

1937–   World War II in China; Japan occupies much of northern and
1945   coastal China.

1944   Japan inflicts devastating losses to the GMD. The CCP is able to avoid the worst of the fighting while also gaining much of the peasantry to their side by effectively portraying themselves as the vanguard against the Japanese.

1946   The CCP creates the People's Liberation Army (PLA) to fight the GMD now that the Japanese have surrendered.

1946–   Civil war; the CCP is victorious; Chiang and remaining GMD forces
1949   flee to Taiwan.

1949   *October 1:* The People's Republic of China (PRC) is formally established in Beijing as a democratic dictatorship.

Cast of Characters

Yuan Shikai (1859–1916): Military official in Qing dynasty who convinced the emperor to step down. Under Sun Yat-sen's acceptance, became president, then seized power and attempted to found a new dynasty.

Sun Yat-sen (1866–1925): Father of modern China who advocated the creation of a modern republic, which led, in part, to the end of the Qing dynasty. When the old regime fell, he was an active force at trying to create a unified republic (which did not occur until after 1949).

Chiang Kai-shek (1887–1975): Nationalist military and political leader who took command of the GMD after the death in 1925 of Sun Yat-sen. Led attempts at purging the left wing of the GMD and the CCP in 1927, continuing the civil war. After his defeat he fled to Taiwan and continued to claim mainland China.

Mao Zedong (1893–1976): Communist military and political leader who unified China in 1949 for the first time in decades and brought relative political stability to the country, absent of external interferences in the country's affairs. He led the CCP from the Long March until his death.

Further Reading

Diflik, Arif. 1989. *The Origins of Chinese Communism.* New York: Oxford University Press.
Pepper, Suzanne. 1978. *Civil War in China: The Political Struggle, 1945–1949.* Berkeley: University of California Press.

Sheridan, James E. 1975. *China in Disintegration: The Republican Era in Chinese History, 1912–1949*. New York: Free Press.

Wilbur, C. Martin. 1983. *The Nationalist Revolution in China, 1923–1928*. Cambridge, MA: Cambridge University Press.

Wu, Odoric Y.K. 1994. *Mobilizing the Masses: Building Revolution in Henan*. Stanford, CA: Stanford University Press.

The Cuban Revolution (1959)

Fulgencio Batista seized power in Cuba in 1952, months before he was likely to lose the presidential election. Batista had led a coup twenty years earlier, had been elected president, and had later been voted out of office. When he seized power in 1952, he significantly restricted constitutional liberties. Under Batista's reign, significant economic changes to the Cuban economy continued. "Sugarcane came to account for 80 to 90 percent of all of Cuba's exports, and for a third of the island's total income," almost all of which was sold in the US market (Wolf 1999: 257). Under Batista, the production of sugar became increasingly centralized and dominated by US-owned companies. By 1959, nearly a fifth of Cuba's soil was owned by the twenty-eight largest producers of sugarcane. US companies controlled nine of the ten largest sugar mills and twelve of twenty in the next size class, so that US-owned companies controlled the production of "about 40 percent of the island crop, and controlled 54 percent of the island's grinding capacity" (1999: 256). Batista's rule became increasingly neopatrimonial, as the economic benefits generated from export went almost exclusively to those who could support his rule (including the United States).

In response to the coup, "one of the disappointed candidates from that election, Fidel Castro, who had stood for a congressional seat, organized a 1953 attack on the Moncada military barracks" (Wickham-Crowley 1992: 16). The attack failed and Castro was imprisoned; he was later exiled to Mexico, where he organized a group of mostly Cuban exiles. The group, which included Che Guevara, was called the 26th of July Movement (M-26) because the original 1953 attack had taken place on July 26. The eighty-two guerrillas in the M-26 had trained for less than a year when they boarded the *Granma* and sailed from Mexico to Cuba. They planned to attack military outposts in a coordinated effort while others led a general strike and urban protests.

The *Granma* was delayed and off course when it landed on December 2, 1956. The small band was quickly surrounded, and all but 15–20 men were killed by the army. This group retreated into the hills of the Sierra Maestra (on the eastern tip of Cuba, farthest from the urban areas of Havana on the west coast). Over the next two years, they evaded Batista's forces and gradually gained more followers as Batista became more ruthless in his repression of the peasantry. By the summer of 1958, despite not having more than several hundred guerrilla soldiers, Castro controlled much of the Sierra Maestra. In response, Batista launched an operation to retake control of the mountains and destroy M-26. From June through August a series of battles between the military and M-26 moved control over the region back and forth. By the end of August, it was clear that Batista's campaign was failing, and M-26 took the offensive by moving out of the mountains toward larger urban areas. Between August and December, M-26 took control of more towns in eastern Cuba and began to negotiate with military leaders in the larger urban areas. Two wings of the guerrilla group pushed west and took Yaguajay and Santa Clara. The next day, January 1, 1959, Batista fled the country. Within a week, Castro's forces had taken control of Santiago de Cuba (the main eastern city) and Havana (the capital) without a fight.

Castro moved to quickly purge Batista loyalists from the government, killing hundreds of policemen, soldiers, and others charged with crimes against the Cuban population committed under the Batista regime. Guevara was appointed the supreme prosecutor of these public trials and was largely responsible for deciding their fate. Given the extensive control of US-owned companies, Castro moved to nationalize all foreign-owned lands in August 1960 and implemented significant land reform to break up plantations for redistribution into cooperatives. It was not until this time that the United States became active in opposing Castro, and as a result, it was not until this time that Castro was overtly Marxist. Given the US embargo and the Cold War, the Soviet Union made rapid inroads in supporting the Castro regime. In April 1961, after the failed Bay of Pigs invasion, Castro proclaimed Cuba socialist. By 1965, Castro had consolidated power, integrating a number of leftist groups into his government.

After 1961, Cuba had an enormous impact on revolutionary movements in Latin America. Part of this was due to the fact that it was a shining example of success in the area where that was least likely to occur. As Wickham-Crowley argues, "The thought processes of future guerrillas were probably remarkably neat: if Cuba can carry out a socialist revolution under the very nose, and against the resistance, of *yanqui* imperialism, then why not here as well, where the U.S. presence is so much less pervasive?" (1992: 32). The Cuban example was supplemented with Cuban support for revolutions. Guevara's work as a guerrilla leader in Africa and Latin America is an example of how Cuba worked to export the revolutionary project to other countries. "An enormous number of Latin Americans made the trip to Cuba, which quickly came to resemble a revolutionary Mecca where potential guerrillas would be spiritually prepared—and often militarily trained—for revolutionary struggle" (1992: 31).

Time Line

1952   Fulgencio Batista seizes power in Cuba months before he was likely to lose the presidential election.

1953   *July 26:* Fidel Castro organizes an attack on the Moncada military barracks.

1955   Castro is exiled to Mexico, where he forms M-26 to overthrow Batista.

1956   *December 2:* M-26, a small band of guerrilla fighters aboard the *Granma,* lands in Cuba, is surrounded, and all but 15–20 men are killed by the army; the rest escape into the mountains.

1958   *Summer:* Castro controls much of the Sierra Maestra.

        June–August: Battles between the military and M-26 in Sierra Maestra.

        August: M-26 takes the offensive by moving out of the mountains toward larger urban areas.

        August–December: M-26 takes control of more towns in eastern Cuba and begins to negotiate with military leaders in the larger urban areas.

1959   *January 1:* Batista flees the country.

        January 7: Castro's forces take control of Santiago de Cuba and Havana without a fight.

1960   *August:* Castro moves to nationalize all foreign-owned lands and implements significant land reform to break up plantations for redistribution into cooperatives.

1961   *April 15:* United States bombs airfields in Cuba and launches the Bay of Pigs invasion over the next three days.

        April: Cuba proclaims itself socialist.

1965   Castro has largely consolidated power, integrating a number of leftist groups into his government.

Cast of Characters

Fulgencio Batista (1901–1973): President of Cuba or power behind the president from 1930 to 1944 and 1952 to 1959, when the revolution occurred. He had been elected, then retired, then ran for office again. When it was clear that he would lose, he seized power in a coup.

Fidel Castro (1926–): President of Cuba following the revolution in 1959 and remained in power until 2008. Served as a guerrilla role model for many Latin American revolutionaries.

Che Guevara (1928–1967): Argentine Marxist who was active in revolutionary and socialist movements throughout Latin America and Africa. After working in the Jacobo Arbenz government in Guatemala, he moved to Mexico, where he met Fidel Castro and became one of the chief architects of the successful guerrilla revolution in Cuba.

Further Reading

Anderson, John Lee. 1998. *Che Guevara: A Revolutionary Life*. New York: Grove/Atlantic.

Debray, Regis. 1967. *Revolution in the Revolution? Armed Struggle and Political Struggle in Latin America*. New York: Monthly Review Press.

Kampwirth, Karen. 2002. *Women and Guerrilla Movements: Nicaragua, El Salvador, Chiapas, Cuba*. University Park: Pennsylvania State University Press.

Ruiz, Ramon Eduardo. 1968. *Cuba: The Making of a Revolution*. Amherst: University of Massachusetts Press.

Wickham-Crowley, Timothy P. 1992. *Guerrillas and Revolution in Latin America: A Comparative Study of Insurgents and Regimes Since 1956*. Princeton, NJ: Princeton University Press.

The Nicaraguan Revolution (1979)

The revolution in Nicaragua occurred during the height of the Cold War, when much of the world was divided between the Soviet Union and the United States. Nicaragua, a country of about 3 million people in the late 1970s, was the largest Central American country and the most sparsely populated. The prototypical "banana republic," it was occupied by US military forces for much of the first thirty years of the twentieth century. When US forces finally left, it was only after creating a strong National Guard that was dominated by Anastasio Somoza Garcia. Somoza seized power in a coup in 1936 and either he, his heirs, or those controlled by them ruled Nicaragua until the 1979 revolution.

Anastasio Somoza Debayle, the last of the Somoza dynasty, was probably the most brutal and corrupt. He held power from 1967 until 1979 in various ways (he was not president the entire time but was in control of the National Guard, so he effectively retained control of the government). A massive earthquake struck the capital city of Managua on December 23, 1972, killing tens of thousands of people and left hundreds of thousands homeless. As foreign aid poured into the country, Somoza took the opportunity to funnel the money to his supporters, rebuild housing for loyalists, make real estate investments based on the tragedy of the earthquake, and even sell donated reconstruction supplies.

Several prominent groups rose to challenge the Somoza regime. In 1961, the FSLN was formed and remained relatively unknown and isolated in its attempt to start a rural guerrilla war. The FSLN gained international attention when, in 1974, FSLN commandos raided a party attended by many high-level government workers (barely missing the US ambassador). In exchange for the hostages from that incident, Somoza agreed to release FSLN prisoners, pay $5 million, and publicize FSLN propaganda on the state-owned radio and television stations. After the hostages were released, Somoza declared martial law and cracked down on the press. In 1974 the Democratic Union of Liberation (UDEL) was formed by Pedro Joaquin Chamorro, a prominent opposition activist and newspaper editor.

With the election of Jimmy Carter in 1976 as the US president, a shift in US foreign policy occurred, pushing repressive regimes to improve their human rights record or face cuts in foreign aid. Thus, in September 1977, Somoza lifted martial law, and a month later the United States restored military aid to Nicaragua. The lifting of press censorship, however, allowed opposition groups to have a stronger voice in condemning the regime. In October 1977, Los Doce (the Group of Twelve) issued its first public statement calling for the resignation of Somoza and the inclusion of FSLN in provisional government. Los Doce was a group of prominent opposition leaders, business leaders, religious leaders, and leaders of the FSLN. The diverse class backgrounds indicated that a broad coalition of opposition was forming.

A key turning point in mobilizing the opposition was the assassination of opposition leader Pedro Joaquin Chamorro on January 10, 1978. Tens of thousands attended his funeral services, and rioting occurred in Managua. Two weeks later, the democratic opposition party that he had formed called for a general strike to pressure the government into investigating Chamorro's assassination and to remove Somoza from power. The strike had mixed success but was called off on February 5. Throughout the country small communities began to resist the National Guard and from February 20 to 28, a crowd in the Monimbo barrio gathered for a memorial mass for Chamorro. The National Guard tried to break up the demonstration, but the people built barricades, rioted, and held off the National Guard for several days. Using heavy firepower and killing hundreds, the National Guard eventually regained control, but the strike and barricade set a precedent that was followed throughout the next few months.

To maintain control of the uprising, on August 22, FSLN commandos took the Nicaraguan Congress hostage, demanding more prisoner releases and money for their safe return. Two days later Somoza complied, and the next day a month-long general strike supported by the Chamber of Commerce began, indicating the broad opposition to Somoza. In September, the FSLN coordinated a series of attacks on National Guard posts throughout the country, to which Somoza responded with another declaration of martial law. The United States sponsored mediation talks between a coalition of democratic opposition groups (not including the FSLN) and Somoza, but the talks dissolved in mid-November 1978. For the next few months, guerrilla and National Guard forces battled throughout Nicaragua.

In June 1979, the democratic opposition and FSLN coordinated a general strike that effectively shut down most urban commerce. During that month, the FSLN slowly gained control of more cities, battling the National Guard for control of each. On July 17, Somoza resigned and fled to Miami, leaving an interim president who also fled the country two days later. On July 20, the FSLN announced the creation of a revolutionary junta to govern Nicaragua.

Time Line

1936–   Anastasio Somoza Garcia rules Nicaragua with support from the
1956   United States.

1961   Sandinista National Liberation Front (FSLN) is founded by Carlos
         Fonseca Amador, Tomas Borge Martinez, and Silvio Mayorga in
         neighboring Honduras.

1963   *March:* First armed action by FSLN suffers massive defeats, as the
         small movement has no popular support in its raids on government
         strongholds.
         June–October: FSLN retreats, as it is almost completely destroyed
         by National Guard forces.

1967   *February 1:* Anastasio Somoza Debayle "wins" presidential elec-
         tion, taking the office after brother Luis Somoza Debayle turns ill.

1968   Second Council of Latin American Bishops meeting in Medellin,
         Colombia, establishes patterns for Vatican II's implementation in
         Latin America, spawning liberation theology.

1972   *December 23:* An earthquake strikes the center of Managua, de-
         stroying the central area and killing tens of thousands of people.

1974   *November:* Democratic Union of Liberation formed by Pedro
         Joaquin Chamorro.
         December 27: FSLN commandos raid a party with many high-
         level government workers (barely missing US ambassador). So-
         moza releases prisoners, pays $5 million, and publicizes FSLN
         propaganda to secure the return of the hostages. Begins martial
         law period.

1976   *November 8:* Carlos Fonseca, ideological leader of the FSLN, is
         killed in a National Guard attack on his mountain camp.

1977   *September 19:* Martial law and press censorship lifted. In response,
         a month later, US president Jimmy Carter conditionally restores
         military aid.

October 14: Los Doce (the Group of Twelve) issues first public document calling for resignation of Somoza and the inclusion of FSLN in provisional government.

1978   *January 10:* Pedro Joaquin Chamorro is assassinated. Tens of thousands attend funeral services, and rioting occurs in Managua.

January 23: UDEL calls for a general strike to investigate Chamorro's assassination and to remove Somoza from power. The strike is called off on February 5.

February 20–28: The National Guard teargasses a crowd in the Monimbo barrio gathered for a memorial mass for Chamorro. They respond by building barricades, rioting, and holding off the National Guard for several days. Eventually the guard takes over, using heavy firepower and killing hundreds. This spontaneous reaction becomes characteristic of the movement for much of the revolution.

April: Tens of thousands of students strike for a month to get the release of political prisoners.

August 22–24: FSLN commandos take the Nicaraguan Congress hostage. Somoza releases prisoners and pays more money to ensure their release.

August 25: Democratic opposition begins a month-long general strike with support of the Chamber of Commerce. Somoza responds by revoking Chamber's charter and arresting striking business leaders.

September 9: FSLN coordinates a variety of attacks on National Guard posts throughout the country. In response, four days later, Somoza declares martial law.

October: US sponsors mediation talks that break down in mid-November.

1979   *June 4:* Joint Democratic opposition–FSLN general strike begins, shutting down urban commerce.

June: Throughout the month the FSLN advances on a number of cities, battling with the National Guard for control of each. Eventually the balance of control tips toward the FSLN.

July 17: Somoza resigns and flies to Miami. Congress names Francisco Urcuyo interim president. In response, the FSLN continues its advance, and Urcuyo flees two days later. A revolutionary junta takes power on July 20.

Cast of Characters

General Anastasio Somoza Garcia (1896–1956): Leader of the Nicaraguan National Guard in 1933 when US marines left for the last time. He overthrew the president, had himself elected president, and established a dynasty that lasted until the revolution.

Anastasio Samoza Debayle (1925–1980): Garcia's son and the last Somoza to rule Nicaragua. Oversaw twelve years of extreme corruption before being ousted by the FSLN.

Carlos Fonseca (1936–1976): One of the three original founders of the FSLN and its chief ideologue.

Pedro Joaquin Chamorro (1924–1978): Leading prodemocracy dissident and editor of the opposition newspaper *La Prensa*. His assassination in January 1978 sparked the revolutionary situation. Founded coalition group Democratic Union of Liberation (UDEL).

Further Reading

Black, G. 1981. *Triumph of the People: The Sandinista Revolution in Nicaragua*. London: Zed.

Booth, John A. 1982. *The End and the Beginning: The Nicaraguan Revolution*. Boulder: Westview Press.

Borge, Tomas, Carlos Fonseca, Daniel Ortega, Humberto Ortega, and Jaime Wheelock. 1982. *Sandinistas Speak*. Ed. Bruce Marcus. New York: Pathfinder Press.

Parsa, Misagh. 2000. *States, Ideologies, and Social Revolutions: A Comparative Analysis of Iran, Nicaragua, and the Philippines*. Cambridge: Cambridge University Press.

Selbin, Eric. 1993. *Modern Latin American Revolutions*. Boulder, CO: Westview Press.

Wickham-Crowley, Timothy P. 1992. *Guerrillas and Revolution in Latin America: A Comparative Study of Insurgents and Regimes Since 1956*. Princeton, NJ: Princeton University Press.

The Iranian Revolution (1979)

By 1953, Prime Minister Mohammed Mossadeq and the Iranian parliament had been gaining power in relation to the constitutional monarch, the shah Mohammad Reza Pahlavi (*shah* means king, and the individual is typically referred to as the shah). In 1951 Mossadeq had led the nationalization of Iranian oil and was involved in moving funding from the military and the shah toward the country's Health Ministry and the poor. In response to a constitutional crisis in 1953, Mossadeq dissolved the parliament, and the shah dismissed Mossadeq. When Mossadeq supporters took to the streets, the shah fled the country. His military supporters were able to regain control, and the shah returned to create a much more repressive regime centered on his personal rule.

Throughout the 1960s, the shah implemented what he called the White Revolution, a rapid modernization campaign orchestrated by the state. It involved redistributing some land, privatizing government-owned industries, granting suffrage to women, and creating a literacy corps to reduce illiteracy and manage compulsory education. The point of these reforms was to gain support in rural areas as well as to encourage urbanization, where the shah held greater control. The unintended consequence of the reforms was an alienation of the Islamic clergy, who had been large landowners and many of whom disapproved of women's voting and attending school with men. Ayatollah Ruhollah Khomeini, a charismatic member of the clergy, was a vocal voice of opposition to the shah's reforms, focusing particularly on the way the reforms seemed to favor Western influence over traditional Iranian (or Persian) interests. In response to his opposition, the shah jailed and then exiled Khomeini, who fled to Iraq, where he remained a vocal voice of opposition.

Despite the opposition, the reforms were largely successful in modernizing Iran's economy and brought significant economic growth to the country. Oil exports, Iran's biggest export and the primary source of income for the shah, rose from $1 billion in the 1968–1969 period to $20 billion in the 1975–1976 period. The reforms were a failure, however, in terms of creating more widespread support for the shah. Through the 1970s, as the economy expanded, more of the surplus enriched those close to the shah. He became increasingly dependent upon the military and secret police (SAVAK), foreign investors, and the United States. The shah created a one-party state and relied on SAVAK to crush any opposition.

With the election of Jimmy Carter as US president in 1976, the US-Iranian relationship began to change. Carter pushed the shah to reduce the egregious human rights violations in exchange for continued support (the United States bought much of Iran's oil, and Iran used the oil money to buy US military technology). As a result, the shah released more than 300 political prisoners in February 1977, which had the ironic effect of encouraging more pressure for liberalization within Iran.

To try to silence its critics, in early 1978 the government singled out Khomeini (who had called for committees of opposition to be formed in mosques from his exile in Iraq) in a slander campaign. The campaign backfired and by singling out Khomeini, he became the symbolic voice of opposition. Religious students in the seminary city of Qom demonstrated, and at least ten were killed by police forces. This triggered a wave of demonstrations, government repression, and further demonstrations. One of the biggest examples of this cycle occurred on September 8, 1978. The shah had publicly agreed to some political reforms that would give more power to the parliament, then reversed them and declared martial law. This included banning the right to assemble. Some 15,000 people had gathered in Jaleh Square in Tehran unaware of the declaration of martial law. They were met with brutal repression; it is estimated that thousands may have been killed (the official number was eighty-six).

Again, the shah sought to sideline Khomeini and pressured neighboring Iraq to expel him. To the shah's chagrin, the international press greeted Khomeini in Paris and eagerly broadcast his calls for revolution to the world. Khomeini's strategy in opposing the military, the shah's primary support, was not through armed confrontation but through martyrdom. He reasoned that military forces would be ashamed to fire on their own people if they did not pose a threat and that this would encourage military defections. This strategy was combined with workers' strikes that effectively shut off Iran's oil. Throughout November and December of 1978, demonstrations, strikes, and protests increased, and the government effectively failed to respond. Carter indicated that the United States would not intervene to support the shah.

On January 16, 1979, the shah fled the country, hoping to replicate his 1953 coup. Khomeini returned in February and appointed a government of opposition. A battle between pro- and antishah military erupted and by February 11, the opposition forces had largely won. There were many clergy with differing ideas about how the new government should be structured, but Khomeini, because of his popularity in opposing the shah, quickly consolidated power by creating an Islamic Revolutionary Council to oversee government policy while a new government was formed. He also called for a nationwide referendum on whether to establish an Islamic Republic, which passed with a reported 98 percent approval.

After the referendum, two events shaped the outcome of the Iranian Revolution. The first was the US hostage crisis, followed by the war with Iraq. The hostage crisis was set off by the shah's flying to New York City for medical treatment of his terminal cancer in October 1979. More militant youth within Iran viewed this as the beginning of a conspiracy to bring back the shah. As a result, 450 young militants stormed the US embassy in Tehran, taking fifty-three US officials hostage. The event had the effect of radicalizing the regime. The Iran-Iraq War is discussed in Chapter 8.

Time Line

1953   With US help, Prime Minister Mohammed Mossadeq is ousted, and the shah establishes a dictatorship.

1960s   Shah implements a White Revolution of modernization from above.

1963   Ayatollah Khomeini becomes an outspoken critic of the modernization campaign; is jailed and exiled in 1964.

1977   US president Jimmy Carter makes US aid dependent on improved human rights in Iran.

1978   *January 7:* The official press runs a libelous story attacking Khomeini. Angry students and religious leaders protest in the holy city of Qom. Demonstrators were killed, setting off a cycle of antishah violence on each successive fortieth day of Muslim mourning.

February 18: Forty days later, protesters march in many cities to honor the fallen and to protest against the rule of the shah. Violence erupts in Tabriz; more than 100 demonstrators are killed.

March 12: The shah orders 346 prisoners to be released on the 100th anniversary of his father's birth.

March 29: Another fortieth-day memorial takes place, with protests across the nation. Luxury hotels, theaters, and other symbols of the shah are destroyed; security forces intervene, killing many.

August 20: A packed movie theater in Abadan catches fire after its doors are locked; 377 people die. The government blames Islamic Marxists; the shah's opponents accuse SAVAK of setting the fire.

August 27: Prime Minister Jamshid Amouzegar resigns.

September 8: Martial law is imposed in Tehran and other cities. Massive protest breaks out in Tehran; the regime uses tanks, helicopters, and machine guns to crush the protest. One hundred and twenty-one people are killed and 200 are wounded. This day becomes known as Black Friday.

September 24: Under pressure from the shah, Iraq expels Khomeini, who arrives in Paris on October 10.

October 2: Civil service strikes spread throughout Iran.

October 25: The shah releases 1,125 political prisoners.

October 31: Some 37,000 oil workers begin strikes.

November 5: Antishah demonstrators in Tehran set fire to the British Embassy, hundreds of shops, hotels, liquor stores, banks, restaurants, and buses. Ten demonstrators are killed, and the army does little to intervene.

November 6: The prime minister's cabinet resigns and is replaced by a military government. Several newspaper editors are arrested, and censorship is reimposed, prompting a newspaper strike.

November 7: The military government arrests thirty-three persons, including former ministers and the ex-SAVAK chief, on charges of corruption and abuse of power.

December 10: Hundreds of thousands of antishah demonstrators march peacefully. The military government permits the march to stave off bloody clashes.

1979   *January 1:* Shapour Bakhtiar promises parliament that his government will shut off oil to Israel and South Africa, dissolve SAVAK, free political prisoners, and closely cooperate with religious leaders.

January 4: Bakhtiar, named prime minister by the shah, announces his acceptance conditional on the shah's absence.

January 16: The shah leaves Iran.

January 19: More than 1 million pro-Khomeini demonstrators march in Tehran demanding the overthrow of Bakhtiar.

February 1: Khomeini makes a triumphal return, cheered by more than 1 million people in Tehran.

February 3: Khomeini vows to launch a "holy war" against Bakhtiar unless he resigns and makes way for an Islamic republic but stresses that he prefers the situation be resolved peacefully.

February 5: Khomeini names seventy-year-old Mehdi Bazargan as prime minister of his provisional government.

February 9: Air cadets supporting Khomeini battle imperial troops for control of training base. In two days of fighting, 210 are killed and 870 wounded in Tehran.

February 10: Troops return to their barracks and Iran's military commander announces support for Khomeini. Bakhtiar resigns in favor of Bazargan.

March 30–31: Iranians vote on whether Iran should be an Islamic Republic.

November 4: Students in Tehran take a number of officials at the US Embassy hostage. Bazargan resigns as prime minister.

December 2–3: New constitution is approved in referendum.

1980   *March:* Cultural revolution begins with crackdown on media, universities, and various bureaucracies.
September 22: Iraq invades Iran.

Cast of Characters

Shah Mohammad Reza Pahlavi (1919–1980): Leader of Iran from 1941 to 1979. Created a modernization campaign of land reform and women's emancipation as well as the repressive SAVAK (secret police). The shah made Iran into a one-party state in 1975, which allowed him to rule with autocratic power.

Ayatollah Ruhollah Khomeini (1900–1989): First came into political relevance in 1964 when he denounced the shah and after this was one of the shah's most visible opponents. While in exile from Iran he wrote *Guardianship of the Islamic Jurists,* a book that condemned the shah and called for an Islamic theocracy to be put in place. The constitution formed after the revolution made him the supreme leader.

Mehdi Bazargan (1907–1995): Worked as one of the planners of the 1979 Iranian Revolution through his organization, Freedom Movement of Iran, and later served as the interim prime minister. Was more committed to democratic reforms and objected to many proposals of the more conservative religious leaders. Resigned at the end of 1979 in response to the Iranian hostage crisis and continued conflicts with religious authorities.

Shapour Bakhtiar (1914–1991): Iranian politician who was a member of the opposition to the shah. In 1978 he was appointed as prime minister by the shah as a concession to the opponents of the shah's regime, an appointment that Bakhtiar took as a means of preventing a takeover by the militant opposition. He was pushed from power by Khomeini.

Further Reading

Abrahamian, Ervand. 1982. *Iran Between Two Revolutions*. Princeton, NJ: Princeton University Press.

Debashi, Hamid. 1985. *Ideology and Discontent: The Ideological Foundation of the Islamic Revolution in Iran*. New York: New York University Press.

Milani, Mohsen. 1994. *The Making of Iran's Islamic Revolution: From Monarchy to Islamic Republic*. 2nd ed. Boulder, CO: Westview Press.

Parsa, Misagh. 1989. *Social Origins of the Iranian Revolution*. New Brunswick, NJ: Rutgers University Press.

Wright, Robin. 2000. *The Last Great Revolution*. New York: First Vintage Books.

The Philippine Revolution (1986)

The revolution in the Philippines effectively began with the assassination of the opposition politician Benigno Aquino in 1983 and was irreversible once Ferdinand Marcos's pervasive fraud in the 1986 election was made public. The international context of the revolution in the Philippines was the Cold War. The Philippines were a strong US ally in Southeast Asia and hosted the largest US naval and air base outside of the United States. After the loss of Vietnam, the United States buttressed support for any allies in the region, including the Philippines and Indonesia, two countries with active communist insurgencies.

Ferdinand Marcos was elected president of the Philippines in 1965. He won reelection in 1969, under the constitution that allowed only two terms in office. During his second term, he staged an attack on his defense minister, Juan Ponce Enrile, and using this as provocation, declared martial law in 1972 to deal with the threat of the communist insurgency. Although the threat was real, the attack was staged, and Marcos effectively used martial law to quell all opposition and remain in power.

One of the leading voices of opposition was Benigno Aquino, who was jailed for seven years and then allowed to go to the United States for medical treatment. In 1981, Marcos lifted martial law but retained the repressive apparatus he had built, and in the subsequent elections, under an amended constitution, he won reelection. As parliamentary elections drew near, Aquino and other opposition leaders prepared for a coordinated campaign. Upon Aquino's return to the Philippines in 1983, he was assassinated as he stepped off the plane. Marcos was widely viewed as ultimately behind the assassination, and Aquino's funeral spurred hundreds of thousands to take to the streets in mourning and protest.

Within a month, the mourning ceremonies quickly turned into anti-Marcos demonstrations. Over the next two years, the demonstrations increased and became more widespread across groups of society. In addition, the communist insurgency also increased in its effectiveness. The New People's Army (NPA) was waging a guerrilla campaign throughout the Philippine countryside. Marcos responded by increasing military strikes against guerrilla camps and supporters. For all of 1985, an average of fourteen people were killed every day in the fight between the NPA and the military. The United States, which actively supported Marcos, saw his age, his health, his fraudulent elections, the demonstrations, and the insurgency as liabilities that might lead to a crisis that the communists could exploit to come to power. As a result, the United States pressured Marcos to hold elections to gain some legitimacy and to choose a legitimate vice president to succeed him should he die in office.

On November 3, 1985, Marcos announced on US television that an election would be held the following January (though it was pushed back to February). Marcos was sure that he would win the election because the opposition was fractured—there were several viable candidates who would run against him, splitting the opposition vote. On the day before the filing deadline, Corazon Aquino, wife of the slain opposition leader, and Salvador Laurel, leader of the largest opposition political party, agreed, however, to run on a unified ticket (with Aquino as the candidate for president). The ticket unified much of the opposition, and Aquino's presence mobilized Filipinos; the final campaign rally had more than half a million in attendance.

The election was held on February 7, 1986, and it was clear that there was widespread fraud. In anticipation of the fraud, a nongovernmental monitoring organization was created to monitor polling stations and watch the ballots. According to independent exit polling, Aquino was ahead. After a week of ballot tabulation, however, the National Assembly, which was controlled by Marcos, proclaimed Marcos the winner of the presidential election. In response, on February 16, Aquino led a rally during which she organized a nationwide strike and boycott of all companies owned by Marcos and his cronies (which was an extensive list, so pervasive was his corruption). The boycott seemed to be working, and participation in the strike was extensive.

In response to the situation, on February 23, the minister of defense, Juan Ponce Enrile, and Fidel Ramos, a high-ranking officer in the Reform the Army Movement, initiated a coup to remove Marcos. Loyalists found out about the coup, however, and tried to arrest the leaders, who fled to a military base in the middle of Manila. There, they appealed to Manilans to come to their defense and denounced the Marcos regime as fraudulent. The Catholic Church, which had become increasingly active in condemning the repression of the Marcos regime, played a huge role in encouraging Manilans to surround the military base in defense of the defectors by broadcasting the pleas and instructions for nonviolent resistance over Radio Veritas, one of the few independent news sources in Manila.

In an equally important move, the clergy took an active role in organizing the demonstrations outside the base. The protesters prayed and sang hymns and national songs; when the military arrived, the protesters begged them to join the opposition. When faced with nuns, priests, and the whole spectrum of Philippine society, the military forces quickly joined the defectors. For four days Manilans surrounded the base, nonviolently repelling any attempt at capturing the increasing group of defectors. Throughout the protest, Marcos called on loyalists to defend the regime and even ordered planes to try to fire on the base (even though it was surrounded by hundreds of thousands of civilians). The United States quickly pulled support for Marcos and encouraged him to leave.

On February 25, Corazon Aquino was sworn in as president of the Philippines while Ferdinand Marcos fled the country. Under Aquino's tenure, a new constitution was drafted, and significant reforms were made within the political structure, though little social or economic change occurred.

Time Line

1983   *August 21:* Benigno Aquino is assassinated as he returns to the Philippines from his exile in the United States. Over the next ten days, hundreds of thousands participate in various aspects of his funeral ceremonies.

September 9: Candlelight vigil of tens of thousands in memory of Aquino turns into anti-Marcos demonstration.

September 16: First explicitly anti-Marcos demonstration that incorporates business class takes place in Makati business district. This is followed by widespread demonstrations with hundreds of thousands participating.

1984   *May 14:* Legislative and local elections are held amid widespread violence.

August 21: Hundreds of thousands march on anniversary of Aquino's assassination.

1985   *November 3:* Marcos announces the election to be held in January 1986 (this is later pushed back to February).

December 11: Filing deadline for candidates in presidential election. Aquino and Laurel agree to run on a unified ticket.

1986   *February 7:* Presidential elections begin.

February 15: The National Assembly proclaims Marcos the winner of the presidential election.

February 16: Corazon Aquino begins nationwide strike and boycott.

February 22: Military officers Juan Ponce Enrile and Fidel Ramos attempt a coup, then retreat to Camps Crame and Aguinaldo and call for Marcos to resign.

February 23: Thousands of Manilans surround the military camps to protect the defectors from the military. The crowds are able to keep the military from firing on the defectors and to erode Marcos's power base in the armed forces.

February 25: Aquino is sworn in as president of the Philippines. Marcos flies to Clark Air Base and then to Hawaii.

Cast of Characters

Ferdinand Marcos (1917–1989): President of the Philippines who remained in power through fraudulent elections and amassed enormous personal wealth despite the poverty of his country.

Benigno Aquino (1932–1983): Opposition politician who served as senator but was arrested under martial law, then fled the country for surgery in the United States. Upon his return he was assassinated, sparking the revolutionary situation in the Philippines.

Corazon Aquino (1933–2009): Widowed wife of Benigno Aquino and eventual president of the Philippines after the revolution.

Salvador Laurel (1928–2004): Leader of democratic opposition political party; ran as vice president with Corazon Aquino against Ferdinand Marcos in the 1986 snap election.

Cardinal Jaime Sin (1928–2005): Archbishop of Manila, the country's largest diocese, who was active in promoting peaceful alternatives to the brewing civil war in the Philippines. Was instrumental in condemning the Aquino assassination and electoral fraud and in bringing together Aquino and Laurel for a unified democratic opposition party as well as bringing the masses to the streets.

Juan Ponce Enrile (1924–): Defense minister of the Philippine Army. Defected with Fidel Ramos to spur the velvet revolution.

Fidel Ramos (1928–): Lieutenant general in Philippine Army. Defected with Juan Ponce Enrile to spur the velvet revolution.

Further Reading

Chapman, William. 1987. *Inside the Philippine Revolution*. New York: W. W. Norton.

Johnson, Bryan. 1987. *Four Days of Courage: The Untold Story of the People Who Brought Marcos Down*. New York: Free Press.

Jones, Gregg R. 1989. *Red Revolution: Inside the Philippine Guerrilla Movement*. Boulder, CO: Westview Press.

Kessler, Richard J. 1989. *Rebellion and Repression in the Philippines*. New Haven, CT: Yale University Press.

Wright, Martin, ed. 1988. *Revolution in the Philippines? A Keesing's Special Reports*. Chicago: St. James Press.

The Tiananmen Square Prodemocracy Movement (1989)

One way to understand what is truly relevant in revolution is to also look at failed revolutionary movements. The process of revolution in the successful cases looked very similar to what was happening in China in 1989, up to the point at which the regime cracked down on the dissidents and ended the revolutionary situation.

The roots of the 1989 student demonstrations in Tiananmen Square go back to the years just after the fall of the Qing dynasty and the end of World War I. The new and unstable republic had been formed with the hope that a modern government would rid all vestiges of foreign domination. The terms of the Treaty of Versailles made clear that that was not to be the case, as Japan was given control over Shandong, a historically Chinese area controlled by Germany. In response, students in Beijing set out a list of demands, and 3,000 protested the government on May 4, 1919. The government arrested many of the protesters, which spurred further demonstrations that were supported by many of those dissatisfied with the government, and the center of dissent moved from Beijing to Shanghai, the business capital of China. The government eventually conceded, released the students, and did not sign the Treaty of Versailles; they were unable to stop Japanese occupation of Shandong, however.

The May 4th Movement, as it came to be known, was a symbol for student activism to hold the government accountable. The tradition was expressed again in 1978, when students in Beijing pushed the government to include political reforms in its modernization campaign (by painting large posters that were hung in Beijing on what came to be known as the democracy wall). One of the key leaders of the Communist Party who was associated with the democracy wall was Hu Yaobang, once viewed as a possible successor to Deng Xiaoping (the successor to Mao Zedong and architect of China's rapid economic reforms).

The 1989 Tiananmen Square prodemocracy movement was directly tied to the democracy wall movement, as it began with the death of Hu on April 15, 1989. Students took the opportunity of Hu's death to stage demonstrations. As Hu was one of the Communist Party's central figures, the government did not want to stop commemoration gatherings; the students used the gatherings, however, as a platform for calling for democratic reforms. On April 18, thousands of students staged a sit-in at the Great Hall of the People, the seat of government, to demand greater democracy, a free press, and more money for education. As police actively broke up the demonstrations, they began to spread to other cities as well. The police repression led to a student boycott that also spread nationwide.

In an attempt to stop the protests, an editorial in the *People's Daily* condemned the student demonstrations, painting them as aimed at overthrowing the government and socialist system. This enraged the students, who saw themselves as advocating reforms that would make the government better; they even used pictures of Mao as an ideal figure who was not corrupt, as the current government had become. The following day, more than 150,000 students and supporters illegally filled Tiananmen Square. In response to the protests, the official Communist Party newspaper published an overview of the two weeks of protests to pacify students, and government officials met with student leaders to discuss their demands.

On May 4, 1989, the seventieth anniversary of the first student demonstration in Tiananmen Square, hundreds of thousands of students marched from all over Beijing to Tiananmen, which was officially closed. To encourage pressure on reforming the government, 1,000 Chinese students began a hunger strike in Tiananmen Square, marking the beginning of the continuous occupation of the square. It was no coincidence that this began the day before Mikhail Gorbachev was scheduled to arrive. Welcoming ceremonies of foreign dignitaries traditionally take place in Tiananmen, and Gorbachev's visit was the first visit of a Soviet premier since a chill in Sino-Soviet relations in the early 1960s. The students in Tiananmen cheered Gorbachev's efforts at political opening in the Soviet Union.

By May 17, more than one million people crowded the square in support of the fasting students, with similar fasts and demonstrations occurring throughout China. In response, troops from the People's Liberation Army were called in. Generals stationed in Beijing said they would not suppress the demonstrations. On May 20, for the first time since the civil war, martial law was declared in Beijing; military trucks were unable to get to the heart of the city, however, because of roadblocks set up by students and their supporters. The protests continued while the government appeared to do little.

Finally, on June 3, the decision was made to end the demonstrations. An internal split between reformists and conservatives was decided in favor of the conservatives, led by Deng Xiaoping (though he held no formal office within the party). Around 9 p.m. troops from outside of Beijing began to enter the city. When they met roadblocks, they violently dispersed the crowd (including opening fire). By 2 a.m. the next morning, the troops arrived at Tiananmen Square and were firing on crowds nearby. Two hours later, the troops had negotiated an orderly exit with the students, who marched back to their schools. The official death toll of the crackdown was 241, though reliable estimates range from 400 to 800. Over the next few days, troops completely dominated Beijing, and police and military forces arrested hundreds accused of attacking soldiers as well as leaders of independent student and worker associations. The following week, severe censorship was imposed and thousands more were arrested throughout China.

Chinese repression became more systematic later in June. Given that students began the movement, the government ordered colleges to set up new political education programs so that students would learn to "love socialism and love the army" and accept official condemnation of the protests. The media liberalization that allowed some coverage of the protests was repealed, and Chinese news organizations were told to forget about press freedom and concentrate on "correct" Marxist ideas. The summer ended with the requirement that all government employees who graduated from college in 1985 or later work one to two years in "grassroots units" to improve their political understanding to avoid repeated future misconceptions.

Time Line

1989   *April 15:* Hu Yaobang dies.

April 17: Thousands of students march in Beijing and Shanghai.

April 18–21: Thousands of students demonstrate in Beijing and other cities; some of the demonstrations are broken up by police. Students stage a sit-in at the Great Hall of the People, the seat of government, to demand greater democracy, a free press, and more money for education.

April 24: Students across China begin an indefinite school boycott.

April 26: Tens of thousands of students march, collect money for their movement, create posters, and give public speeches—all of which are illegal without state permission. An editorial in the *People's Daily* condemns the student demonstrations, painting them as aimed at overthrowing the government and socialist system.

April 27: More than 150,000 students and supporters cross police lines to fill Tiananmen Square.

April 28: The official Communist Party newspaper publishes an overview of the two weeks of protests to pacify students.

April 29: Students and high-level government officials meet to discuss the past two weeks.

May 4: On the seventieth anniversary of the first student demonstration in Tiananmen Square, hundreds of thousands of students march from all over Beijing to Tiananmen, which is officially closed. Smaller marches take place in many other cities, and journalists begin a campaign for freedom.

May 12: The party agrees to hold talks with an independent student group on the student demands for sweeping democratic reforms and an end to official corruption.

May 13: About 1,000 Chinese students began a hunger strike in Tiananmen Square; their supporters refuse to leave, beginning the occupation of the square. Thousands flock to their support over the next few days.

May 15: Mikhail Gorbachev arrives; his welcoming ceremonies are moved from Tiananmen to the airport.

May 17: More than one million people crowd the square in support of the fasting students. Similar fasts and demonstrations occur throughout China.

May 18: Troops begin to arrive from outside of Beijing as generals stationed in Beijing say they will not suppress the demonstrations.

May 20: Martial law is declared in Beijing. Military trucks are forced to turn around when students and supporters block their way into Beijing.

May 24: China ends satellite broadcasts, eliminating foreign reporting.

June 3: Troops emerge from the Great Hall of the People and are surrounded by protesters. They disperse them with tear gas and clubs. Around 9 p.m. troops begin to enter the city and are met with roadblocks. They violently disperse the crowd (including opening fire).

June 4: By 2 a.m. troops have arrived at Tiananmen Square and are firing on crowds nearby. By 3 a.m., they have the square surrounded. At 5 a.m. the students make an orderly retreat from the square. Over the next few days, troops completely dominate Beijing.

June 7: The troops who cleared the square leave central Beijing, firing at random as they leave.

June 10: Chinese news announces the arrest of 400 people accused of attacks on soldiers enforcing martial law, including several leaders of independent student and worker associations.

June 15: The first death sentences are handed down for instigating riots. The first executions are held June 21.

Cast of Characters

Deng Xiaoping (1904–1997): Most powerful leader in China even though the highest-ranking position he held during the prodemocracy movement was chairman of the Central Military Commission of the Communist Party. Deng was purged twice by radicals during the 1966–1976 Cultural Revolution and then staged a comeback that transformed China from a country dominated by ideological battles into one with pragmatic, market-oriented economic policies.

Hu Yaobang (1915–1989): Member of the Central Committee that headed the Chinese Communist Party. Had been dismissed as party general secretary (the hand-picked successor to Deng) in 1987 for not doing enough to stop democratization protests during a student movement. His death was an opportunity for students to conduct and participate in public mourning ceremonies during which they could express opposition to the conservative wing of the party and support for the reformists that Hu represented.

Zhao Ziyang (1919–2005): General secretary of the Chinese Communist Party after 1987 (following Hu Yaobang) and had been the nation's leading advocate of rapid economic reforms. Was in line to replace Deng as behind-the-scenes leader but was purged for sympathizing with the students.

Jiang Zemin (1926–): Enlarged Politburo chose him as Zhao Ziyang's successor as party general secretary in June 1989. Implemented many of the repressive actions that halted the prodemocracy movement.

Further Reading

Calhoun, Craig. 1994. *Neither Gods nor Emperors: Students and the Struggle for Democracy in China*. Berkeley: University of California Press.
Cheng, Chu-yüan. 1990. *Behind the Tiananmen Massacre: Social, Political, and Economic Ferment in China*. Boulder, CO: Westview Press.
Hicks, George, ed. 1990. *The Broken Mirror: China After Tiananmen*. Chicago: St. James Press.

Liang, Zhang, Andrew J. Nathan, and Perry Link, eds. 2001. *The Tiananmen Papers*. New York: PublicAffairs.

Wasserstrom, Jeffrey N. 1991. *Student Protests in Twentieth-Century China: The View from Shanghai*. Stanford, CA: Stanford University Press.

Wasserstrom, Jeffrey N., and Elizabeth J. Perry, eds. 1994. *Popular Protests and Political Culture in Modern China*. 2nd ed. Boulder, CO: Westview Press.

The South African Revolution (1994)

South Africa is unique among cases of revolution for many reasons: it was already an independent democracy, and yet the antiapartheid movement was very similar to other antidictatorial democratic movements; the revolution forced the end of a government, and yet the government was a key actor in the transition to universal suffrage.

The history of South Africa is a history of new peoples coming into the area. A variety of African groups moved into the area in the twelve centuries before European explorers arrived. In 1652, the Dutch East India Company founded a colony on the Cape of Good Hope and brought Dutch settlers to the region. English settlers came 100 years later, pushing the Dutch away from the coastal areas. The British gained control over the region following the Boer War (1899–1902; the Boers, who spoke Afrikaans, were the ancestors of the Dutch) after the discovery of diamonds and gold. During British control, many South Asians were brought into the area as laborers. Thus, when South Africa was granted dominion status (autonomy within the British Empire), there were four relatively distinct groups of people: white (including British and Afrikaners), black (encompassing the various African groups indigenous to the region), Indian or South Asian, and colored (descendants of the offspring of both Africans and Europeans). As the whites implemented legal domination over the others, resistance began to arise. In January 1912, the South African Native National Congress (which later became the African National Congress, or ANC) was formed to petition the government for reforms.

In 1948 the National Party, an Afrikaner-dominated political party, won national elections and began to implement white domination under a system called apartheid. Over the next decade, the apartheid government passed laws forbidding mixed marriages, required all citizens to be registered in one of the four racial categories, organized land ownership by race, established Bantustans or homelands for blacks and required that they live on the marginal lands of South Africa (which constituted only 13 percent of the landmass of South Africa), created separate educational systems, and ensured that only whites could vote. Resistance to the apartheid system became more vocal from more sources. Leadership of the ANC became more militant in the late 1940s and worked with other groups, including the Communist Party and the Indian Congress, to press for freedoms. The government reaction to these actions was typically brutal.

A more moderate Pan African Congress (PAC) organized a pass law demonstration in 1960 in Sharpeville. (Pass laws required blacks to carry identification that listed their legal residence and place of work or school.) South African police opened fire on the demonstrators, killing 69 and wounding another 200. In response to this and other crackdowns on demonstrations, more militant wings formed from traditional groups to engage in sabotage, including Umkhonto we Sizwe or "Spear of the Nation," associated with the ANC, and the PAC's Azanian People's Liberation Army. As a result of this increased militancy, the government imprisoned many leaders in the 1960s (including Nelson Mandela) and banned both the ANC and PAC. With much of this leadership in prison, the locus of resistance shifted to union activity. Throughout most of the 1960s and 1970s, unions and strikes were illegal, but they had become increasingly effective at pressing for moderate economic reforms. This energized the nonviolent movement to press for more radical changes. In 1976, 20,000 students marched in Soweto to protest the separate educational system and the requirement that their classes be taught in Afrikaans. Again the government cracked down, killing more than 1,000 students. The protests and repression gained increasing international attention.

As a result of international pressure, in 1983 the government drafted a new constitution that provided separate parliaments for each racial group, except for blacks, who were denied suffrage. Blacks took to the streets in the townships (because blacks were supposed to live in Bantustans but were also needed for work in the cities, large illegal townships had risen up around the periphery of many urban areas). In 1984, the South African military joined police in putting down the demonstrations in the townships, and thus the repression became even more brutal. The exiled ANC called for an international boycott of South Africa while at the same time organizing guerrilla training in neighboring African countries to lead sabotage attacks in South Africa. The highly professionalized and well-equipped South African Defense Force (SADF) followed the guerrillas into other countries and killed many of them. In this context a stalemate emerged. Blacks could not militarily defeat the SADF and did not ever advocate a bloody civil war, but the National Party could not maintain control given the international pressure and domestic turmoil.

During the late 1980s, clandestine contacts between ANC and National Party leaders began to discuss a future for South Africa. In September 1989, F. W. de Klerk (a slightly more moderate National Party candidate) was elected president of South Africa. The new president acknowledged that the National Party could not continue the apartheid system as it had in the past.

He intended a gradual evolution of "the nation's political system from the situation of white dominance to one that would involve wider power sharing among the country's designated racial groups," but "the evolutionary transformation he foresaw would not permit the possibility of indigenous African majority rule" (DeFronzo 2007: 386). De Klerk began to relax some of the strict segregation laws, but much of this was cosmetic. Of more importance was the fact that within a year he had removed the ban on the ANC and Communist Party and freed many political prisoners, including Nelson Mandela.

Violence escalated as talks about the future of South Africa continued in fits and starts. Some negotiations included just the major parties (including the government, ANC, PAC, and Inkatha, a Zulu-nationalist party), others were bilateral negotiations, and still others included a multiparty forum with more than twenty-six parties and organizations. As the negotiations continued, so did the boycotts, strikes, and demonstrations as well as government repression in terms of disappearances, murders, and crackdowns. Violence among black groups also increased as Inkatha attacked the ANC, often with the complicity of police forces.

The groups involved in the negotiations finally agreed to an interim constitution, bill of rights, scheduled elections, and an executive council to run the government from the end of 1993 until a new government was elected. The first fully democratic elections were held April 26–29, 1994, and the ANC won 62.5 percent of the vote, with Nelson Mandela elected president. The interim constitution was in effect until May 8, 1996, when a new constitution was adopted by the legislative assembly, though it retained the main features of the interim constitution and, most important, retained the multiracial composition of the legislative assembly.

Time Line

1948   Policy of apartheid is adopted when National Party wins elections.

1952   ANC joins with others to begin passive resistance campaign.

1959   PAC is founded.

1960   *March 21:* Sharpeville massacre occurs as state represses a protest of the pass laws.

1961   *May 31:* South Africa becomes an independent republic.

December 16: First sabotage acts by ANC's armed wing, Spear of the Nation.

1964   Riviona trials in which ANC leader Nelson Mandela and others are sentenced to life in prison for guerrilla activity.

1976   *June 16:* Soweto uprising in which more than twenty students are killed as they protest the apartheid education system.

1983   Tricameral reforms creates a white, colored, and Indian parliament (blacks would still not be represented).

1984–   Township revolts spur a declaration of state of emergency.
1989

1987   Strike by 250,000 African mine workers.

1989   F. W. de Klerk succeeds P. W. Botha as president. Meets Mandela. Public facilities desegregated. Many ANC activists freed.

1990   *February:* De Klerk lifts the ban on the ANC.
February 11: Mandela is released after twenty-seven years in prison.

1991   Start of multiparty talks. Repeal of remaining apartheid laws.

1992   *March:* White-only referendum held to determine whether talks on a new constitution should continue. Whites vote 68 percent in favor of continued negotiations.

1993   Interim constitution.

1994   *April 27:* Nelson Mandela is elected president as ANC wins 62 percent of the vote.

1996   Truth and Reconciliation Commission, chaired by Archbishop Desmond Tutu, begins hearings on human rights crimes committed by the former government and liberation movements during apartheid.
Parliament adopts new constitution.

Cast of Characters

Robert Sobukwe (1924–1978): Political activist. Originally with the ANC, but in 1959 founded the PAC. Arrested in conjunction with pass law protests and jailed for nine years.

Nelson Mandela (1918–): First president of South Africa in multiracial elections and leader of ANC opposition during apartheid. Arrested at the Rivonia trials in 1963. Shared the 1993 Nobel Peace Prize with F. W. de Klerk for their efforts to end apartheid.

Desmond Tutu (1931–): First black South African Anglican archbishop of Cape Town. He was a vocal activist for nonviolent resistance and took part in calming the Soweto riots. Received the Nobel Peace Prize in 1984 for his stance on nonviolence and headed the Truth and Reconciliation Commission after apartheid ended.

F. W. de Klerk (1936–): Last president of South Africa under apartheid and leader of the National Party. Shared the 1993 Nobel Peace Prize with Nelson Mandela for their efforts to end apartheid. Served as deputy president to Nelson Mandela from 1994 until 1996.

Further Reading

Frankel, Philip, Noam Pines, and Mark Swilling, eds. 1988. *State, Resistance, and Change in South Africa*. London: Croom Helm.

Grundy, Kenneth W. 1993. "South Africa's Tortuous Transition." *Current History* 92 (May): 229–233.

Gurney, Christabel. 2000. "'A Great Cause': The Origins of the Anti-Apartheid Movement, June 1959–March 1960." *Journal of Southern African Studies* 26, no. 1 (March): 123–144.

Lawson, George. 2005. *Negotiated Revolutions: The Czech Republic, South Africa, and Chile*. Burlington, VT: Ashgate Publishing.

Marias, Hein. 1998. *South Africa, Limits to Change: The Political Economy of Transformation*. Cape Town, South Africa: University of Cape Town Press.

Mermelstein, David, ed. 1987. *The Anti-Apartheid Reader: The Struggle Against White Racist Rule in South Africa*. New York: Grove Press.

Sommer, Henrik. 1996. "From Apartheid to Democracy: Patterns of Violent and Nonviolent Direct Action in South Africa, 1984–1994." *Africa Today* 43, no. 1: 53–76.

Wood, Elizabeth. 2000. *Forging Democracy from Below: Insurgent Transitions in South Africa and El Salvador.* Cambridge, MA: Cambridge University Press.

The Rwandan Revolution (1994)

Most westerners know Rwanda because of the genocide that occurred there in 1994. The magnitude of the atrocities masks the fact that the genocide occurred within the context of a revolutionary situation. In 1990, Rwanda had a population of 7.5 million people packed into a small country, giving it the highest population density in Africa. There are two primary ethnic groups in Rwanda: the Hutus (comprising 85 percent of the population) and Tutsis (15 percent). This ethnic balance is rather unique in Africa, because it is common to have dozens of ethnic groups living in the same country and because the two groups live intermingled with no separate historical homeland.

Historians note that before the colonial era the relationships between the two groups were rather peaceful and the distinctions slight. The colonial era polarized the differences when Belgium gained control of what was then known as Ruanda-Urundi in 1923 after World War I. The Belgians supported a Tutsi monarchy through whom they ruled. They also eliminated a variety of local political positions that had mostly been occupied by Hutus, beginning the process of widespread political marginalization of the Hutu majority. In 1935, Belgium began labeling ethnic groups on identification cards, a process that helped legitimize and even bureaucratize ethnic distinctions that became a key factor in the conflicts over the rest of the century. Hutu resistance became organized in 1957, and a peasant revolt in 1959 fueled the decolonization process.

When Rwanda became independent in 1962, there was a complete reversal of ethnic power, with little other changes. "A centralized Tutsi monarchy had become an equally elitist Hutu-led republic . . . a Tutsi social system that had ingested the beliefs of the European colonists on their racial superiority and right to rule became a Hutu majoritarian state that regarded the Tutsi as foreign invaders who had colonized the state in an earlier period" (Adelman 1998: 437). Upon independence, Hutu violence against Tutsis was severe, with hundreds of thousands of refugees and tens of thousands of Tutsis killed. The refugees fled to neighboring Burundi, Zaire, Uganda, and Tanzania. In 1973, when tensions flared again and there were renewed anti-Tutsi riots, defense minister Juvenal Habyarimana seized power. With a new constitution, Habyarimana remained in power as president until the revolution in 1994.

During Habyarimana's rule, Tutsi persecution declined significantly, but he never allowed refugee repatriation. As his tenure deepened, his government became more corrupt and opposition became more vocal, even within the Hutus. At the same time, Tutsis who had fled to Uganda had been instrumental in helping Yoweri Museveni seize power in 1986. The refugees, though active in the Ugandan military, remained a distinct refugee population, pushing for repatriation. On October 1, 1990, several of these Tutsi refugees within the military "deserted and invaded Rwanda as the Rwandese Patriotic Army (RPA), the militant wing of the Rwandese Patriotic Front (RPF)" (Adelman 1998: 437).

The Rwandan civil war was fought between the RPF and the Rwandan government from September 30, 1990, to July 19, 1994. The fighting of the civil war was primarily between the Hutu government forces (including the presidential guard and army) and the Tutsi-dominated RPF. Throughout the last year of the war, radio stations of both sides called for extreme brutality and violence against the opposing group. An example of the type of propaganda by both sides is illustrated in a news report in March of 1994:

> At FM 106, RTLM radio is broadcasting what passes in Rwanda for political commentary:
> "You cockroaches [a common characterization of Tutsis] must know you are made of flesh! We won't let you kill! We will kill you!"
> At 6200 on your shortwave dial, Radio Muhabura, appropriately named after a local volcano, is thundering back:
> "Habyarimana (the president) never understands if you do not use weapons! Only weapons and guns make him understand!" (Mugabo 1994)

On August 4, 1993, the Arusha Peace Accords were signed, which outlined power sharing with Tutsi forces, "the rule of law, the role of the president, a transition process to democracy, and integration of the armed forces" (Adelman 1998: 438). In response to these concessions, Hutu extremists formed the Coalition for the Defense of the Republic (CDR). Under the guise of mobilization in response to rebel activity, the CDR armed and trained Interhamwe ("those who fight together") militia. It was this group that orchestrated and carried out the mass killings that surpassed the rate at which Nazis killed Jews during World War II (Waller 2007: 225).

Hutu extremists allegedly assassinated the president by shooting down his plane on April 6, 1994. This began the genocide during which the CDR organized the mass killing of Tutsis and moderate Hutus by the Interhamwe militia but also included the retaliatory violence that occurred as the RPF gained the upper hand in the civil war. In the span of less than four months, it is estimated that 800,000 people were killed within Rwanda. The genocide ended July 19, 1994, when the RPF took control.

The international context of the Rwandan Revolution did little to restrain the violence that occurred. US and UN forces had been attacked during a nation-building UN mission in Somalia in October of 1993 and were in the process of pulling out of the relief operation when the genocide occurred. During the genocide itself, the United Nations sent in an initial peacekeeping force of 2,500 and then deliberated for weeks about their role before reducing the level of troops by 90 percent.

Time Line

1923 Belgium gains control of Ruanda-Urundi.

1935 Belgium begins labeling ethnic groups on identification cards.

1957 Hutu resistance becomes organized.

1959 Peasant revolt fuels the decolonization process.

1962 Rwanda becomes independent.

1973 Amid anti-Tutsi riots, defense minister Juvenal Habyarimana seizes power.

1986 Tutsis who had fled to Uganda are instrumental in helping Yoweri Museveni seize power.

1990 *October 1:* RPF, led by Paul Kagame, invades Rwanda, beginning four-year civil war.

1993 *August 4:* Arusha Peace Accords are signed between government and RPF.

October: UN and US troops take on casualties in Somalia and begin withdrawal of peacekeeping mission.

1994 *April 6:* President Habyarimana is assassinated when his plane is shot down. *Interhamwe* militia begin genocide.

July 19: RPF takes control of Rwanda, ending the genocide.

Kagame installs Pasteur Bizimungu, a Hutu, as president (he is deposed in 2000, and Kagame assumes power when Bizimungu becomes overly critical of the government).

Cast of Characters

Juvenal Habyarimana (1937–1994): While serving as defense minister in Rwanda, led a coup overthrowing the president in 1973. He remained in power as president until 1994, when he was assassinated, sparking the genocide.

Yoweri Museveni (1944–): An officer in the Ugandan military who fought against Idi Amin and then Milton Obote, whom he overthrew and replaced as president.

Paul Kagame (1957–): Tutsi who fled persecution in Rwanda. Became head of military intelligence in the Ugandan military, then formed the RPF and led the guerrilla war against the Rwandan government. Installed himself as president in 2000 and won democratic elections in 2003.

Further Reading

Dallaire, Roméo, Brent Beardsley, and Samantha Power. 2005. *Shake Hands with the Devil: The Failure of Humanity in Rwanda.* New York: Carroll and Graf Publishers.

Destexhe, Alain. 1995. *Rwanda and Genocide in the Twentieth Century.* London: Pluto Press.

Melvern, Linda. 2004. *Conspiracy to Murder: The Rwandan Genocide.* New York: Verso.

Prunier, Gérard. 1995. *The Rwanda Crisis: History of a Genocide.* New York: Columbia University Press.

The Serbian Revolution (2001)

Slobodan Milosevic was a high-ranking member in the Communist Party of Serbia and orchestrated significant reforms throughout the late 1980s. With the fall of communism in Eastern Europe, he was elected president of Serbia within the Yugoslav federation. Slovenia, Macedonia, Croatia, and Bosnia-Herzegovina all seceded from the union (the first three in 1991; Bosnia-Herzegovina in 1992), each with increasingly brutal resistance from Serbia, led by Milosevic. In 1992, Yugoslavia became the Federal Republic of Yugoslavia (with Vojvodina, Kosovo, Montenegro, and Serbia as the constituent republics).

In 1996, a coalition of opposition political parties won a clear victory in Serbian municipal elections, but Milosevic refused to acknowledge his party's defeat. A nonviolent campaign eventually forced Milosevic to allow the opposition to be seated. The broad coalition that had formed in opposition to Milosevic quickly dissolved, and politics returned to normal, with Milosevic dominating the political arena. Shortly thereafter (July 1997), owing to term limits, Milosevic stepped down as president of Serbia and was elected president of the Federal Republic of Yugoslavia. As president, he ordered military forces to quell an independence movement in Kosovo that eventually led to a NATO bombing campaign in Montenegro and Serbia. After the seventy-eight-day bombing campaign, Milosevic agreed to limited autonomy for Kosovo.

Prior to the bombing campaign, on October 10, 1998, in response to repressive university and media laws introduced earlier that year, a group of students from the University of Belgrade formed a group called Otpor, Serbian for "resistance." Building on the success and analyzing the mistakes of the 1996–1997 nonviolent campaign, they created an innovative organization that called for the removal of Milosevic and the establishment of democracy and the rule of law. Otpor's strategy was a mixture of nonviolent tactics derived from Gene Sharp and a kind of cheerful insolence, methodically mocking the state's power and renouncing any ambition to political office themselves (1984). Steve York commented that

> every nonviolent movement has as its first obstacle the problem of overcoming fear. The *Otpor* kids were brave. They expected to be arrested, but they prepared for arrest with all sorts of publicity stunts and by training their activists how to behave when interrogated, by recruiting lawyers to help, by building solidarity. They calculated that their arrests, combined with their use of humor and ridicule, if sustained long enough, would persuade ordinary people to overcome their fear. . . .

[Some of the tactics Otpor utilized included rock concerts,] guerrilla
theatre in the streets, a lunar eclipse observation featuring the gradual
obliteration of Milosevic's image, a New Year's Eve party in which the
year 2000 was rung in with the names and pictures of those who were
killed in Milosevic's wars. . . . In the spring of 2000, with scheduled elections a year away, *Otpor* mobilized its national network, using neighborhood kids as organizers, building an email network, distributing leaflets,
drafting quick response plans to meet the repression and arrests which
they expected. Increasingly threatened by *Otpor's* successes, the state information minister went on national television to declare Otpor a terrorist
organization. *Otpor* responded by sending out thousands of clean-cut kids,
well-known in their communities, wearing T-shirts with the words: "*Otpor*
Terrorist." (York and Zimmerman 2008)

Milosevic called for early elections to undermine and split the growing
opposition. This actually encouraged a coalition of opposition around a single candidate, Vojislav Kostunica. The coalition, fueled by Otpor's slogan—
"otov Je,"or "He's Finished!"—grew astronomically. It also organized the
training of 30,000 volunteer election monitors assigned to some 10,000
polling places to prevent fraud. By the end of election day, the independent
monitors were able to show that Kostunica had won. Milosevic-dominated
government tallies indicated that a runoff was necessary because neither
candidate had won a majority of the vote.

In response, Kostunica called for a general strike. The opposition gained
support from much of Serb society, including workers, police, and the students who had begun the opposition campaign. "Ten days after the election,
hundreds of thousands of Serbs—miners, farmers, men and women from
all walks of life—converged angrily on the capital, in convoys that clogged
the highways in every direction" (York and Zimmerman 2008). The opposition had worked with police to ensure that the protests were nonviolent but
not repressed. Unable to shut down the demonstrations, on October 6, 2000,
Milosevic conceded defeat and stepped down. Six months later, Milosevic
was arrested and later extradited to The Hague by the International Criminal Tribunal for the Former Yugoslavia for crimes against humanity, war
crimes, and genocide for his role during the wars in Croatia, Bosnia, and
Kosovo. His trial began February 12, 2002, but it ended without a convic-
tion, as he died of a heart attack while in custody five years later.

Time Line

1989   Slobodan Milosevic becomes president of Serbia.

1991   Slovenia, Macedonia, and Croatia break away from Yugoslavia.

1992   Bosnia-Herzegovina breaks away from Yugoslavia.

Yugoslavia becomes the Federal Republic of Yugoslavia.

1996   In Kosovo, the Kosovo Liberation Army (KLA) begins attacking Serbian police.

Opposition coalition clearly wins municipal elections, but Milosevic refuses to acknowledge defeat. For eighty-eight days, nonviolent protests bring Serbia to a halt, forcing Milosevic to grant the opposition their victory.

1997   *July:* Milosevic is elected president of Yugoslavia.

1998   *March:* Milosevic sends troops to Kosovo; KLA resistance meets the Serb troops.

October: Government passes repressive media restrictions and laws that affect university students.

October 10: Otpor is formed in response to new laws.

1999   *March 24:* Peace talks collapse; NATO launches airstrikes throughout Serbia for seventy-eight days.

June 9: UN negotiates a peace agreement between Serbs and KLA.

May: Milosevic is indicted for war crimes.

2000   *July 6:* Parliament agrees to change the constitution, allowing Milosevic to run for another term.

July 27: Government calls early elections for September.

August: Opposition coalesces in Democratic Opposition of Serbia (DOS) to elect consensus candidate Vojislav Kostunica

September 24: Federal presidential elections are held; Kostunica wins, but Milosevic calls for a recount and refuses to release the results.

September 29: Campaign of strikes and civil disobedience against the government begins with miners who supply most of Serbia's electricity.

October 5: More than one million people participate in strike and demonstrations in Belgrade, occupying government buildings and working with police to allow the protest to continue peacefully.

October 6: Milosevic resigns.

October 7: Kostunica is sworn in as president.

2001   *April 1:* Milosevic is arrested and handed over to international
        criminal tribunal.

Cast of Characters

Slobodan Milosevic (1941–2006): President of Serbia and then of Yugo-
    slavia. Under his tenure, Yugoslavia broke up into its constituent re-
    publics, and Serbia played a pivotal role in the brutal civil wars
    associated with that. Was overthrown in a nonviolent revolution.

Vojislav Kostunica (1944–): A law professor who was fired for criticizing
    the president (Josip Tito) and went on to found the Democratic Party of
    Serbia in 1992. Was the coalition candidate, opposed Milosevic, and
    won the election that ousted him.

Further Reading

Daalder, Ivo H. 2000. *Winning Ugly: NATO's War to Save Kosovo.* Wash-
    ington, DC: Brookings Institution Press.
Sell, Louis. 2002. *Slobodan Milosevic and the Destruction of Yugoslavia.*
    Durham, NC: Duke University Press.
Welton, Neva, and Linda Wolf. 2001. *Global Uprising: Confronting the
    Tyrannies of the 21st Century: Stories from a New Generation of Ac-
    tivists.* Gabriola Island, BC: New Society Publishers.
York, Steve, and Miriam Zimmerman. 2008. *Bringing Down a Dictator.*
    http.//www.aforcemorepowerful.org.

East Timorese Independence (1974–2002)

Portuguese merchants and clergy solidified colonization of the eastern half of the island of Timor in 1749 after a hundred years of struggle with the Dutch (for the western half) and the indigenous population (Taylor 1999). Portugal maintained the colony for its strategic location as well as for sandalwood and, later, coffee. Portugal's control was over half of the island of Timor, just 400 miles off the coast of Australia. The other half was part of the Dutch-controlled East Indies until Indonesia's independence in 1949. In 1974, as Portugal's dictatorship crumbled, so too did its hold on its colonies. As Portugal began decolonization, it allowed the creation of political parties in East Timor in May 1974 (Niner 2001). Two parties emerged as leading the independence movement: the Timorese Democratic Union (UDT) and the Revolutionary Front for an Independent East Timor (commonly known as Fretilin). Between March and July 1975 the Portuguese Decolonization Commission organized local elections to select an executive council to coordinate general elections for a Constitutional Assembly to convene in October 1976. Fretilin won most of the seats of this council. Following several anti-Fretilin rallies in East Timor's capital of Dili on August 9 and 10, 1975, UDT mounted a coup. For several days, fighting raged in the streets of Dili, resulting in a death toll of 1,500 to 3,000. During this fighting Fretilin formed an armed wing, Falintil (Armed Forces for the National Liberation of East Timor), to remove the coup leaders and attempt to create stability (Niner 2001: 17).

During this process, the Indonesian government, under President Suharto, had been trying to destabilize leftist parties by means of anticommunist propaganda and by recruiting West Timorese to infiltrate UDT. UDT leader Francisco Lopes da Cruz encouraged Suharto to intervene militarily and began a full invasion in September. By December 1975 the Indonesian military controlled much of the country and invaded Dili. Thousands were killed, and tens of thousands of East Timorese fled to the mountains behind Fretilin lines. Within months, 35,000 Indonesian troops were stationed in East Timor. Suharto wanted East Timor because of the threat that independence next door might prove subversive in Indonesia. This was a very real concern for Indonesia, as it was a collection of thousands of islands spread over thousands of miles. In 1976, Indonesia proclaimed that it had integrated East Timor as its twenty-seventh province, though it never received international recognition of the integration. After three years of significant military resistance, Indonesia had succeeded in decimating the guerrilla fighters and had largely consolidated control in the urban areas. In the process, international human rights groups estimate that some 200,000 (of an original population of 800,000) people died from the fighting, famine, and disease that resulted from disrupted food supplies. A status quo was maintained throughout most of the 1980s, with the Indonesian military essentially governing East Timor. For most of the decade it was closed to foreigners while Indonesia encouraged its citizens to move to East Timor and invested heavily in roads, schools, and other buildings, though this was predominantly viewed as benefiting only Indonesians and solidifying their control over the territory (Taylor 1999).

In 1989, with the announcement that the pope would visit East Timor, Indonesia began to open the territory to outsiders. During the next three years, international attention to East Timor was sporadic as dissidents held protests and guerrillas continued to wage war with the Indonesian army. In 1991, thousands of students, protesting the recent killing of a student as well as the decision of a Portuguese parliamentary delegation to cancel its scheduled visit, marched through the streets of Dili. The protest ended when Indonesian troops opened fire in the Santa Cruz cemetery, killing at least 200. The massacre gained international attention because two US reporters were beaten at the scene, and a British journalist was able to smuggle footage of the massacre to London, where it was broadcast to the world. In response to the protests, Indonesia engaged in widespread repression. The plight of the Timorese became an international cause célebre, and UN, Portuguese, and human rights activists around the world applied pressure on Indonesia to reform. In 1996, the Nobel Committee fueled the cause by awarding the Peace Prize to Carlos Filipe Ximenes Belo, the Catholic bishop of East Timor, and Jose Ramos-Horta, who traveled the world advocating for East Timorese independence, for their efforts to bring peace to the troubled territory. The UN was also active in mediating talks between Portugal (which was still recognized internationally as the ruling authority of East Timor) and Indonesia to allow for a referendum on the province's future.

The talks, international pressure, and human rights condemnations were fruitless until Suharto resigned in 1998. Although the issue of East Timor was a part of the reason Suharto was forced from office, it was minor compared to the combination of crises that plagued the last years of his administration. When Suharto stepped down, his vice president, B. J. Habibie, replaced him and was widely viewed as likely to continue Suharto's policies. To the surprise of most involved, Habibie announced that he would allow autonomy, though not independence, for East Timor. This quickly turned into allowing a referendum on autonomy. Again he stunned international observers when he said that if the East Timorese voted no on autonomy, he would allow independence. In the span of a few months, because of Habibie's decisions, the Indonesian policy had gone from integration to allowing a UN-organized referendum on independence. As Richard Tanter argues, "Whether Habibie believed a ballot would safely yield a clear majority for Indonesia, whether he bowed to pressures of Indonesia's international financial donors, or whether he believed it was time to cut the country's losses in a hopeless and debilitating cause and allow the East Timorese a path to independence, is not clear. What is clear is that Habibie's use of his limited personal authority broke the stalemate that had long prevailed in East Timor" (2001: 189).

The referendum was held on August 30, 1999, after delays caused by violence and intimidation by anti-independence militias. The militias were most likely armed, and even staffed, by the Indonesian military. Despite the violence, 78.5 percent of registered East Timorese voted for independence from Indonesia. In response, armed militias rampaged through urban areas and villages, killing hundreds and forcing more than half of the population into the mountains or refugee camps in West Timor (many of which were controlled by the militias). International condemnation of the conflict rose to such a fevered pitch that the UN Security Council authorized an international force to restore order after just a few hours of debate. Led by Australia, an international coalition quickly took control of Dili and over the month of October gained control of most of the territory. On October 19, 1999, the Indonesian legislature approved the referendum and voted to allow East Timor to become independent. After three years of UN supervision, on May 20, 2002, East Timor became the first new country of the twenty-first century.

Time Line

1974   *April 25:* The Carnation Revolution of Portugal leads to the process of decolonization of East Timor.

1975   *July 17:* Colonial control is scheduled to end in October 1978.

July 29: Fretilin wins in local elections.

August 11: Opposition party, Timorese Democratic Union (UDT), launches a coup to take power from Portugal. By September, Fretilin has forced the UDT into West Timor.

November 29: Indonesia signs a declaration with UDT to formally integrate East Timor into Indonesia.

December 7: Indonesia invades East Timor.

1976   *January 13:* Indonesian military forms a provisional government that invites Indonesia to proclaim sovereignty over East Timor.

       May 31: Indonesian military forms a Popular Assembly that approves a petition to Indonesian president Suharto for full integration.

       July 17: Suharto signs a bill integrating East Timor into Indonesia. The UN General Assembly rejects this annexation and calls for self-determination.

       November 19: Indonesian relief workers report that up to 100,000 people have been killed since the invasion.

1989   *October 12:* Pope John-Paul II visits Dili, celebrating an open-air mass where a small demonstration takes place that is quickly and violently dispersed by police.

1991   *November 12:* Thousands of students march to Santa Cruz cemetery in Dili to commemorate the killing of a civilian at the hands of the Indonesian military. In response, the military opens fire and kills at least 200. The entire event is recorded by Western media and broadcast to the world.

1996   *October 11:* Nobel Peace Prize is awarded to Carlos Filipe Ximenes Belo and Jose Ramos-Horta for their efforts to bring peace to East Timor.

1998   *May 21:* Suharto resigns after massive popular, violent demonstrations plague Indonesia. His vice president, B. J. Habibie, replaces him.

       June 9: Habibie announces that he would allow autonomy, though not independence, for East Timor.

1999   *January 27:* Habibie announces that if the East Timorese vote no on autonomy, he would allow independence. Fighting between pro- and anti-Indonesian groups intensifies, lasting until UN peacekeepers arrive and gain control.

       February 10: Jose "Xanana" Gusmao is released from prison to house arrest.

       March 12: UN agrees to administer vote on autonomy proposal. The Security Council resolution supporting the vote is passed June 11.

       July 16: UN begins voter registration for August referendum.

August 30: Referendum takes place after months of widespread violence and intimidation by paramilitary groups.

September 4: UN announces that 78 percent of registered voters rejected the autonomy proposal, opting instead for full independence. Pro-Indonesian paramilitary forces immediately begin a rampage.

September 5: Bishop Belo's compound, which had housed thousands of refugees, is attacked; dozens are killed, and all are forced to leave.

September 8: Xanana Gusmao returns to East Timor.

September 10: International condemnation of Indonesia's response to the referendum grows as paramilitary forces destroy much of East Timor. Military aid is stopped, planned loans are scrapped, and there are widespread calls to allow international peacekeepers to stop the violence.

September 13: Habibie agrees to an international peacekeeping force to implement the referendum.

September 14: All but twelve staffers are airlifted from the last remaining UN compound.

September 20: The first contingent of peacekeeping troops arrives from Australia to a gutted Dili.

September 27: The Indonesian Armed Forces formally yield responsibility for security to the UN in East Timor.

October 19: Indonesian legislature approves the referendum and allows East Timor to become independent.

October 22: Xanana Gusmao returns to Dili. UN peacekeepers reach and establish control in the last East Timorese towns after a month of occupation.

2002   *May 20:* East Timor becomes the first new country of the twenty-first century.

Cast of Characters

Suharto (1921–2008): President of Indonesia from 1966 to 1998. Was instrumental in the invasion of East Timor and demanded it remain a part of Indonesia.

B. J. Habibie (1936–): Became president of Indonesia in 1998 when

Suharto stepped down. Reversed Suharto's policy on East Timor and allowed for a referendum on autonomy administered by the UN as well as the insertion of UN peacekeeping troops.

Carlos Filipe Ximenes Belo (1948–): Catholic bishop of East Timor who was awarded the Nobel Peace Prize, with Jose Ramos-Horta, in 1996 for his work at bringing peace to East Timor.

Jose Ramos-Horta (1949–): Traveled the world advocating for East Timorese independence. Was awarded the Nobel Peace Prize, with Bishop Belo, in 1996 for this work.

Jose "Xanana" Gusmao (1946–): Leader of Falintil. He rose through the ranks through strategic prowess and by surviving as the top leaders before him were captured or killed. He was captured and imprisoned in 1992 but was able to retain control of the movement from jail.

Further Reading

Cristalis, Irena. 2002. *Bitter Dawn: East Timor: A People's Story*. London: ZED Books.

Fernandez, Clinton. 2004. *Reluctant Saviour: Australia, Indonesia, and the Independence of East Timor*. Melbourne, Australia: Scribe Publications.

Greenlees, Don, and Robert Garran. 2003. *Deliverance: The Inside Story of East Timor's Fight for Freedom*. Sydney, Australia: Allen and Unwin.

Martin, Ian. 2001. *Self-Determination in East Timor: The United Nations, the Ballot, and International Intervention*. Boulder, CO: Lynne Rienner Publishers.

Nevins, Joseph. 2005. *A Not So Distant Horror: Mass Violence in East Timor*. Ithaca, NY: Cornell University Press.

Smith, Michael G., and Moreen Dee. 2003. *Peacekeeping in East Timor: The Path to Independence*. Boulder, CO: Lynne Rienner Publishers.

Taylor, John G. 1999. *East Timor: The Price of Freedom*. Annandale, NSW, Australia: Pluto Press.

Tiffen, Rodney. 2001. *Diplomatic Deceits: Government, Media, and East Timor*. Sydney, Australia: University of New South Wales.

The Nepalese Revolution (1996–2008)

In 1996, a former agricultural science teacher named Prachanda began a communist insurgency in opposition to the monarchy of Nepal. The members of a communist party, known as the Maoists, styled themselves after the Shining Path movement in Peru and their namesake, Mao Zedong, asserting that the only way to create a republic was through a prolonged people's war. Their "people's war" was based in the poor rural areas of Nepal, where they recruited their members, many of them poor farmers dissatisfied with the level of economic assistance they got from the government. One-third of the Nepalese population lived in poverty; most of the rural population consisted of subsistence farmers. The largest sector of the Nepalese economy was tourism, which, with the insurgency and political conflict, dropped significantly.

Throughout the first years of the movement the Maoists were a minor threat to the government, which was fairly stable under King Birendra's rule. The violence began to escalate first in 2000 when the Maoist rebels stole modern weapons from Nepalese police and army storage bunkers.

On June 1, 2001, the crown prince of Nepal opened fire on his family at dinner, killing his father, mother, siblings and other members of the royal family, before finally killing himself. The crown prince's uncle, Gyanendra, ascended to the throne and in November of that year declared a state of emergency. This allowed the Nepalese military to replace police efforts in battling the Maoists.

Maoist violence reached a peak in 2002. Further, the tactics were often particularly brutal. Human rights groups, such as Amnesty International, called international attention to atrocities committed by both the government and the Maoists. A report in April 2002 claimed that during one skirmish police were captured by Maoists, stripped of their clothing, blindfolded, and forced to march naked before finally being beheaded.

The Maoists also combined nonviolent tactics with their violence. For example, they called several strikes and set up roadblocks around the capital city of Katmandu, preventing goods such as gas, fruits, vegetables, grains, and many other foodstuffs from getting to the population. The Maoists threatened people who defied the strikes, preventing them from going to work or shopping. In this way, nonviolent noncooperation was forced with the threat of violence.

In 2003, the Nepalese government accepted a cease-fire offer from the Maoists and began peace talks, after which the violence decreased dramatically. The talks broke down in 2004 when the government refused to compromise with the rebels on the issues of redrafting the constitution and examining the monarchy. In February 2005, King Gyanendra seized absolute power by dismissing parliament. He cut the nation off from any communication with the outside world by shutting off cellular phone and Internet service, censoring broadcasts over the state-run radio station, and diverting flights scheduled into the country. He also curtailed civil liberties throughout the year and a half that he was in absolute control, often imposing curfews, illegalizing the right to protest, and jailing protesters without trial. Members of the old parliament formed a Seven Party Alliance (SPA) that coordinated opposition to the king and signed a "twelve-point agreement" of understanding with the Maoists that outlined their opposition to the king and a commitment to democracy and economic reforms.

In response to King Gyanendra's seizing control, mass prodemocracy protests erupted throughout Nepal, concentrated in the cities and climaxing in April 2006. The initial trigger was April 4, 2006, when the king banned all forms of public meetings to stop a planned strike and protests called by the SPA. In response, hundreds of thousands took to the streets of Katmandu, the capital city, in a nonviolent demonstration. Even the Maoists vowed to not target the capital city during the first wave of protests, a sign many viewed as support for the nonviolent movement. As the month wore on, what had been student-dominated protests became a series of nationwide strikes representing almost every class and affiliated group in Nepal's cities and often in rural Nepal as well. The protests also became increasingly violent, with police forces' repression of demonstrators followed by riots in response. By mid-April, violence was common in terms of throwing stones, burning tires, and attacking police and those not complying with the strikes. The Nepal-based representative of the UN High Commissioner for Human Rights, Ian Martin, commenting on the situation, said "democratic rights do not exist. The opportunities for peaceful protests have been closed down" (Rosenberg 2006).

On April 25, 2006, King Gyanendra agreed to reinstate the parliament, and a month later the parliament voted to curtail the power of the monarch, creating a secular state. In the following two years, the Maoists won a majority in parliamentary elections, and the new assembly voted overwhelmingly to abolish the monarchy in May 2008.

Time Line

1996   Maoist communist insurgency begins in opposition to the monarchy of Nepal.

2000 Violence escalates when the Maoist rebels steal modern weapons from Nepalese police and army storage bunkers.

2001 *June 1:* Crown prince of Nepal kills king, other members of the royal family, and himself. Gyanendra ascends to the throne.

November: State of emergency is declared.

2003 Government accepts a cease-fire offer from the Maoists and begins peace talks.

2004 Talks break down.

2005 *February:* Gyanendra seizes absolute power by dismissing parliament. Seven Party Alliance (SPA) is formed from old parliament.

November 22: Twelve-Point Agreement is signed between Maoists and SPA.

2006 *April 4:* King bans all forms of public meetings.

April: Hundreds of thousands take to the streets of Katmandu in nonviolent demonstrations. Over the month, strikes become more common as does violent rioting at demonstrations.

April 25: Gyanendra agrees to reinstate the parliament.

May 18: Parliament votes to curtail the power of the monarch, creating a secular state.

2008 *April 10:* Maoists win a majority in new Constituent Assembly elections.

May 28: Assembly abolishes the monarchy and ratifies a new constitution.

Cast of Characters

King Birendra (1945–2001): Ruled Nepal from 1972 until 2001, when he was killed by his son. In 1990, following demonstrations, Birendra had agreed to the drafting of a new constitution that limited his role to a constitutional monarch.

King Gyanendra (1947–): Assumed the throne in Nepal after the killing of the king and much of the royal family. To quell the Maoist insurgency, took control of the government by dismissing parliament. These actions spurred popular opposition that toppled the constitutional monarchy.

Prachanda (1954–): Leader of the Maoist insurgency in Nepal. Orchestrated the 1996 uprising and 2005 alliance with SPA. As leader of the Communist Party of Nepal, became prime minister under the new constitution when his party won a majority of seats in the Constituent Assembly.

Further Reading

Lawoti, Mahendra. 2005. *Towards a Democratic Nepal: Inclusive Political Institutions for a Multicultural Society.* Thousand Oaks, CA: Sage Publications.

Parajulee, Ramjee P. 2000. *The Democratic Transition in Nepal.* Lanham, MD: Rowman and Littlefield.

Riaz, Ali, and Subho Basu. 2007. *Paradise Lost? State Failure in Nepal.* Lanham, MD: Lexington Books.

Thapa, Deepak. 2003. *Understanding the Maoist Movement of Nepal.* Kathmandu, Nepal: Centre for Social Research and Development.

Bibliography

Ackerman, Peter, and Christopher Kruegler. 1994. *Strategic Nonviolent Conflict: The Dynamics of People Power in the Twentieth Century.* Westport, CT: Praeger Publishers.

Adelman, Howard. 1998. "Rwandan Civil Wars (1959–1994)." In *The Encyclopedia of Political Revolutions,* ed. Jack Goldstone. Washington, DC: Congressional Quarterly, 436–438.

Ash, Timothy Garton. 1999. *History of the Present: Essays, Sketches, and Dispatches from Europe in the 1990s.* London: Allen Lane.

BBC News. 2006. "Profile: Ugandan Rebel Joseph Kony." June 28. http://news.bbc.co.uk.

Berejikian, Jeffrey. 1992. "Revolutionary Collective Action and the Agent-Structure Problem." *American Political Science Review* 86, no. 3 (September): 647–657.

Bergesen, Albert J. 2008. *The Sayyid Qutb Reader: Selected Writings on Politics, Religion, and Society.* New York: Routledge.

Berryman, Phillip. 1984. *The Religious Roots of Rebellion: Christians in Central American Revolutions.* Maryknoll, NY: Orbis Books.

Booth, John A., and Patricia Bayer Richard. 2006. "Revolution's Legacy: Residual Effects on Nicaraguan Participation and Attitudes in Comparative Context." *Latin American Politics and Society* 48, no. 2: 117–142.

Brinton, Crane. 1965. *The Anatomy of Revolution.* New York: Vintage Books.

Bronner, Stephen Eric. 2004. *Reclaiming the Enlightenment.* New York: Columbia University Press.

Burrowes, Robert J. 1996. *The Strategy of Nonviolent Defense: A Gandhian Approach.* Albany: State University of New York Press.

Center for the Study of Civil War. 2006. *UCDP/PRIO Armed Conflict Dataset.* Uppsala Conflict Data Program (UCDP), Department of Peace and Conflict Research, Uppsala University and the Centre for the Study of Civil War at

the International Peace Research Institute, Oslo (PRIO). http://www
.prio.no.

Chamorro, Violeta. 1996. *Dreams of the Heart: The Autobiography of President Violeta Barrios de Chamorro of Nicaragua.* New York: Simon and Schuster.

Chang, Sidney H., and Leonard H.D. Gordon. 1991. *All Under Heaven: Sun Yat-sen and His Revolutionary Thought.* Stanford, CA: Hoover Institution Press.

Coleman, James S. 1990. *Collective Action and the Civil Rights Movement.* Chicago: University of Chicago Press.

Combs, Cindy C. 2006. *Terrorism in the Twenty-First Century.* 4th ed. Upper Saddle River, NJ: Pearson Prentice Hall.

Davies, James. 1962. "Toward a Theory of Revolution." *American Sociological Review* 6, no. 1: 5–19.

DeFronzo, James. 2007. *Revolutions and Revolutionary Movements.* 3rd ed. Cambridge, MA: Westview Press.

DeFronzo, James. ed. 2006. *Revolutionary Movements in World History From 1750 to the Present.* Santa Barbara, CA: ABC-CLIO Inc.

Douglas, Ed. 2005. "Inside Nepal's Revolution." *National Geographic Magazine,* November, 54.

Eckstein, Susan. 2003. "The Impact of Revolution on Social Welfare in Latin America." In *Revolutions: Theoretical, Comparative, and Historical Studies,* 3rd ed., ed. Jack Goldstone. Belmont, CA: Thomson Wadsworth, 120–135.

Edeen, Alf. 1994. "The Soviet Civil Service: Its Composition and Status." In *The Encyclopedia of Political Revolutions,* ed. Jack Goldstone. Washington, DC: Congressional Quarterly, 204–213.

Edmisten, Patricia Taylor. 1990. *Nicaragua Divided: La Prensa and the Chamorro Legacy.* Pensacola: University of West Florida Press.

Farazmand, A. 1987. "The Impacts of the Revolution of 1978–1979 on the Iranian Bureaucracy and Civil Service." *International Journal of Public Administration* 10, no. 4: 337–366.

Faroohar, Manzar. 1989. *The Catholic Church and Social Change in Nicaragua.* Albany: State University of New York Press.

Fisher, Roger, and William Ury. 1991. *Getting to Yes: Negotiating Agreement Without Giving In.* Boston: Houghton Mifflin.

Fonseca Amador, Carlos. 1982. "Nicaragua: Zero Hour." In Tomas Borge, Carlos Fonseca, Daniel Ortega, Humberto Ortega, and Jaime Wheelock, *Sandinistas Speak,* ed. Bruce Marcus. New York: Pathfinder Press, 23–42.

Foran, John. 1997. "Discourses and Social Forces: The Role of Culture and Cultural Studies in Understanding Revolutions." In *Theorizing Revolutions,* ed. John Foran. Boulder, CO: Westview Press.

————. 2005. *Taking Power: On the Origins of Third World Revolutions*. New York: Cambridge University Press.

Foran, John, and Jeff Goodwin. 2003. "Dictatorship or Democracy: Outcomes of Revolution in Iran and Nicaragua." In *Revolutions: Theoretical, Comparative, and Historical Studies*, 3rd ed., ed. Jack Goldstone. Belmont, CA: Thomson Wadsworth, 107–120.

Foreign Policy and the Fund for Peace. 2010. "The Index of Failed States." July/August. http://www.foreignpolicy.com (accessed August 21).

Fournier, Anna. 2007. "Patriotism, Order, and Articulations of the Nation in Kyiv High Schools Before and After the Orange Revolution." *Journal of Communist Studies and Transition Politics* 23, no. 1: 101–117.

Freedom House. 2010. *Freedom in the World 2010*. www.freedomhouse.org (accessed October 18).

Friere, Paulo. 2006. *Pedagogy of the Oppressed*. New York: Continuum.

Gilpin, Robert. 1987. *The Political Economy of International Relations*. Princeton, NJ: Princeton University Press.

Goldstone, Jack A. 1980. "Theories of Revolution: The Third Generation." *World Politics* 32, no. 3: 425–453.

Goldstone, Jack. 1994a. "Is Revolution Individually Rational? Groups and Individuals in Revolutionary Collective Action." *Rationality and Society* 6, no. 1: 139–166.

————. 1994b. "The Comparative and Historical Study of Revolutions." In *Revolutions: Theoretical, Comparative, and Historical Studies*, 2nd ed., ed. Jack Goldstone. Fort Worth, TX: Harcourt Brace College Publishers, 1–17.

————. 1998. "Reform." In *The Encyclopedia of Political Revolutions*, ed. Jack Goldstone. Washington, DC: Congressional Quarterly, 415–417.

————. 2003. *Revolutions: Theoretical, Comparative, and Historical Studies*. 3rd ed. Belmont, CA: Thomson Wadsworth.

Goldstone, Jack, ed. 1994. *The Encyclopedia of Political Revolutions*. Washington, DC: Congressional Quarterly.

Goodwin, Jeff. 2001. *No Other Way Out: States and Revolutionary Movements, 1945–1991*. Cambridge: Cambridge University Press.

Goodwin, Jeff, and James M. Jasper. 1999. "Caught in a Winding, Snarling Vine: The Structural Bias of Political Process Theory." *Sociological Forum* 14, no. 1: 27–53.

Gorman, Stephen M. 1981. "Power and Consolidation in the Nicaraguan Revolution." *Journal of Latin American Studies* 13, no. 1: 133–149.

Gould, Roger V. 2006. "Workers." In *The Encyclopedia of Political Revolutions*, ed. Jack Goldstone. Washington, DC: Congressional Quarterly, 526–529.

Gurr, Ted Robert. 1970. *Why Men Rebel*. Princeton, NJ: Princeton University Press.

Hagopian, Mark N. 1974. *The Phenomenon of Revolution.* New York: Dodd, Mead.

Hale, Henry E., and Rein Taagepera. 2002. "Russia: Consolidation or Collapse?" *Europe-Asia Studies* 54, no. 7: 1101–1125.

Halliday, Fred. 1998. "Islamic Fundamentalism." In *The Encyclopedia of Political Revolutions,* ed. Jack Goldstone. Washington, DC: Congressional Quarterly, 263–265.

———. 2003. "Counter-Revolution." In *Revolutions: Theoretical, Comparative, and Historical Studies,* 3rd ed., ed. Jack Goldstone. Belmont, CA: Thomson Wadsworth, 136–140.

Hamilton, Richard. 1998. "Bourgeoisie." In *The Encyclopedia of Political Revolutions,* ed. Jack Goldstone. Washington, DC: Congressional Quarterly, 47–48.

Havel, Vaclev. 1992a. "Politics and Conscience." In *Open Letters: Selected Writings 1965–1990,* ed. Paul Wilson. New York: Vintage Books, 249–271.

———. 1992b. "The Power of the Powerless." In *Open Letters: Selected Writings 1965–1990,* ed. Paul Wilson. New York: Vintage Books, 125–214.

———. 1992c. "Thinking About Frantisek K." In *Open Letters: Selected Writings 1965–1990,* ed. Paul Wilson. New York: Vintage Books. 363–372.

———. 1992d. "Two Letters from Prison." In *Open Letters: Selected Writings 1965–1990,* ed. Paul Wilson. New York: Vintage Books, 232–236.

Hobbes, Thomas. 1996. *Leviathan,* ed. J. C. A. Gaskin. Oxford: Oxford University Press.

Hodges, Donald C. 1986. *Intellectual Foundations of the Nicaraguan Revolution.* Austin: University of Texas Press.

Hoffer, Eric. 1951. *The True Believer: Thoughts on the Nature of Mass Movements.* New York: Harper and Row.

Hull, N.E.H., Peter C. Hoffer, and Steven L. Allen. 1978. "Choosing Sides: A Quantitative Study of the Personality Determinants of Loyalist and Revolutionary Political Affiliation in New York." *Journal of American History* 65, no. 2: 344–366.

Huntington, Samuel. 1968. *Political Order in Changing Societies.* New Haven: Yale University Press.

Janis, Irving. 1982. *Groupthink.* 2nd ed. Boston: Houghton Mifflin.

Jefferson, Thomas. 2010. "The Object of the Declaration of Independence." Thomas Jefferson Legacy. Library of Congress. www.loc.gov/exhibits/jefferson (accessed October 18).

Joffe, George. 2006. "Islamic Fundamentalist Revolutionary Movement." In *Revolutionary Movements in World History from 1750 to the Present,* ed. James V. DeFronzo. Santa Barbara, CA: ABC-CLIO, 452–464.

Johnson, Chalmers. 1973. *Autopsy on People's War.* Berkeley: University of California Press.

Karnow, Stanley. 1998. "Ho Chi Minh." *Time*. April 13.

Katouzian, Homa. 1989. "The Political Economy of Iran Since the Revolution: A Macro-Historical Analysis." *Comparative Economic Studies* 31, no. 3: 55–77.

Katz, Mark N. 1997. *The Diffusion of Revolutionary Waves*. London: Macmillan Press.

Katz, Mark N. ed. 2001. *Revolution: International Dimensions*. Washington, DC: CQ Press.

Keane, John. 2000. *Vaclav Havel: A Political Tragedy in Six Acts*. New York: Basic Books.

Kelly, Jonathan, and Herbert Klein. 2003. "Revolution and the Rebirth of Inequality: Stratification in Postrevolutionary Society." In *Revolutions: Theoretical, Comparative, and Historical Studies,* 3rd ed., ed. Jack Goldstone. Belmont, CA: Thomson Wadsworth, 86–93.

Keohane, Robert O., and Joseph S. Nye. 2001. *Power and Interdependence*. 3rd ed. New York: Longman.

Khomeini, Imam. 1981. *Islam and Revolution: Writings and Declarations of Imam Khomeini*. Trans. Hamid Algar. Berkeley, CA: Mizan Press.

Kimmel, Michael S. 1990. *Revolution: A Sociological Interpretation*. Philadelphia, PA: Temple University Press.

Kuran, Timur. 1991. "Now Out of Never: The Element of Surprise in the East European Revolution of 1989." *World Politics* 44, no. 1: 7–48.

Lawson, George. 2005. *Negotiated Revolutions: The Czech Republic, South Africa, and Chile*. Burlington, VT: Ashgate Publishing.

Lichbach, Mark I. 1994. "Rethinking Rationality and Rebellion. Theories of Collective Action and Problems of Collective Dissent." *Rationality and Society* 6, no. 1: 8–39.

Lieberthal, Kenneth. 2004. *Governing China: From Revolution Through Reform*. 2nd ed. New York: W. W. Norton.

Lipset, Seymour Martin. 1970. *Revolution and Counter-Revolution: Change and Persistence in Social Structures*. Garden City, NY: Anchor Books.

Locke, John. 1690. *Second Treatise of Government,* ed. C. B. Macpherson. Repr., Indianapolis, IN: Hackett Publishing, 1980.

Lohmann, Susanne. 1994. "The Dynamics of Informational Cascades: The Monday Demonstrations in Leipzig, East Germany, 1989–91." *World Politics* 47, no. 1: 42–101.

Mabeko-Tali, Jean-Michel. 2006. "Angolan Revolution." In *Revolutionary Movements in World History from 1750 to the Present,* ed. James V. DeFronzo. Santa Barbara, CA: ABC-CLIO, 61–70.

Mannheim, Karl. 1936. *Ideology and Utopia*. New York: Harcourt, Brace.

Markoff, John. 1998. "Peasants." In *The Encyclopedia of Political Revolutions,* ed. Jack Goldstone. Washington, DC: Congressional Quarterly, 392–394.

Marx, Karl. 2003. "Manifesto of the Communist Party." In *Revolutions: Theo-retical, Comparative, and Historical Studies*. 3rd ed., ed. Jack Goldstone. Belmont, CA: Thomson Wadsworth, 23–31.

Meier, August. 1970. "Who Are the 'True Believers'?—A Tentative Typology of the Motivations of Civil Rights Activists." In *Protest, Reform, and Re-volt: A Reader in Social Movements*, ed. Joseph R. Gusfield. New York: John Wiley and Sons, 473–483.

Meisner, Maurice. 1998. "Intellectuals." In *The Encyclopedia of Political Rev-olutions*, ed. Jack Goldstone. Washington, DC: Congressional Quarterly, 243–245.

Moaddel, M. 1993. *Class, Politics, and Ideology in the Iranian Revolution.* New York: Columbia University Press.

Moghadam, Valentine M. 2003. "Gender and Revolutions." In *Revolutions: Theoretical, Comparative, and Historical Studies,* 3rd ed., ed. Jack Gold-stone. Belmont, CA: Thomson Wadsworth, 94–107.

Moore, Barrington. 1966. *Social Origins of Dictatorship and Democracy.* Boston: Beacon Press.

———. 1978. *Injustice: The Social Bases of Obedience and Revolt.* White Plains, NY: M.E. Sharpe.

Moore, Will H. 1995. "Rational Rebels: Overcoming the Free-Rider Problem." *Political Research Quarterly* 48 (June): 417–454.

Mugabo, Manasse. 1994. "Ethnic Clashes on Airwaves." Associated Press. March 12.

Muller, Edward N., and Karl-Dieter Opp. 1986. "Rational Choice and Rebel-lious Collective Action." *American Political Science Review* 80, no. 2: 471–488.

Niner, Sarah. 2001. "A Long Journey of Resistance: The Origins and Struggle of CNRT." In *Bitter Flowers, Sweet Flowers: East Timor, Indonesia, and the World Community,* ed. Richard Tanter, Mark Selden, and Stephen R. Shalom. Lanham, MD: Rowman and Littlefield, 15–30.

Olson, Mancur. 1965. *The Logic of Collective Action: Public Goods and the Theory of Groups.* Cambridge, MA: Harvard University Press.

Pagnucco, Ron. 1993. "Teaching About Agency and Structure in Nonviolent Social Change." *Journal for Peace and Justice Studies* 5, no. 2: 97–107.

Park, Robert Ezra. 1955. *Society.* Glencoe, IL: Free Press.

Parsa, Misagh. 2000. *States, Ideologies, and Social Revolutions: A Compara-tive Analysis of Iran, Nicaragua, and the Philippines.* Cambridge: Cam-bridge University Press.

Political Instability Task Force. 2009. "Historical State Conflicts, Crises, and Transitions, 1955–2004." Center for Global Policy, School of Public Pol-icy, George Mason University. http://globalpolicy.gmu.edu/pitf/index.htm (accessed October 18).

Rashid, Ahmed. 2001. *Taliban: Militant Islam, Oil, and Fundamentalism in Central Asia.* New Haven: Yale University Press.

Rosenberg, Matthew. 2006. "Nepal Security Forces Shoot Pro-democracy Protesters, Killing at Least 4." Associated Press. April 19.

Rothchild, Donald. 1998. "Ethnic Conflict." In *The Encyclopedia of Political Revolutions,* ed. Jack Goldstone. Washington, DC: Congressional Quarterly, 161–163.

Sambanis, Nicholas. 2006. "It's Official: There Is Now a Civil War in Iraq." *New York Times,* July 23.

Sarkees, Meredith Reid. 2000. "The Correlates of War Data on War: An Update to 1997." *Conflict Management and Peace Science* 18, no. 1: 123–144.

Schock, Kurt. 2003. "Nonviolent Action and Its Misconceptions: Insights for Social Scientists." *PS: Political Science and Politics* 36, no. 4: 705–712.

Scott, James. 1976. *The Moral Economy of the Peasant: Rebellion and Subsistence in Southeast Asia.* New Haven: Yale University Press.

Selbin, Eric. 1993. *Modern Latin American Revolutions.* Boulder, CO: Westview Press.

———. 2006. "Elites, Intellectuals, and Revolutionary Leadership." In *Revolutionary Movements in World History from 1750 to the Present,* ed. James V. DeFronzo. Santa Barbara, CA: ABC-CLIO, 254–257.

Sewell, William, Jr. 1985. "Ideologies and Social Revolutions: Reflections on the French Case." *Journal of Modern History* 57, no. 1: 57–85.

Sharp, Gene. 1984. *The Politics of Nonviolent Action.* Boston: Porter Sargent Publishers.

Skocpol, Theda. 1979. *States and Social Revolutions: A Comparative Analysis of France, Russia, and China.* Cambridge: Cambridge University Press.

———. 1994a. *Social Revolutions in the Modern World.* Cambridge, MA: Cambridge University Press.

———. 1994b. "Old Regime Legacies and Communist Revolutions in Russia and China." In *Revolutions: Theoretical, Comparative, and Historical Studies,* 2nd ed., ed. Jack Goldstone. Fort Worth, TX: Harcourt Brace College Publishers, 233–252.

Smithey, Lee, and Lester R. Kurtz. 1999. "'We Have Bare Hands': Nonviolent Social Movements in the Soviet Bloc." In *Nonviolent Social Movements: A Geographical Perspective,* ed. Stephen Zunes, Lester R. Kurtz, and Sarah Beth Asher. Malden, MA: Blackwell Publishers, 96–124.

Snyder, Robert. 1999. "The End of Revolution?" *The Review of Politics* 61, no. 1: 5–29.

Steger, Manfred. 2000. *Gandhi's Dilemma: Nonviolent Principles and Nationalist Power.* New York: St. Martin's Press.

Straus, Scott. 2005. "Darfur and the Genocide Debate." *Foreign Affairs* 84, no. 1: 123.

Taber, Robert. 1970. *The War of the Flea: A Study of Guerrilla Warfare Theory and Practice*. New York: Citadel Press.

Tanter, Richard. 2001. "East Timor and the Crisis of the Indonesian Intelligence State." In *Bitter Flowers, Sweet Flowers: East Timor, Indonesia, and the World Community,* ed. Richard Tanter, Mark Selden, and Stephen R. Shalom. Lanham, MD: Rowman and Littlefield, 189–207.

Tarrow, Sidney. 1998. *Power in Movement: Social Movements and Contentious Politics*. 2nd ed. Cambridge: Cambridge University Press.

Taylor, John G. 1999. *East Timor: The Price of Freedom*. Annandale, NSW, Australia: Pluto Press.

Taylor, Michael. 1987. *The Possibility of Cooperation*. New York: Cambridge University Press.

Thompson, Mark R. 2004. *Democratic Revolutions: Asia and Eastern Europe*. New York: Routledge.

Tilly, Charles. 1978. *From Mobilization to Revolution*. Reading, MA: Addison-Wesley Publishing.

———. 1995. *European Revolutions, 1492–1992*. Cambridge, England: Blackwell Publishers.

———. 2004. *Social Movements, 1768–2004*. Boulder, CO: Paradigm Publishers.

Tocqueville, Alexis de. 1998. *The Ancien Regime and the French Revolution*. Chicago: University of Chicago Press.

Trimberger, Ellen Kay. 1978. *Revolution from Above: Military Bureaucrats and Development in Japan, Turkey, Egypt, and Peru*. New Brunswick, NJ: Transaction Books.

Truth and Reconciliation Commission of Peru. 2003. "Press Release 226: TRC Final Report Was Made Public on August 28 2003 at Noon." http://www .cverdad.org.pe/ (accessed July 11, 2007).

Tsebelis, George. 1990. *Nested Games: Rational Choice in Comparative Politics*. Berkeley: University of California Press.

Tucker, Aviezer. 2000. *The Philosophy and Politics of Czech Dissidence from Patocka to Havel*. Pittsburgh, PA: University of Pittsburgh Press.

Tullock, Gordon. 1971. "The Paradox of Revolution." *Public Choice* 11: 89–99.

UNU-WIDER World Income Inequality Database, Version 2.0c. 2008. http://www.wider.unu.edu/.

US Declaration of Independence. 1987. *The Founders' Constitution*, Vol. 1. Chicago: University of Chicago Press. http://press-pubs.uchicago.edu/founders/documents/v1ch1s5.html (accessed October 18).

Van Inwegen, Patrick. 2006. "Velvet Revolution: An Actor-Based Model." *Peace and Change* 31, no. 2: 175–203.

Waitzkin, Howard. 1983. "Health Policy and Social Change: A Comparative History of Chile and Cuba." *Social Problems* 31, no. 2: 235–248.

Waller, James. 2007. *Becoming Evil*. 2nd ed. New York: Oxford University Press.

Walt, Stephen M. 1996. *Revolution and War.* Ithaca, NY: Cornell University Press.
———. 1999. "Rigor or Rigor Mortis? Rational Choice and Security Studies." *International Security* 23, no. 4: 5–44.
Walton, John. 1998. "Rebellion and Revolt." In *The Encyclopedia of Political Revolutions,* ed. Jack Goldstone. Washington, DC: Congressional Quarterly, 413–415.
Weber, Max. 1958. "Politics as a Vocation." In *From Max Weber: Essays in Sociology,* eds. and trans. H. H. Gerth and C. Wright Mill. New York: Oxford University Press, 77–128.
———. 1968. *Economy and Society,* Vol. 1. New York: Bedminster Press.
———. 2003. "Charisma, Bureaucracy, and Revolution." In *Revolutions: Theoretical, Comparative, and Historical Studies,* 3rd ed., ed. Jack Goldstone. Belmont, CA: Thomson Wadsworth, 33–36.
Wendt, Alexander E. 1987. "The Agent-Structure Problem in International Relations Theory." *International Organization* 41, no. 3 (Summer): 335–370.
Whyte, Martin King. 1994. "Inequality and Stratification in China." In *Revolutions: Theoretical, Comparative, and Historical Studies,* 2nd ed., ed. Jack Goldstone. Fort Worth, TX: Harcourt Brace College Publishers, 213–233.
Wickham-Crowley, Timothy P. 1992. *Guerrillas and Revolution in Latin America: A Comparative Study of Insurgents and Regimes Since 1956.* Princeton, NJ: Princeton University Press.
———. 1997. "Structural Theories of Revolution." In *Theorizing Revolutions,* ed. John Foran. New York: Routledge.
Wittkopf, Eugene, and Christopher Jones with Charles Kegley. 2008. *American Foreign Policy: Pattern and Process.* 7th ed. Belmont, CA: Thomson Wadsworth.
Wolf, Eric R. 1999. *Peasant Wars of the Twentieth Century.* Norman: University of Oklahoma Press.
World Research Institute. 2010. "Economics, Business, and the Environment— GDP: GDP per capita, current US dollars." *EarthTrends.* www.earthtrends .wri.org/text/economics-business/variable-638.html (Accessed October 18).
York, Steve, and Miriam Zimmerman. 2008. *Bringing Down A Dictator.* http:// www.aforcemorepowerful.org (accessed August 7, 2008).
Zimmerman, Matilde. 2000. *Sandinista: Carlos Fonseca and the Nicaraguan Revolution.* Durham, NC: Duke University Press.
Zunes, Stephen. 1999. "The Role of Nonviolent Action in the Downfall of Apartheid." *Journal of Modern African Studies* 37, no. 1: 137–169.
Zunes, Stephen, and Lester R. Kurtz. 1999. "Conclusion." In *Nonviolent Social Movements: A Geographical Perspective,* ed. Stephen Zunes, Lester R. Kurtz, and Sarah Beth Asher. Malden, MA: Blackwell Publishers, 302– 322.

Index

About the Book

Understanding Revolution concisely, but thoroughly, explains one of the most fundamental sources of political change in the modern world. Designed to be accessible to undergraduate students, the book systematically explores such questions as:

- What should be defined as a revolution?
- Is there a "typical" pattern to the course of a revolution?
- What are the roles of ideologies, structures (e.g., the state, class structures, the international system), and individuals in shaping revolutions?
- What causes groups to mobilize behind revolutionary leaders?
- What happens after a revolutionary group assumes power, or fails?

The discussion highlights points of agreement and debate within the social science literature, and brief case studies of revolutions and revolutionary movements bring concepts to life.

Patrick Van Inwegen is assistant professor of political science at Whitworth University.